CONTENTS

1   INTRODUCTION   1
The impact of computers on our lives   1
A reluctance to embrace the technology   2
A typical school and two typical teachers   2
The broad focus of the project   3

2   THE PLACE, THE PEOPLE, THE PROGRAMME OF EVENTS   4
The school   4
The staff   4
The children   5
Computer equipment in the school   5
The participating teachers   5
An outline plan of the study   5

3   MATTERS OF METHODOLOGY   7
Ethnography or participant observation? Matters of definition   7
Quantitative measures   10
Qualitative measures   14
Getting to know the teachers   16
The teachers' accounts   18
The headteacher's account   19
Getting to know the children   19

4   RECENT AND RELEVANT RESEARCH   23
Computing in primary schools   23
First-hand experiences in other classrooms   24
The effect of having a 'home computer'   26
Wordprocessors and other content-free software   26
The benefits of group work   27
Teachers' resistance to innovation in the classroom   28
The implications of the National Curriculum   29

The role of information technology in the primary school 30
How well prepared are our two teachers at Broadwood? 32

5   MAKING A START 33
Choosing the programs 34
The computer as a tool, not as an end in itself 34
Tools, not training packages 34
Expert in what? 35
Teacher training: previous experience and available resources 36
School resources 37
If at first you don't succeed . . . 39
Meeting teacher needs: the revised training programme 40
Why did the teachers appear not to take up researchers' suggestions? 42
An introduction to a database 45
Using the database – a turning point? 46
Interrogating the database 48
Testing the children 49
The role of headteacher and parents 50
Organising a parents' evening 50

6   HORSES FOR COURSES – Different programs for different purposes:
a chronicle of events 52
Spring term 1987 52
Summer term 1987 64
Autumn term 1987 73
What do the teachers and researchers think? Some retrospective accounts 91
The headteacher's reaction to the project 112

7   PROFILES OF PROGRESS? 114
An experiment in changing self-images 114
Accounting for change: children's explanations 120
Accounting for change: researchers' observations 122
A profile of improvement 124
A profile of deterioration 126

8   MAINTAINING MOMENTUM 128
The project and the National Curriculum 128
A checklist of essential skills 129
What did we learn about training? 135
Providing adequate support 136
How did the teachers cope with a limited number of computers? 137
How will they maintain the momentum? 141

Appendix I 143
Appendix II 152
References and Bibliography 157
Index 161

1
INTRODUCTION

The Impact of Computers on our Lives

Despite the all-pervasive nature of information technology in contemporary life, few people as yet (and teachers are no exception) fully comprehend the extent of its influence and intrusion into the very fabric of their daily lives. It seems to us of paramount importance that teachers in particular should acquire a 'better-than-average' understanding of the uses and implications of information technology if we are looking to schools to ensure that future generations are computer literate, competent citizens of twenty-first-century society.

Let's be quite clear what we mean, and what we don't mean, by the term 'computer' or 'information literate'. In comparison with the number of people who will need to be competent users of information and information technology in the workforce of the 1990s, the number of highly trained technicians, systems analysts and computer programmers will be very small indeed. The uses of information-handling devices based upon microtechnology are developing and spreading so fast that soon there will hardly be a job which does not depend, in one form or another, on its application. Very often of course we don't even realise that what we are doing actually involves the new technology; what is certain however, is that our efficiency in using it is very much enhanced by a familiarity with its ways. Our immediate concern here is not so much with how a specific aspect of information technology 'works' as such, but how best we can use it to achieve the purposes we have in mind. In brief, a familiarity with the potential of the new technology leads us to newer, quicker and more efficient ways of doing things and, in some cases, to a realisation that we are now able to accomplish what previously was totally beyond our grasp. In the classroom context this is particularly true of such things as simulations, wordprocessors, desktop publishers and databases. Being well informed about this or any other new technology means, of course, that we now have the choice of whether to use it or not. If we understand its strengths and its weaknesses, what a new technology does well, what it does badly and how it can be abused, we are in a better position to decide when, where, and how it should be used.

What we are concerned with here, then, is not the preparation of technicians or experts; rather, the guidance of potential users of information technology towards informed and effective decision-making about their particular requirements. The need to raise the computer or information literacy of the population has finally been enshrined in the legislation of the 1988 Education Reform Act. The consequent implementation of the National Curriculum will locate information technology as a central and vital part of school life for all those between the ages of 5 and 16.

A Reluctance to Embrace the Technology

Despite the remarkable advances achieved by MEP, MESU, the local education authorities and numerous colleges and universities up and down the country, many teachers remain untouched by the introduction of information technology to schools. Whilst initially this could be attributed perhaps to the compartmentalisation of subjects within the curriculum, such that those teachers who had expertise, interest and equipment often tended to be in secondary school mathematics and science departments, this is now no longer the case. Computers are distributed throughout many schools. Thanks moreover to the highly successful 'Micros in Schools' scheme initiated by the Department of Trade and Industry, there are more computers available than ever. That is not to say there are enough. Some secondary schools have had the added bonus of TVEI funds to supplement their provision of information technology, but many small primary schools still depend on the goodwill of parents to raise money to purchase further hardware and software. That there are more computers in schools than ever before does not mean there are enough for one in every classroom.

It's reasonable to assume therefore that one reason for the reluctance to get involved may well be a continuing problem of access. This is not the whole story by any means, however. As our account unfolds in forthcoming chapters, readers will come to see, as we did, that people need time to identify uses of the technology for themselves. Telling people that information technology is for them does not necessarily work. On the contrary it may well serve to strengthen resolutions not to get involved whatever happens! We have colleagues who still insist on producing everything in longhand, whose manuscripts are covered with correcting fluid and fitted together with sticky tape like a jigsaw. Their main stock in trade consists of a pencil and a pair of scissors. This seems woefully inefficient to those of us who have mastered the wordprocessor. Essentially, the point is that one really has to *want* to attain computer literacy before it seems worth attempting that steep climb up the learning curve. You have got to identify a use, an advantage to yourself, even if subsequently you discover how unrealistic your initial expectations were.

A Typical School and Two Typical Teachers

For the purposes of our study it was important to select a school which would be reasonably representative of its kind. Broadwood Primary School, in our estimation, was typical although it must be said that not every headteacher would be prepared to tolerate the intrusion of a research team and not every teacher would agree to be observed, told what to do, questioned, and have his/her lessons disrupted by our constant comings and goings. Naturally we tried to blend into the surroundings as much as possible and make a positive contribution to classroom life by encouraging our two research assistants to become as much a part of the action as possible. It was as important for the school staff to feel that they were getting something out of the exercise as it was for us to try out our ideas and to collect our data. Having said this it will be evident that the chosen school came from a subset of self-selected schools in the area which were or would have been willing to cooperate.

Other factors also applied. Since our project was to be part of a European collaboration between Great Britain, France and Belgium, certain things had to be common to the chosen schools in all three countries. Thus, we all were obliged to choose a school that had not previously been used for experimental work in the past. Moreover, we all agreed to concentrate on the 9–11-year-olds with at least one female teacher. The choice of just one school and two of its teachers does not provide data that can be readily subject to statistical analysis. Over the period of a year, however, it does permit ample opportunity for study in depth. The choice of school, as a school typical of its kind, is important in that it allows us to make a small amount of cautious generalisation and to offer conclusions and suggestions which might be relevant to teachers in many other schools similar to Broadwood Primary.

The Broad Focus of the Project

Chapter 3 includes an explanation of the term 'ethnographic' that appears in the sub-title of the book and an outline of the methodology that guided our research. For the moment, it is sufficient to say a few words about the broad focus and intention of the project.

The central aim of the research was to understand the ways in which teachers and pupils came to grips with the computers that we introduced into their classrooms from 1987 onwards. Understanding teachers' and pupils' behaviour towards the computer meant observing them, talking to them and, most importantly, getting them to talk to us about their experience.

The teacher talk and pupil talk that is the bedrock of our study can be thought of as 'accounting'. Accounting refers to speech which accompanies action. Such speech is intended to make action intelligible and justifiable in occurring at the time and the place that it does. By way of example, Leah's sudden and seemingly aggressive lunge at her companion at the computer in Mrs. Green's classroom one morning was explicated by the words, 'You don't need two l's in "child" ', and in consequence, her action ceased to be offensive to her classmate, Felicity, and was readily understandable to us as observers.

Coping with Computers is replete with numerous sequences of teachers' (and, to a lesser extent, pupils') accounting for their actions (and inactions!) during the course of the study. The task of the researchers is to make teachers' and pupils' accounts meaningful to you, our readers, by locating them within the context of constant change that constituted life in classrooms at Broadwood Primary School. In brief, *Coping with Computers* is an account of accounts.

2
THE PLACE, THE PEOPLE, THE PROGRAMME OF EVENTS

The School

Broadwood Primary School is situated between two contrasting housing estates on the outskirts of a small thriving market town in the East Midlands. To the south is a large sprawling council estate leading down to the University campus. To the north bordering on to open farmland and woodland, there is a relatively new estate of owner-occupied detached and semi-detached houses, some suited for large families and others designed for first-time buyers. Both estates form part of Broadwood's catchment area and provide a ready supply of children. No falling roles here. At the time we began our study there were approximately 250 children between the ages of 5 and 11 years in the school. Originally built to house fewer than this, Broadwood Primary has several rather unsightly mobile classrooms on the ample playing field adjacent to the main school building. They cannot be seen from the front entrance. The main school building is of a purpose-built open-plan design with infant class areas at one end gradually moving up the age groups to the upper juniors at the other.

The Staff

The school staff is almost entirely female, having a non-teaching head, eight full-time teachers, five ancillary workers and one male teacher, the deputy head. In addition to this, and common in many British primary schools, a small number of parents, invariably women, are to be found working with small groups of children under the supervision of one of the qualified teaching staff.

Posts of special responsibility exist for language development, library and resources, art, craft and design technology, mathematics, science, environmental studies and computing, coordination of studies between infant and junior classes and expressive arts.

The Children

Because of the varied nature of the school's catchment area, some children come from quite severely socially disadvantaged families. For example, at the time of the study, 40% of children qualified for free meals, 30% of families had more than four children, 30% of the families had only one natural parent or were single-parent families and 23% were involved in some way with the social services. Despite the potentially disruptive nature of some of these children, discipline in the school is good.

Computer Equipment in the School

When we began our research the school only had one computer, a BBC model B with disc drive but no printer. In order to encourage computer-based activity further in the school, two more computers of the same type were loaned by the University so that the two participating teachers could each have a computer permanently installed in her class area. Both classes were vertically grouped third and fourth year (9–11-year-olds), situated adjacent to one another at one end of the main school building. The open-plan design meant that activities in each area were visible for all to see, something which proved to be very useful as the project developed.

The Participating Teachers

Our two teachers were both experienced, having been at Broadwood for some time. Joan had trained as a mature student some nine years previously and held a post of special responsibility for library and resources. Although she had attended a course on using the computer in the library, and had experimented with a handful of drill-and-practice programs in the classroom, she had no formal training or experience with the computer in the classroom, nor did she have a computer at home. Pauline had also trained as a mature student some four years previously. Her post of special responsibility was for reading and language development. Although she had a personal computer at home, she had had very little experience of using it. In the classroom setting, her experience had been confined to the same handful of drill-and-practice programs used by Joan.

An Outline Plan of the Study

It was our intention to spend a whole year with Pauline and Joan in their classrooms, helping them to learn about and integrate information technology into their curriculum. At the same time we wanted to identify a small group of children who, whilst having positive views of themselves as learners, had unusually low self-images in relation to using the computer. It was our intention to encourage the two teachers to provide special help and encouragement for these children, in the form of extra computer time or the opportunity to work with children who had particularly positive attitudes towards computers in order to see just what improvement that might make to our 'target' pupils' views of themselves.

For this purpose we employed two part-time research assistants, both experienced primary school teachers, to work alongside Pauline, Joan and the children. The research assistants were to collect information for the project and play the role of parent/helpers under the direct supervision of the two teachers. In chronological order the stages of the project were as follows:

September 1986 Work in the classroom was supposed to start but there was a holdup in the funding from the EEC. Training sessions started with the two teachers visiting the University on several occasions. Fieldwork was postponed until January.

January 1987 Jane, our first research assistant, joined us and observations began in the two classrooms. Each teacher had a computer permanently installed in her area. During January all children in the two classes were tested and the special 'target' group identified. The teachers were informed of the test results and asked to provide special treatment for the target group. Training continued in school during lunch breaks. Children were observed at the computer using a systematic observation instrument, C.O.M.I.C.

April 1987 Both teachers underwent a focused interview to ascertain their feelings about the progress of the work.

May 1987 Sue, our second research assistant, joined the team to work in school with Jane. Systematic observations continued. Training was switched to the University every Wednesday afternoon. This proved more successful, away from the pressures of school. All children were tested again.

September 1987 A new batch of third years joined both classes. These were tested for the first time. Systematic observations continued. A parents' evening was held to inform them about the work and to encourage their participation.

November 1987 Teachers and research assistants were asked to begin writing (independently) their own accounts of the introduction and use of all computer programs. Systematic observation continued.

December 1987 Teachers' and researchers' accounts were completed. Observations ceased on the last day of term.

3
MATTERS OF METHODOLOGY

Ethnography or Participant Observation? Matters of Definition

The first task in this chapter is to explain our choice of the word 'ethnographic' as it appears in the sub-title of the book. We then have something to say about the ways we set about collecting and analysing our data.

Ethnography, according to Geertz (1973), is both the process and the product of the study of human culture; a succinct definition that has appeal and application. Because it is the process and the product of change in pupils and teachers that is the focus of our study, the word ethnographic seems to encapsulate the essence of our research interest in the course and content of transformations that occurred in two Leicestershire classrooms during 1987 and 1988. And yet we have misgivings about using a grandiose word like ethnography to describe our account of what took place at Broadwood Primary School. This is no false modesty on our part. In a recent analysis, Woods (1986) distinguishes between two approaches to ethnography. On the one hand there are those who see ethnography as exclusively descriptive of particular situations and, in consequence, limited by the distinctive nature of the information it uncovers. On the other hand, Woods asserts, there are those who prefer to see ethnography as 'generalizing, comparative and theoretical'. The two approaches, the *idiographic* and the *normative* are not, of course, mutually exclusive though we share Woods' view that there are few notable exceptions to a general atheoretical trend in contemporary ethnographic research. Our study is no exception in that, like many others, it belongs to a descriptive genre that seeks primarily to map out areas of classroom life that have had little exploration to date. Perhaps it would be wiser to eschew the term ethnography altogether and settle for an alternative descriptor of data collection and analysis. Since participating and observing are the essential activities in the methodology we chose to use at Broadwood Primary School, participant observation might better describe our approach.

Bryman (1988) defines participant observation as the sustained immersion of the researcher among those whom he or she seeks to study with a view to generating a rounded, in-depth account of the group, organization, or whatever, a sober explanation striking precisely that note of balance and moderation to which we aspire in setting out this account of happenings at Broadwood School. And yet, it leaves us hankering after an essential 'process and flux' of events that was a *daily actuality* in the lives of pupils, teachers and observers during the course of the project. For ethnography, as Taft (1988) reminds us, is not equivalent to participant observation in so far as researchers' involvement in the normal activities of a group should be treated as a case of partial acculturation in which they acquire an insider's knowledge of the group through their direct experience with it. These experiences, Taft asserts, provide investigators with tacit knowledge which helps them understand the significance to the group members of their own behaviour and that of others, enabling researchers to integrate their observations about the behaviour with information gained from other sources such as records, documents or interviews with informants. Ethnography, then, involves more than participant observation as defined earlier. The fact that researchers have a role within the group, Taft observes, not only requires them to be conscious of their own influence, but may also give them an emotional stake in a particular research outcome. We raise this specific issue in a later chapter (see page 85). For the moment, suffice it to say that deliberations about terminology were resolved by our decision to settle for the word ethnographic in the sub-title of the book as best representing both the spirit that guided our purposes and the piecemeal product that has resulted from our year-long intrusion into the lives of pupils and staff at Broadwood Primary School.

All in all, the research team spent in excess of 600 hours in the classrooms of Pauline Green and Joan Brown. As participant observers, Sue Gray and Jane White recorded fieldnotes covering some 200 or more hours of working with pupils at the computer, discussing happenings and events with Pauline and Joan, recording interactions on C.O.M.I.C. profiles and testing and interviewing target children on two occasions. The observers' fieldnotes were shared with us at regular intervals and became a focus of discussion among the research team about the direction of the study and the feelings of its adult and pupil participants. As we show in Chapters 5 and 6, the on-going records of events in the two classrooms alerted us both to progress and to problems, enabling us to take specific issues back to the teachers and thus to accommodate and to change emphases, expectations or procedures in light of exigencies as they occurred. We are reminded here of the essentially social nature of educational research:

> Social research must be treated as a process in which the researcher constructs lines of action over time to try to achieve his goals in the situations which face him; negotiating with others, and making trade-off decisions between imperfect alternatives. In turn, these lines of action structure his options in the future and thereby shape the nature of his findings.

Hammersley's (1983) cogent comment precisely pinpoints the unpredictability of ethnographic research. Our study is no exception. Inevitably, the end result of the social activity that we here choose to call ethnographic research is that Informants and hosts tell their stories, and in turn, the ethnographers have their own tales to tell (Atkinson, (1980). Of necessity, the tale we propose to tell in this chapter begins with some 'whys' and 'whats' of practices and procedures in data collection and analysis.

The Choice of Both Quantitative and Qualitative Measures

It is inappropriate here to enter into a protracted debate about competing epistemological positions associated with the use of quantitative and qualitative techniques of data collection. Interested readers are referred to the excellent account in Bryman (1988).

It is equally unsatisfactory, however, simply to signal accord with Taft's (1988) observation that ethnographic studies gain credibility when they combine both subjective and objective methods, and then proceed to set out a quantitative–qualitative research 'stall' for our readers' delectation.

We employed a variety of quantitative and qualitative methods of data collection for the following reasons. First, we believe that in specific instances, quick, quantitative techniques of data gathering are appropriate (in respect of, for example, pupils' attitudes, self-images, and patterns of interaction) particularly in view of the ethical and logistic problems raised by protracted intrusions into the lives of pupils in school.

Second, and equally importantly, a judicious use of quantitative and qualitative approaches to data collection allows us to address fundamental issues of methodological rigour concerning ethnographic studies. Those issues centre upon the question of verification.

Verification

The 'climate of distrust' (Fairbrother, 1977) said to surround ethnography arises in no small degree from what its critics proclaim as its lack of methodological rigour – in particular, the absence of those statistical techniques of verification that are available to the positivistic researcher (Ball, 1988). But verification techniques *are* available in ethnographic research. Two of the most common, *respondent validation* and *triangulation*, were employed throughout the present study.

Respondent validation involved us in sharing with pupils and teachers our accounts of the classroom events we observed in order to ascertain that our interpretations of those happenings corresponded with the viewpoints of the actors themselves. Triangulation is commonly held to be the application and combination of several research methodologies in the study of the same phenomenon (Denzin, 1988). Strictly speaking, however, that definition refers to methodological triangulation, one of four basic types of triangulation identified in the literature: *data* triangulation, *investigator* triangulation, *theory* triangulation and *methodological* triangulation.

Methodological triangulation involved us in using interaction coding schedules, questionnaires, self-concept scales, sociometric measures, interviews, teacher ratings and research assistants' observations to increase the accuracy of our interpretation of changes occurring in six specially selected pupils in each of the two classrooms at Broadwood Primary School. Furthermore, methodological triangulation required us to work with Pauline's and Joan's written accounts of their experiences with the computer, together with the observations that Sue and Jane made of computer use in the teachers' classrooms, and the intensive, focused interviews of Pauline and Joan undertaken from time to time by Derek Blease. In this way we were able to produce our account of the transformation that took place in the thinking and the practice of the two teachers during the course of the research.

Quantitative Measures

We selected a number of quantitative measures to elicit pupils' self-images as learners, their determination to achieve academically, their choice of workmates and their views of themselves as computer users. In addition, we sought teachers' predictions of pupil self-images, constructed a questionnaire about out-of-school computer use which could be crudely quantified and, finally, adapted a systematic observation schedule specifically for the study.

Academic Self-Image (Barker-Lunn, 1970)

This short measure of children's views of themselves in terms of their school work was originally constructed from the responses of 400 children randomly selected from a large, representative sample of 2,300 boys and girls in fourth-year primary school classrooms. The scale has had wide use in British studies, is interesting and easy to complete and has high internal consistency (alpha-coefficient = 0.88). The nine-item scale contains such items as shown in Figure 3.1.

	Response		
	Hardly ever	**Sometimes**	**Never**
I get lots of sums wrong	☐	☐	☐
	Yes	**Not sure**	**No**
My teacher thinks I'm clever	☐	☐	☐

Figure 3.1   Academic self-image: nine-item scale

Self-Peer Ranking of Achievement Motivation (Holmes, 1971)

A self-peer ranking method of measuring determination to achieve in school was adapted in format and wording from that outlined by Holmes and Tyler (1968) and Holmes (1971). The original scale, developed for use with older students, produced a correlation of 0.33 ($p = 0.005$) between class grades and self-ranked need to achieve. The format of our adapted measure is set out below. A pupil's self-peer rank score is simply the number of fellow pupils to whom he/she gives a zero rating.

NAME: _____

Here is a list of all the boys and girls in your class.
First, cross out your own name on the list.
Now look carefully at each name in turn.

If you think that a particular boy or girl *generally tries harder than you do at school work* put a 1 next to his or her name.

If you think that a particular boy or girl *generally tries less hard than you do at school work* put a 0 next to his or her name.

Be sure to write either a 1 or a 0 next to each name on the list.

Choice of Workmates

At the bottom of the self-peer ranking of achievement motivation measure was the question:

WHOM DO YOU LIKE TO WORK WITH IN CLASS?
WRITE IN THREE NAMES

_____   _____   _____

This measure of pupils' choice-status within their classrooms was intended to provide an 'insider's view' of the sociometric status of class members with respect to their work groups, to be used *inter alia*, alongside observers' ratings and teachers' assessments to construct compatible computer-work 'environments' for target pupils (see page 119). Each work-choice carried one point, research evidence suggesting that there is little to choose between the use of weighted or unweighted scores (Gronlund, 1955; 1959). A pupil's choice-status was determined by:

$$\text{Choice} = \frac{\text{Number of persons choosing individual}}{N - 1}$$

where N = The number of persons in the group.

The choice-status data enabled us to construct two further sociometric indices (Proctor and Loomis, 1951) intended to throw further light on the classroom environments. These were a measure of group cohesiveness where

$$\text{Cohesion} = \frac{\text{Number of reciprocated choices}}{\text{Total possible number of reciprocated choices}}$$

(where choice is restricted to x permitted choices, the total possible number of reciprocated choices is $xN/2$) and a measure of the integrativeness of a group where

$$\text{Integration} = \frac{1}{\text{Number of persons receiving no choices}}.$$

These indices were computed for both classrooms in January and May 1987. On neither occasion did they provide any differentiation between the classes. They do not, therefore, feature in any of our analyses.

Pupils' Views of Themselves as Computer Users

An important criticism of many measures of self-concept is that they are constructed by researchers who impose upon respondents descriptions of the self that are theirs rather than the subject's. Scales that permit a respondent to describe his/her unique self in terms of his/her unique self-perceptions go a long way to answering such criticism. Our adaptation of Kilpatrick and Cantril's (1965) self-anchoring scaling technique goes only some way along that road.

Seven aspects of working with a computer were drawn up by the researchers together with carefully matched statements to illustrate them to which pupils could readily respond.

The aspects of computer work were:

1.   keyboard skills
2.   playing games
3.   knowledge of the computer
4.   following instructions
5.   success with computer-based exercises
6.   relations with group
7.   motivation/interest

The seven aspects were illustrated by the following statements:

1.   Pressing the right keys most of the time.
2.   Doing well at computer games.
3.   Knowing all about how to use the computer.
4.   Understanding what the computer wants you to do.
5.   Getting the right answers to the computer's questions.
6.   Helping other pupils understand how to use the computer.
7.   Wanting to use the computer.

Each of these seven statements was placed in a 'box' at the top of a ten-rung ladder, the top rung (10) indicating *the very best*, the bottom rung (0) *the very worst*. Pupils were asked to put a tick on the ladder to indicate where they saw themselves at that moment in time. Part of the self-anchoring scale is illustrated in Figure 3.2. In addition to separate scores (0–10) for each of the seven statements, an overall self-image as computer-user score was computed for each pupil.

The very best	10
	9
	8
	7
	6
	5
	4
	3
	2
	1
The very worst	0

Figure 3.2   *Understanding what the computer wants you to do*

Logbooks of Computer Use in School

On each occasion that pupils worked at the classroom computer(s) they were required to enter their name, the date, the name of the program used and the amount of time spent at the computer. Observers monitored the early stages of this recording duty until they were satisfied that it was being accurately carried out. Inspection of the logbooks of both classes suggests that the children responded to the task in exemplary fashion.

Out-of-School Computer Access and Use

An indication of pupils' access to and use of a computer out-of-school was obtained by means of the following questionnaire. Points were awarded as indicated on the measure, pupils' scores ranging from 0 to 8.

1. Do you have a computer at home?

Y	N
1	0

2. Does it belong to you or someone else in the house?

Y	N

3. If it is someone else who is it? _____

4. If you share the computer at home, with whom do you share it? _____

5. How often do you use the computer at home?

every day	times a week	times a month
3	2	1

6. Do you use a computer anywhere else than at home or school?

Y	N
1	0

7. If yes, where is it? _____

8. How often do you use it?

every day	times a week	times a month
3	2	1

Teacher Ratings of Pupils

Our general impression of different 'climates' in the two classrooms at Broadwood Primary School was confirmed by discussions with the observers, Sue and Jane. Without putting too fine a point on it, Pauline's approach was more relaxed, less directive and less sanctioning than Joan's. Pupils in Mrs. Brown's classroom knew exactly how she rated most aspects of their performance and behaviour!

One of the ways in which we tried to derive an indirect assessment of the learning environments of the pupils in Pauline's and Joan's classes was to ask both teachers to predict the names of those pupils who had rated themselves highest and lowest on the various self-image measures that had been collected at the beginning of the project. The task given to Mrs. Green and Mrs. Brown related to children's self-images of academic ability, their determination to succeed, their popularity as work partners and their views of themselves as computer users.

Our hunch was that in Joan's more directive classroom, where children were more frequently in receipt of positive and negative sanctions, there would be a greater degree of concordance between pupils' self-images and Joan's predictions than in the less directive classroom of Pauline. The results of the analysis are given on page 156.

C.O.M.I.C. (Categories for Observing Microcomputer use in Classrooms)

C.O.M.I.C. is a systematic observation schedule we designed to record the proportion of time children spend on various tasks when using the computer. (See Appendix I for a detailed description.) There are twelve observation categories in all, subdivided into two groups, one for 'on task' behaviour including system management, using the software, performing computer-related tasks, and interaction with others, and the other for 'off task' behaviour including interaction with others and performing non-computer-related tasks. On each occasion the observer sits where the children can be clearly seen and heard, the target child being the one operating the computer. The categories of behaviour are recorded at regular ten-second intervals, thus leaving sufficient time to write brief descriptive details about the context and interaction between members of the group throughout the session. Observations can continue for as long as twenty to thirty minutes at a time.

The data are treated in exactly the same way as the Flanders Inter Action Categories (Flanders, 1970). That is to say, observation tallies are arranged in pairs so that each event becomes the second part of one pair and the first part of the next. Individual pairs are then counted up and entered on a 12×12 grid to reveal an overall profile of the types and frequencies of behaviour whilst a particular program is in use. Thus, C.O.M.I.C. profiles enabled us to compare and contrast proportions of time expended in operating the hardware or using the software across the various programs introduced into Pauline's and Joan's classes.

Qualitative Measures

Discussions with our observers, Sue and Jane, and a perusal of their fieldnotes suggest that, overall, they had spent roughly half their time in school engaged in collecting what, loosely, could be called quantitative data and the other half in producing qualitative observational records. We say 'roughly' and 'loosely' because it is impossible to be more exact about these matters. By far and away the greatest part of the time spent assembling quantitative data was in connection with the production of numerous C.O.M.I.C. interaction schedules. But since these themselves were liberally annotated with on-the-spot comments on particular happenings or events, it is futile and foolhardy to attempt to disentangle quantitative from qualitative data in this regard.

Observers' Diaries

Sue and Jane produced detailed records of happenings at Broadwood Primary School in the form of diaries, sometimes on a daily basis. These were invaluable sources of data in helping us understand the ebb and flow of events in Pauline's and Joan's classrooms and the discontinuous nature of their 'progress' with computers. Sue's diary for the week commencing June 23rd 1987 contains the following:

> Jane and I discussed the dangers of becoming so confident and competent that the teachers would not bother to carry out or try out the programs for themselves. . . . There is a definite need to restrain enthusiasm and be backward in coming forward. . . . Pauline felt guilty at not starting anything new and felt distracted by having a sick child at home. . . . I took my lead from Joan who seemed keen to complete her INFORM information. . . .

Researchers' On-Going Accounts and Observations

We too made a practice of identifying and commenting on what we regarded as significant events as they occurred, particularly so when they appeared out of keeping with our preconceptions or expectations. Often our accounts are compiled from observers' diaries and their informal discussions with Pauline and Joan. Here, for example, are our observations on the teachers' rationale for constructing computer work groups at the beginning of the project.

Grouping children to use the computer (20/25.2.87)

Having obtained pupils' responses to measures of academic self-image, achievement motivation, choice-status and self-ranking on computer use, we then invited their teachers to give us the names of five children in their classes whom they rated *highest* on each of these characteristics and five whom they rated *lowest*. Pupils' self-ratings and teachers' estimations were then compared. Statistically, the accuracy of both teachers in identifying 'high' and 'low' children on one or more of the profiles was beyond chance occurrence, one of the teacher's success being significantly better than that of her colleague. Once we had completed the scoring of each child's set of profiles, the results were given to the teachers.

Somewhat naively we expected that Mrs. Brown and Mrs. Green would want to make immediate use of the information we made available in order to constitute pupil groups for working on the computer. This was not the case.

The diary records of the classroom observers show that, initially at least, allocation of non-target children to work groups was made more or less on an ad hoc basis – 'those who would not mess about', or 'those who had finished their sewing', or 'because these three hadn't done well enough last time'. Observers' notes show that groups of three frequently developed problems. [Tann (in Simon and Willcocks, 1981) found that teacher-selected mixed-sex groups were grudgingly tolerated at best or totally non-functioning at worst.]

> The boy disagreed fairly consistently with the choices agreed upon by the two girls. On the basis that two to one is a majority, the girls' choices were usually implemented. Occasionally the boy rushed in first and entered his choice before the girls could do

anything about it. Kristian felt rather fed-up and wished that he was sharing with one or two other boys.

The observer sat with Benjamin, Brian and Sonia. . . . The children reached consensus fairly amicably to begin with but Sonia began to feel left out and dissatisfied. Her suggestions were consistently ignored until she said, 'Shall I just watch you two then and write what *I* want in *my* notebook?' A few minutes later she said to the observer, 'It's been a disaster. I shouldn't have come with these two but Mrs. Brown chose us.'

Richard and Wayne ignored Timothy and discussed their answers together. He tried to be included but they ignored his suggestions. He quickly gave up trying to be involved and looked around the room, daydreamed, gazed out of the window, sang little ditties made up from words on the computer screen and used his clipboard as a steering wheel. . . . When the first summary came up on the screen, Richard and Wayne began to take notes. 'I'm not going to bloody write that!' said Tim.

The observer probed the teachers about the basis of their allocation of pupils to computer groups. '*How is it decided who works with whom?*'
   Mrs. Green feels that she has to choose this year. This, she asserts, is because she has a high proportion of older boys who would sit in front of the computer and do nothing if they were allowed to choose their own partners. This is one reason why mixed sex groups are constituted in Pauline's classroom.
   Mrs. Brown has a different mix of children. Her choices vary according to the situation, she explains. Sometimes friendship choices are made. Occasionally, if a few children have finished their other activities, they use the computer. In such instances, she allows up to four children to work in a group.

Seeing Through the Eyes of Others

The *sine qua non* of qualitative research is, in Bryman's (1988) words, an express commitment to viewing events, action, norms and values from the perspective of the people being studied.... The strategy of taking the subject's perspective is often expressed in terms of *seeing through the eyes of the people you are studying*. Whilst this approach implies long periods of participant observation, Bryman continues, other methods, notably in-depth, unstructured interviewing are also employed.

Our commitment to seeing events through the eyes of teachers and pupils involved us, *inter alia*, in both participant observations and interviews. Perhaps an account of our methods ought to begin with some outline of our initial encounters with staff and pupils.

Getting to Know the Teachers

Familiarity with school ethnographies makes one acutely aware of the importance of initial encounters; first impressions carry positive or negative charges whose potencies persist long into the life of research projects. Thus our early visits to Broadwood Primary were marked by several self-reminders of the pejorative images that some university staff manage to create in the minds of their colleagues in school (Freeman, 1986). We had no wish to be seen as 'day-trip' researchers (Denscombe, 1983), using 'snap-shot approaches' (Stones, 1986) – here today and gone tomorrow with the data!

We were conscious, too, of the dangers of appearing in the guise of those research metaphors so eloquently described by Jenkins (Shipman, 1974). We wanted to avoid 'gift of grace', 'cargo cult' and 'free sample' images despite the fact that we were intent upon alerting the teachers to the educational potentials of several novel computer programs and that we had a modest yet welcome amount within our research budget specifically designated for spending within the school on computer equipment and/or computer-related materials.

We were fortunate in one sense that we had no need to establish a 'way-in' (Beynon, 1983) to the school. That had already been done for us by a former colleague who had used a program called MICRO MAP with children in Mrs. Brown's and Mrs. Green's classes and had negotiated with Mrs. Black, the headteacher, to undertake a microcomputer project in the school should a research bid prove successful. Initial overtures for an EEC-sponsored research project had been made by him. When he and his whole research team were 'headhunted' overnight by an industrial concern, the present authors completed negotiations for the EEC contract and undertook the joint planning of a research programme with the University of Liège and L'Ecole de Science de l'Homme, Paris.

But now, our ease of entry to Broadwood Primary carried with it, in effect, a commitment in advance to a research location that might not have been our first choice had we had charge of planning the study from the outset: a conjecture that came to mind again, momentarily, later on in the project. By that time, teachers, observers and researchers were more 'at home' in each other's company. It was a chance remark of Mrs. Green, who said, 'Look – we didn't volunteer for this [the project]. We were *volunteered*', that brought us up sharp. We had been practising our skills in perceptive listening (Pope and Denicolo, 1986) to our colleagues' comments and commentaries for several months. This nugget of knowledge in the course of a casual aside helped explain a great deal of what, until then, had lain just below the surface of our understanding.

Lest the phrase 'getting to know the teachers' sounds somewhat unidirectional and out of keeping with the essence of an ethnographic study, what we wish to convey is better put, perhaps, by Hitchcock (1983): Ethnography must be viewed and documented as a *members' accomplishment* (our emphasis). In 'getting to know the teachers' we were at one and the same time addressing the wider issue of how we, the researchers, observers, teachers and pupils, produced for ourselves actual accounts of the world while also engaged in creating that world (Hitchcock, 1983). In 'getting to know the teachers' we were, initially at least, hard at work in creating our own credibility with them. On that score we operated on several fronts simultaneously. We judged (correctly as it turned out) that both the research assistants appointed to act as observers and ourselves had valuable 'idiosyncratic credit' (Hollander, 1964) that we would do well to cash in, for each of us had held full-time teaching posts in primary schools for at least six years. We lost no time on this matter. Quite by chance, too, at the beginning of the research, one of the authors was teaching secondary science in a local comprehensive in fulfilment of the Council for the Accreditation of Teacher Education (CATE) requirement of 'recent and relevant experience'. By a stroke of good fortune, Mrs. Green's husband taught in the same school. More importantly, perhaps, word had it that the 'recent and relevant' was also 'successful' teaching experience.

In addition, one of us had the pleasant task of introducing Mrs. Brown and Mrs. Green to the various programs that were to be used during the course of the project. One afternoon a week at the University, away from the ever-present pressures of pupils, the teachers were able to get to know us differently, to enter an alternative environment of learning and, perhaps, better judge our claim to some expertise in the research in which we were jointly involved. Time out of school, too, offered valuable occasions to strengthen social relationships. So too did lunch at the University, a social evening for those involved in the research and a three-day visit to Belgium during which time Mrs. Green and Mrs. Brown were able to make an extended visit to Crisnée, a small village where the language-teaching-through-computers project was located in the local primary school.

More than anything else, however, it was our persisting presence in Broadwood Primary School that brought researchers and teachers together. For Mrs. White and Mrs. Gray, our research assistants, were more than mere classroom observers. Their teaching qualifications and experience enabled them to contribute valuable (and, indeed, valued) help on a regular basis with small groups of children working at the computers. In addition, they served as 'parent/helpers' on a school visit to York and as extra pairs of hands on both churchyard visits to Quorn and Thorpe Acre and on the trip to the stately home at Beaumanor Hall.

Getting to know the teachers also involved us in sharing with them the information we had derived from the pupils in respect of their academic self-images, motivation and views of themselves as computer users.

Finally, we employed a range of information-gathering techniques to suit our several purposes during the eleven months we were at the school. Observation schedules, participant observation records, daily diaries, questionnaires, interviews (both structured and informal) and personal statements prepared for us by Mrs. Green and Mrs. Brown at the end of the study comprised the armamentarium of research tools by which to tell our tale of events at Broadwood Primary.

The Teachers' Accounts

Pauline and Joan were encouraged to reflect upon several substantive issues to do with the introduction of computers into their classrooms and to write, openly and honestly, of their fears and frustrations as well as any feelings of success and achievement that they might have experienced during the course of the research.

Their reflections (see Chapter 6) have been particularly helpful to us in piecing together a chronological jigsaw of disparate commentaries, observations and interview data that now serves as our account of the progress of the project at Broadwood Primary School.

By way of example, part of Joan's commentary is set out below:

> Another problem during the Summer Term seemed to be difficulties with the hardware. This proved particularly frustrating as one wasted a lot of time trying to get a program to work, while the children were getting restless and needed our attention. Because we were

inexperienced, we tended to blame ourselves and think we were doing something wrong. It was a relief to discover that the disc or computer was malfunctioning. . . .

The group contained a number of disruptive and rather silly children and some of these children chose to put in some silly statements, either without discussion with their partner, or deliberately. On the program you could make changes, but a whole section of work had to be redone. This was fine if the facts put in were inappropriate, but proved tiresome if the children had made a few spelling mistakes or grammatical errors. For the less able children this wasted a lot of time.

The Headteacher's Account

Our understanding of the teething problems experienced at the beginning of the project was further broadened by Mrs. Black's reflections on events during the first term of 1987:

When I approached Pauline and Joan, their reaction was tentative interest coupled with anxiety at the extra work it was going to produce. At this stage they could not be expected to see the advantage of integration. Indeed, with a particularly difficult group of 4th year boys that year, it was not surprising that they probably regarded the project as just 'one more thing to do'. . . .

Progress seemed slow initially. I felt both teachers were struggling to use the computer – as an afterthought – in their work planning. It was set up from time-to-time in their area – usually on a day when Derek was expected! However, as interest grew it did come out more often. For the first three months it was a burden and both teachers displayed some anxiety and stress. I felt guilty for imposing on them. My own absence from school for five weeks meant I was out of touch and unable to support and encourage.

Getting to Know the Children

We used a variety of ways of getting to know each of the pupils in the study. Most had record cards containing information on their school careers since entry at 5 years of age and these were available for scrutiny. From the outset of the research, moreover, classroom observers maintained a daily diary of events from which we were able to extract a wealth of data on formal and informal behavioural and verbal interactions of pupils with pupils, pupils with teachers and pupils with observers across the full range of classroom activities. Coffee breaks provided opportunities to glean additional information on the family circumstances of individual pupils, of their teachers' feelings and attitudes towards them and, equally importantly, of the 'staffroom view' of the proclivities of particular boys and girls.

During the week following the start of the study, small groups of pupils were extracted from both classes and invited to complete questionnaires designed to provide information about: (1) their self-images as learners; (2) their determination to succeed; (3) their choice of workmates; and (4) their views of themselves as computer users. At a later stage, a further questionnaire elicited details of pupils' opportunities to use computers out of school.

The scales of academic self-image (Barker-Lunn, 1970) and achievement motivation (Holmes and Tyler, 1968; Holmes, 1971) that were finally selected as research instruments (see pages 10–12) had been used successfully in previous studies of primary school pupils. Moreover, a recent study (Crocker and Cheesman, 1988) has confirmed that the youngest pupils in schools quickly acquire knowledge of the academic criteria their teachers employ in evaluating their work and that high levels of agreement exist as to the rank order of children in any particular classroom. The measure of a child's choice-status within a group (Gronlund, 1959) is widely reported in the literature. The self-anchoring scaling technique (Kilpatrick and Cantril, 1965) we adapted to obtain children's ratings of themselves as computer users proved attractive to respondents and easy to complete. However, we were concerned to know not only *how* boys and girls rated themselves on seven aspects of computer use but also *why* they assigned particular values to these various aspects of their skills. Specifically selected children were therefore interviewed and encouraged to explain the basis of the decisions underlying their self-awarded scores.

These pupils' explanations highlight some of the limitations of quantitative measures and the dangers of over-reliance on questionnaire data.

Doing well at computer games

Carl   I only gave myself 7 on that because I thought you meant these games [pointing to the screen]. If it was games at home I'm brilliant at those. I'd have given myself 10.

(Self-rating 7)

Wanting to use the computer

Heidi   If it's reading time and I'm really stuck into a book I hope Mrs. Green doesn't choose me. If I was doing something boring I would want to go on the computer.

(Self-rating 5)

Children's self-assessments and subsequent explanations, teachers' comments on pupils' record cards and observers' diary entries were collated in order to broaden and deepen our understanding of individual boys and girls.

By way of example we have assembled various sources of information on one pupil (Robert) in Mrs. Brown's class who was selected for special attention.

Diary Record

The research assistant observed Gregory and Robert for half an hour before break. They appeared shy and hesitant. They were, in fact, quite capable. Their responses were not very adventurous. They chose to go to the Arctic, saw polar bears and whales and heard ice cracking. (The class topic had recently been about Eskimos). . . . Whenever the computer summarised their choices they copied the summaries meticulously into their notebooks. When asked whether their notes were going to be useful later on (for writing an account or story), they didn't know.

School Record

Robert is a bilingual child. Mother North European. Father Teacher.

5–7 years of age: Conscientious, polite, helpful child. Doing well in all areas of school curriculum. Reading is sound; the most able within his age group at maths. Robert is rather shy and inclined to stammer.

7–8 years of age: Parents worried whether Robert is being stretched enough. Robert very intense at the beginning of term – to the point of tears at times, nervous cough. He is enthusiastic and most industrious. Very neat, small handwriting.

8–9 years of age: Family left Broadwood School for year abroad.

9–10 years of age: Robert returned to Mrs. Brown's class. Handwriting has become extremely small. Always appears tense. Represents school at football, swimming and athletics. Good at all games. Very competitive. Able and intelligent boy.

Teacher's Rating (January 1987)

Robert is one of the five identified by Mrs. Brown as the most-academically able pupils in her class.

Self-Rating as a Computer User (January 1987)

Robert was interviewed informally by one of the observers in order to gain a better understanding of his reasons for awarding himself four 5-out-of-10 and one 4-out-of-10 marks on various elements of the profile. Robert showed himself to be thoughtful and introspective, a systematic (and severe) judge of his personal standing as a computer user. For example, 'doing well at computer games', for which he gave himself 5 marks out of 10, had involved him in making comparisons of his present skills at football games and aeroplanes (i.e. 'dodging enemy planes so you don't get blown up') before coming to the self-appraisal. 'I don't really think I can beat my friends' – hence the 5-out-of-10 score.

'Knowing all about how to use the computer' had also elicited a self-award of 5 out of 10 from Robert. 'I know what keys you have to press', he conceded (he had already given himself 7 out of 10 on this sub-scale), 'but I wouldn't be able to get the program ready'.

C.O.M.I.C. Records

In addition to the systematic interaction data, C.O.M.I.C. profiles also contain verbatim comments of observers on interesting and/or noteworthy incidents occurring during the course of the recording sessions. For example:

17.3.87 (10.15 a.m.): Robert and Gregory are figuring out the hours of work of a butler at Quorn Hall. 'How old are they when they die – 65?' Later, 'what does "prime of life" mean?' They work together carefully and systematically for over an hour, gaining in confidence as they progress.

17.6.87 (10.00 a.m.): Robert is paired with a 4th year girl, Melanie, an able and helpful computer operator. Robert and Melanie worked well together, Robert listening attentively to instructions.

17.6.87 (10.30 a.m.): Robert and Erica act as checkers to Stephen. They explain what is required clearly and Stephen finishes quickly. Robert is now in the teacher-role. Enjoys his new responsibilities.

Robert's Logbook of Computer Use

Whenever they worked at the classroom computer, children were required to enter their names, the date, how long they spent at the computer and the name of the program with which they were involved:

Date	*Program*	*Minutes*
March 17	INHABITANTS	105
March 19	INFORM	35
May 12	INHABITANTS	15
June 16	INFORM	40
June 17	INFORM	60
September 9	AMX ART	60
September 16	PROMPT WRITER	60
September 24	FRONT PAGE	90
October 5	FRONT PAGE	47
October 13	FRONT PAGE	45
October 20	PROMPT WRITER	45
November 8	PROMPT WRITER	30
November 26	AMX ART	45
November 30	EDFAX	30
December 2	EDFAX	75
December 8	AMX ART	30

4
RECENT AND RELEVANT RESEARCH

The qualifying words, *recent* and *relevant*, in the title to this chapter serve both to emphasise and explain our purpose in bringing together summaries of only those studies that bear directly on our attempt to understand the process of events at Broadwood Primary School that followed the introduction of computers into the daily lives of teachers and pupils in two of its classrooms.

The discussion comprises three broad areas:

1. An account of studies to do with the introduction and integration of information technology into the primary school curriculum.
2. Teachers' resistance to change.
3. The implications of the National Curriculum for the integration of information technology in primary schools.

Computing in Primary Schools

The state of computing in British primary schools when our project began is well documented (Bleach, 1986; Cox, 1987). At that time (1986), schools were only very slowly absorbing computers into their curricula. Bleach found that whilst many of her teacher respondents indicated willingness to undertake training, 64% were unable to do more than set up and switch on their machines. Many complained that training courses were not available in their areas and, in consequence, that they had to resort to self-help in their spare time. Of the schools contacted, 64% felt that they were not getting sufficient advice. Good software was in short supply, and given the feeling of inadequacy felt by many teachers, they either did nothing, or they stuck to the more simple, though more limiting, drill-and-practice programs available at the time. The introduction of computers into primary schools was accompanied by materials that had 'an excessive emphasis on prescriptive approaches, often inherited from programmed learning, with very narrow outcomes and a single approach to structuring and presenting the content' (Riding and Buckle, 1987). Rather than being a consequence of hardware limitations, it is suggested that this state of affairs reflected a particular view of the learning process itself. Clearly the successful integration of the computer into the curriculum requires a modification of this viewpoint before the strengths of the new technology can be fully exploited. Riding and Buckle's appraisal accurately reflects the situation we found when we began our study at Broadwood. To that extent at least, Broadwood could be said to be typical of many schools of its type. Moreover, the authors encapsulate precisely our own feelings when they conclude (p. 6):

> A basic principle in integrating computers into the existing curriculum is that technology should only be used where it can be more efficient and effective than traditional methods. Any notion that pupils should sit at computers all day is clearly nonsense. There are many attractive and effective aspects of traditional methods to teaching and learning that will continue to play an important part in the school curriculum. What is important is that the computer-presented tasks and activities are clearly related to the rest of the curriculum.

First-Hand Experiences in Other Classrooms

There have been very few projects such as ours at Broadwood Primary. Having two research assistants in a school for a year is an expensive luxury which few can afford without substantial external funding. There are, however, a small number of accounts, which, together with the findings of several small-scale research projects and some highly illuminating descriptions of classroom practice written by enterprising teachers, create a valuable benchmark by which to measure the effectiveness and reliability of our own work.

The principal objective of the Sheffield Project reported by Ellis (1986) was to produce equal opportunities guidelines for class teachers in primary schools. Nevertheless, it is important in the context of our own study since Ellis worked with teachers in a single pilot school, aiming to give them the information and guidance needed to integrate computers into their normal curriculum and ways of working. The resulting guidelines were subsequently put to the test in four other Sheffield primary schools. The context in which the project started was not dissimilar to our own in so far as many teachers expressed a lack of confidence, a concern about handling and reliability of hardware and the shortage of good software. Where examples of good practice did occur, they were found to be largely dependent upon the expertise of an individual teacher. Ellis identifies several issues related to the successful use of computers in primary schools which parallel our own experience. These include the organisation and management of computing throughout the school and in the classroom, the in-service training of staff and the involvement of parents. Making computer hardware readily accessible, easy to use and transportable is a high priority since teachers' decisions to include computers in classroom activities then involve minimum fuss and trouble. Ellis considers it essential that everyone be kept fully informed of what is available, something, he asserts, that should form a part of regular school-based in-service training. The choice of software should provide as much variety as possible, but in particular, cross-curricular, content-free software such as a database and a wordprocessor ought to be given a high priority in order to attract women teachers and girls.

In the classroom, the computer should occupy a permanent place or work area in order that children are helped to accept it as a normal part of their working environment. All the information about the software should be readily available and it is suggested that instruction sheets be prepared to remind children of how to operate the system.

Group work, according to Ellis, is a good way of encouraging girls to participate in computer activities, promoting discussion and decision-making. Mixed groups became the norm in the Sheffield project following careful consideration of how many and which children worked together to ensure that girls would be actively involved. The grouping of younger children was found to work best in twos, whereas older children worked better in groups of three with a distinct and formal division of labour. The three group tasks identified by Ellis bear a close similarity to the results of our own, independent, investigations of group structure. One child would operate the keyboard, a second would read and check the screen and the third would record any important information. It was important to the children that each had a turn at each task. This organisation was subsequently put to good use enabling more experienced children to teach computer skills to the less experienced. Ellis found that the development of computer skills related very closely to the amount of time individuals spent at the keyboard. Moreover, it was sometimes necessary to group all girls together to avoid the keyboard being dominated by the boys. However, grouping children of similar ability often led to lively and rewarding discussion where the children worked at an agreed pace, with a child rarely being excluded.

Ellis considers parents' involvement to be very important in order that they can come to appreciate how computers are being used 'in a gainful and constructive way and the software the children are using is different from that produced for the home computer market' (Ellis, 1986, p. 16). Whilst the Sheffield parents were invited to visit the schools to see what the children were doing, there was no suggestion that they might become involved in the classroom computer activities as in the present project.

Following a series of six case studies, involving 19 classes in ILEA primary schools over the period of one year, Hall and Rhodes (1986) identified a number of influential factors promoting or inhibiting the uptake of information technology, and examined a number of classroom activities arising from its adoption. Several of these have a direct bearing on our own experience. Among the influences they identified were the highly motivating effect of the computer, the value of group rather than individual work, the importance of ease of access to and use of hardware and software, and the crucial role of in-service school-based training. Disc drives and printers were considered to be essential to facilitate rapid access and high-quality output while the use of wordprocessors encouraged the development of literacy skills.

A primary headteacher's view (High, 1988) reiterates many of the concerns referred to above. As a headteacher, High asserts it is necessary to view the problem from a 'whole school' perspective, so that issues such as ease of access, adequate support and encouragement and reduced teaching loads for those who are undergoing training assume high priority. The increase in activity stimulated by the computer does have its drawbacks however, especially when it comes to allocating consumables such as paper, ribbons and discs, all of which have to be found from within existing resourcing levels.

The Effect of Having a 'Home Computer'

The relation between computer skills in school and the ownership of a computer at home has been the subject of some speculation, and is a focus of interest in our own study. Moore (1987) suggests that school-based computer studies have very little carry-over to outside activities, and that home use has a more powerful influence than school use. This argument has been put forward as one explanation for an apparent reluctance or disinterest observed in girls, as compared with boys, when initially faced with computer-based activities in school. In a survey of 974 fourth- and fifth-year secondary school pupils, 56% of boys and only 22% of girls reported having a computer at home (Culley, 1986, p. 34).

Wordprocessors and Other Content-Free Software

There is much controversy surrounding the issue of wordprocessing and literacy skills. A one-year study of wordprocessor use on holistic writing skills with eighty seventh-grade students from four remedial language arts courses in the USA, conducted by Walton and Hannafin (1988), revealed that learners in the treatment group used a wordprocessor three times a week to complete their writing assignments; control-group students used conventional pen-and-paper techniques. An analysis of writing samples taken at the end of the study suggested that wordprocessing alone was of little consequence for able learners but, proportionally, proved most effective for low-achieving students. These results conform closely to our own observations where both teachers and researchers felt that the maximum benefits of the wordprocessor were to be gained from the activities of correction and editing rather than writing itself. Indeed it was suggested that special correction and editing exercises be devised to cater for the needs of the more-able pupils.

The use of wordprocessors and other content-free software has been seen as a way of encouraging those activities associated with a more progressive curriculum. Group work, where the emphasis is on teamwork, cooperation and discussion, with a minimum of teacher intervention, is a good example that directly parallels the way many adults normally work. This view is strongly supported by Straker (1984), who writes that the computer should be used 'to support, enhance and change the existing curriculum' by allowing children to be in control of their own learning. Stimpson (1988) provides a good example of this from his own class's experience using 'Writer', the wordprocessor used in our own project, and a database. Working in small groups, his class of vertically grouped top infants and first-year juniors used the wordprocessor to create and edit stories together. These were then illustrated with drawings and paintings and bound together as story books. Stimpson (p. 15) comments that stories were longer and more varied with a quality far exceeding that which he would have normally expected: 'Sophisticated punctuation, such as speech marks and apostrophes, which most children had not been taught, were soon learned and correctly applied. The children used dictionaries to check spellings on the first printout'.

Using the database, individual groups worked out their own ways to organise the task of cataloguing the class fiction library.

Each group concentrated on a letter of the alphabet and catalogued those books. The children learned how to use the database to answer questions, and taught other children how to use it as well. . . . The children learned a lot about books, libraries, and cataloguing, and were very quick in their groups to check for accuracy and spot mistakes.

(Ibid.)

The Benefits of Group Work

The benefits of group work when using the computer are recognised by many researchers and teachers. Fletcher (1985) suggests that groups of three children working on a task show 'markedly superior' problem-solving performance to children working individually. In addition he maintains that written and verbal testing of pupils' knowledge does not match their 'hands on' ability to solve problems. The implication of this seems to be that working in groups on computer-based problem-solving tasks gives a better performance than might otherwise be expected.

Richardson (1986) describes ways in which children are encouraged to take more responsibility for planning their own learning in his school, where the computer is used as a constant reference source for all of the school's resources and to which the children refer whenever planning a new learning task or project. Pupils take personal responsibility for the content of learning while the teacher adopts the role of adviser. Much of this, and other computer use, Richardson adds, occurs within the context of group activities, fostering discussion and planning skills that involve children in making a whole series of decisions individually and within groups.

Coming to terms with the computer, its keyboard and disc drive as well as the demands of the software is an activity which can benefit from both group discussion and conversations with the teacher. An analysis of children's questions when using the computer (Shaw *et al.*, 1985) revealed eight categories of questions used by thirty, second-grade children (7–8 years of age), engaged in computer-based activities. Of the eight categories, questions relating to use of the keyboard, data entry and program instructions were the most common, although after the first session at the computer, questions about operating systems increased and those about program instructions declined. Stowbridge and Kugel (1983) suggest that computer-based exercises of the drill-and-practice kind are similar to learning activities with which users are already familiar, whereas activities relating to computer operating systems are completely new and students have no prior experience upon which to call.

In the present study teachers and research assistants often worked as a discussion group, solving problems as they arose by pooling their experience. If this didn't work, they would then ask for help. Our systematic observations of the children using the computer in small groups revealed similar patterns of behaviour although in most cases a greater proportion of time was spent talking to the teacher than to other members of the group (see Appendix I). Walker (1983) believes that the things computers are best at do not fit the majority of teachers' views of what classrooms are about. We have already suggested that individual, independent and active learning are characteristics of microcomputer use at its best. In Walker's view: 'It may be that what computers are best able to support, is not the kind of thing many teachers are really comfortable with – independent learning, open-ended problems, flexible curriculum'.

This observation has implications for the extent to which some teachers are able to adopt and integrate the new technology into their personal repertoire of teaching methods and learning resources. In a two-year case study of microtechnological innovation in two primary schools, undertaken by Wright (1987), groups of teachers were asked to discuss 'instances of developing practice and the nature of school policy about microtechnology as it evolved'. Wright observed that 'both teachers' thinking and school planning reached a plateau achieved mainly by empirical trial-and-error testing'. We believe that such developments occur in a series of *slopes* and *plateaux* as a teacher's learning curve climbs towards the limits of his/her existing model of the teaching/learning process. Wright suggests that 'to go beyond this point teachers need further opportunities to develop their understanding of microtechnology's capacity to transform certain aspects of the primary school curriculum'. It is our contention, however, that *the* fundamental change required is to a teacher's existing conception of the teaching/learning process and of his/her pedagogic role within it. This, we would argue, may help explain why some teachers take to the new technology more readily than others. We explore this issue further in the context of Broadwood Primary School in analysing the results of our classroom observations in Chapter 6.

Teachers' Resistance to Innovation in the Classroom

It may seem somewhat perverse to dwell upon teachers' reluctance to adopt new teaching methods and resources rather than to explore their willingness to develop and improve their skills. The fact remains, however, that despite a wealth of goodwill and enthusiasm in the teaching profession, and a broad interest in the idea of information technology, a characteristic of teacher behaviour is a reluctance to venture into new areas where there might be some risk of things going wrong. There are, of course, perfectly legitimate reasons for this stance. Teachers are under increasing pressure to produce results and therefore reluctant to give up or modify tried and tested methods. For some, it is difficult to visualise any advantages in adopting the new technology. A number of British studies of the implementation of computers in primary schools (Gardner, 1984; Ewen and Roberts, 1985; Opacic and Roberts, 1985; Bleach, 1986) show that the incorporation of the new technology in primary schools has been cautious despite the many claims made in its favour.

Heywood and Norman (1988) suggest that the reasons for teacher indifference towards the new technology fall into three areas: the individual, the organisation and the innovation itself. Using recent developments in attribution theory (Kelly, 1983), they set out to ascertain the nature of teachers' concerns over the introduction of computers into classrooms by eliciting the teachers' own explanations of their beliefs and behaviour. Heywood and Norman identified three groups of teachers who had been using the computer for less than a year or not at all; in brief, teachers much like Pauline and Joan at Broadwood Primary School. Of this group they identified (1) users, (2) under-users and (3) non-users. Some of their findings are summarised in Table 4.1.

Table 4.1   Causal categories

Causal category	Examples
(a) Teacher preference against computer-assisted learning	'I don't like it, I don't feel that micros add anything to teaching'
(b) Positive teacher confidence	'I'm happy with it' 'I'm confident with it'
(c) Non-teacher pressure	'The children like it' 'The head is pushing it'
(d) Teacher overload	'I'm too busy to set it up' 'Too many other things to do'
(e) Inadequate confidence/competence	'I'm afraid of using it' 'I've not had enough training'
(f) Negative/inappropriate use	'Poor software' 'We've had a history of breakdown'
(g) Positive/appropriate use	'There's new and exciting software' 'It's a good teaching aid'
(h) Problems with access	'We've only one plug in the classroom' 'The timetable makes access difficult'

[*Source*: Adapted from Heywood and Norman (1988) p. 39.]

Under-user and non-user groups more often blamed inadequate confidence/competence for their reluctance and displayed less positive attitudes whereas the users' group exhibited more positive attitudes. The authors conclude that the major cause of reluctance and concern is to do with a lack of confidence and competence and that a perceived increase in workload is not the prime problem. Our own findings offer strong support for Heywood and Norman's conclusions.

The Implications of the National Curriculum

Nothing will have more potent influence on what British teachers do in their classrooms in the 1990s than the dictates of the National Curriculum which comes into force for all 5 and 11-year-olds in the areas of mathematics, and science from September 1989. Each of these subject areas of the curriculum contains attainment targets in information technology which must be met by law. All teachers will have to include aspects of the new technology in their work in one form or another.

Many teachers will welcome these national requirements as heralding the movement of information technology into the mainstream of education. Among the many advantages brought to the classroom by the new technology few would disagree that opportunities for children to work cooperatively, to discuss and share ideas and to achieve outcomes that are the product of teamwork should rank high. From the pupils' point of view, classroom activities such as these are educationally exemplarily just as long as such learning experiences remain outside of any assessment of pupils' individual performances. That is to say, just as long as children have nothing to lose by sharing their ideas with their classmates.

In 1983, before the idea of the National Curriculum was broached, it was recognised (Brine, 1983; Hawkins, 1983) that, whilst computers remain outside the mainstream of the curriculum, children will consult together over their work. What we now need to know is what will happen when children realise that they are working to a series of attainment targets relating specifically to their performance in information technology. 'What will happen when the work is serious and grades depend on it and children compete for grades?' (Olson, 1988, p. 5).

Concern over this issue and the statutory nature of the dictates of the National Curriculum are reason enough for us to examine what will be required of primary school teachers in some detail. What will teachers be required to include in their classroom activities, what will they need to know about, not just with a passing acquaintance, but in some detail?

The Role of Information Technology in the Primary School

In mathematics, the use of a computer arises in two areas – firstly at level two of Attainment Target 11: Shape and Space, where it is suggested that LOGO be used to develop an understanding of 'instructions for turning through right-angles' and the recognition of 'different types of movement: straight movement (translation); turning movement (rotation); flip movement (reflection)' and at level five when learning to 'specify location by means of coordinates' (NCC, 1988(b), pp. 55–6).

Secondly, at levels four and five of Attainment Target 12: Handling Data, where the interrogation of a computer database is required and, subsequently, to 'Insert and interrogate data in a computer database, and draw conclusions' (*ibid*. pp. 57–8).

The Statutory Instruments published alongside the NCC document make it quite clear that all of these requirements will affect primary school teachers since levels 1–3 in all fourteen attainment targets relate to the first key stage, 5–7 years, and levels 2–6 relate to the second key stage, 7–11 years. There is no doubt that children in these age groups are capable of such work. Indeed, our own experiences in school with 9–11-year-olds in the present study demonstrate this with respect to the database.

The attainment targets for science are equally as specific, setting out what will be expected of children in key stages 1, 5–7-year-olds, and 2, 7–11-year-olds. For the 5–7-year-olds, 'Children's normal work in all areas should involve where appropriate the use of information sources and computers. When appropriate, they should have the opportunity to use tape recorders and television to broaden their experience of science' (NCC, 1988(a), p. 39).

For the 7–11-year-olds, 'Children should have the opportunity to use and investigate the transmission and storage of information using computers, sensors, and the telephone. Children should use these in experiments and to store, retrieve and present their work' (*ibid*. p. 42).

In English (DES, 1988(b)), it is felt that information technology has a particular role to play in language development for 5–11-year-olds, but no attainment targets are specified:

> It is not appropriate to recommend specific attainment targets in Information Technology. Information Technology can help with language development, but the use of the hardware, or of specific software, could never in itself be central. It is possible, however to formulate areas of knowledge, skills and understanding which are central to English teaching. The English classroom should be one place where pupils learn to:
> . . . use Information Technology to send and receive messages (eg. by using electronic mail);
> . . . use Information Technology to help in the production and reception of written language for different audiences (e.g. by using desktop publishing, spelling checkers, style checkers, thesauri, etc);
> . . . show a critical understanding of some of the ways in which information can be manipulated (eg. by data bases, mail merge programs), and therefore show increasing discrimination in their interpretation of such information. (Electronic mail, for example, can link classes elsewhere in the country or in other countries, and can furnish additional very powerful ways of providing children with real audiences for their writing. Such links have already been made and used by teachers.) In general, English teachers should encourage children to study the ways in which language is used in the context of new technologies. And Information Technology in English falls, perhaps, into four main broad categories:
>
> 1. structuring and designing documents, with all the implications which this has for language in learning;
> 2. manipulation of ideas;
> 3. giving children access to a wider range of real audiences;
> 4. developing study skills and information handling.

The working group for design and technology had a rather different brief from those of the other subject groups. It was their task not only to consider the role of information technology in the design and technology curriculum, but also to consider information technology's cross-curricular implications (DES, 1988(a)): 'More specifically, the average 7 year old should be able to: store, retrieve, modify and use information with the aid of Information Technology (e.g. use suitable software to select, retrieve and modify pictures from a stored set of standard pictures in order to illustrate a story.)' Whereas the average 11-year-old should be able to:

> Capture information, and add it to an existing database, to retrieve information selectively from a database, to examine retrieved information critically in order to identify any obvious aberrant items and to present retrieved information appropriately (e.g. add further information to a database about families, use a bar chart to summarise retrieved information about years of birth.)
>
> (*ibid.*)

Two particular ways are identified in which pupils acquire information-technology capability within the curriculum, some of which have been independently recognised by other groups:

1. In subjects other than design and technology, examples of its appropriate use include language work (e.g. creative writing for an audience, using wordprocessing and electronic mail), investigations (e.g. using a database of census records or the Domesday system), modelling (e.g. using weather data) and simulations (e.g. chemical reaction, population of a colony of animals, erosion of a river valley, economy of a historical community). There are in addition some areas of the

curriculum where the work done would be impracticable without the aid of information technology (e.g. automatic data logging in scientific experiments).

2. Information technology is also an important tool for supporting design and technological activity in numerous ways. Examples of this appropriate use include graphics and art systems as aids to trying out and developing design ideas, database and spreadsheet systems as aids to planning, computer-aided designing and manufacturing systems for creating artefacts, or desktop publishing systems for presentation and reporting.

It is perhaps sufficient, to make the point, to consider the requirements for information technology in mathematics, science, English and design and technology. It must be remembered, however, that similar information technology requirements and attainment targets exist in all areas of the curriculum in one form or another. The intention is that information technology will permeate the whole curriculum. This has far-reaching consequences for primary school teachers into the 1990s and beyond, especially since the statutory testing at the key stages of 7 and 11 will include an assessment of the extent to which individual children have achieved those levels of attainment. How this will affect the children's attitudes to their work, and whether increased competition for rewards will become a barrier to the social potential of computers remains to be seen. In the meantime, every primary school teacher is going to have to acquire a certain minimum level of computer literacy in order to comply with the requirements of the 1988 Education Reform Act.

How Well Prepared are our Two Teachers at Broadwood?

The requirements of the National Curriculum bring into sharp focus the very real need for both pre- and in-service training for all teachers in the field of information technology. Our own experiences in this study indicate that a great deal of on-the-spot support is necessary, especially in the early days. Indeed, perhaps the most poignant question to be answered is whether, after all the training, support, encouragement and hard work put into our project by researchers, teachers and children alike, Pauline and Joan are anywhere near ready to meet or face up to those challenges. We will return to this question in a later chapter.

5
MAKING A START

By now, readers will be aware that a large-scale intervention was proposed into the lives of Pauline and Joan and the pupils in their care. That intrusion, moreover, was to take place during the course of three school terms, a relatively short period of time as it turned out, in light of the considerable training in computer literacy skills that teachers, pupils and research assistants would need to undertake before they could be expected to make progress in their own right. From the outset, therefore, it was vital to 'get things right first time' in selecting and sequencing appropriate practices in computer skills.

Part of the European Commission's brief was that the two teachers finally chosen for the study should have had no previous computer experience in the classroom. This requirement proved difficult to fulfil. A comprehensive in-service training programme initiated by the local education authority and MEP had already had some impact on many Leicestershire teachers though few, perhaps, would claim to be fully computer literate as a result of the exposure. The limited amount of prior experience that Pauline and Joan had acquired was probably typical of other teachers. Pauline had attended a course to do with the use of the computer in managing library resources. Both Pauline and Joan had undertaken a small amount of trial work using three programs produced by former colleagues at the University, albeit on a rudimentary basis, neither of them attempting to develop their general skills of computer literacy. What was evident, and indeed understandable at the beginning of the project, was the lack of confidence in themselves as computer users that both teachers shared and their deep apprehension of the technology itself. Such nervousness precluded any grasp of the computer as an integral part of a repertoire of teaching resources and methods; the idea of integration had never been considered.

The prime task was therefore one of training; first in terms of general computer skills, second by the introduction of a range of program types from which, it was hoped, the teachers could make free choices of what computer applications they wished to integrate into their curriculum planning. Strictly, of course, it is not true to suggest that their choices were 'free' since the selection of available program types was made by the researchers, not the teachers. For this reason, our account must begin with an outline of the types of program selected and the reasons for those choices.

Choosing the Programs

It is inappropriate at this point to give detailed descriptions of particular programs. Readers who decide to put some of the ideas presented here to the test may prefer to use different programs of a similar type or may well find that the ones we employed are no longer available or are incompatible. For this reason, the discussion that follows is confined to types of program. A more detailed description of the actual programs is presented in Chapter 6.

The Computer as a Tool, not as an End in Itself

A guiding principle underpinning the philosophy of the project was that the computer should be integrated into the curriculum to be used as a tool in the achievement of the teachers' educational objectives. Moreover, the researchers were agreed that the teaching of programming for its own sake was inappropriate to the context of this particular piece of classroom research. Pauline and Joan were to be trained in the basic skills of computer literacy to the extent that they could handle the day-to-day management of their new resources comfortably and with confidence. It was our hope that coupled with subsequent hands-on experience alongside the pupils, this rudimentary training would equip the teachers to accept the technology for what it was and encourage them to incorporate it into their regular repertoire of teaching methods and resources. Pauline and Joan were relieved that programming would form no part of the many demands that the researchers were to make on them.

Tools, not Training Packages

Along with others working with children and computers we have concluded that whilst computer-based tutorial and drill-and-practice exercises have a valuable part to play in classroom activities, they tend to be restricting, failing largely to exploit the power and versatility of the medium. Adequate exploitation, in our view, can only be achieved when the computer is used as a tool in the pursuit of specified objectives defined by the users themselves. Naturally, our attention turned towards that content-free software which most accurately mirrored the uses of the technology in the world of work, a serendipitous decision as it was to prove when, later in the project, we set about convincing the parents of the pupils involved of the value of computers in the school curriculum.

We begin our account by describing some work done with drill-and-practice and simulation-type programs which served as starting points for the teachers. Our main emphasis, however, was to develop work using a database, a wordprocessor, a newspaper editor, computer art and a teletext emulator. What all of these program types have in common is that the programs themselves are simply the means by which pupils can create, manipulate and experiment with ideas and concepts of their own. In an important way, too, the programs were to serve as examples whereby Pauline and Joan could begin to develop their understanding of how the new technology might become integrated into their personal philosophies of teaching and learning. Finally, we were concerned that teachers and parents alike should appreciate that the computer was to take its place alongside existing methods and resources. It was not to replace them; rather it was to be used as and when it could be shown to have distinct and definable advantages over more traditional methods of working.

It's often the case in the early stages of working with a new resource that one is more dependent upon hunches or gut-feelings about the worth of a particular activity than one is able to demonstrate specific, verifiable advantages; after all, ideas have to be put into practice before they can be assessed and evaluated. From the very start, however, one of the fundamental principles we tried to impress upon the teachers was that the issues they were to address in their decisions about computer use were educational, not technical. Moreover, as experienced classroom practitioners they were already well-equipped to make judgements about the relative worth of computer-based activities. As time passed and the teachers gained more experience with and confidence in the use of the new technology it was to be expected that their educational judgements would be tempered by a better understanding of the technical strengths and limitations of the medium. Our role, as we saw it, was to guide Pauline and Joan towards that point in time when they could make such decisions for themselves. Our proposed programme of training, then, would entail a high initial input from the research team, gradually tailing off as the teachers took on more and more responsibility for making decisions and solving their own problems.

Expert in What?

But what sort of relationship with the teachers would a 'high initial input from the research team' engender? Would they assume the role of novices and we the experts? Experts in what? Clearly initial technical knowledge and backup had to come from the research team. But from the very outset we were most concerned to recognise the educational expertise of Pauline and Joan. Partners rather than novices was the relationship in which we sought to engage our teacher colleagues. We did not underestimate the difficulties involved in such a stance:

> There is little doubt that, since the introduction of computers into schools began, more and more teachers have become enthused by what they perceive to be its possibilities. However, maintaining that initial flush of enthusiasm is not always easily achieved unless teachers learn how to discriminate between what stands up to scrutiny from an educational standpoint, and what does not. It is not that they do not already possess the knowledge and skills to do so, but it is often the case that the need to apply those skills is overshadowed in their minds by the apparent need to master the plethora of technical language printed in computer manuals and some computer journals.
>
> (Blease, 1986, p. 2)

Nor should the task of a research team in helping teachers become computer literate be underrated.

Teachers, more than anyone else, need to become computer literate, and in so doing to become confident and efficient users. Microtechnology must become as pervasive and integral a part of school life as it is rapidly becoming in the worlds of work and leisure. An important part of the way ahead is for computers to be used and to be seen to be used appropriately in schools; they should not, like so many other things in the school curriculum, be seen merely as things one is taught about.

(*Ibid.* pp. 3–4)

It has been suggested (Evans, 1986) that technical expertise is something that should remain strictly within the domain of the systems-analyst, the programmer and the computer designer whose task it is to make computer operation for the rest of us as simple and as friendly as possible. Technical expertise is no longer the issue; for the time being at least, being an expert computer user is. As time goes by, however, everyone acquires a higher and higher level of user expertise:

The argument about the ease of use of computers means that ultimately, people who are able to use the machine competently are no longer experts (as is the case in banks and industrial institutions nation-wide) – they are simply capable of using the tool that is provided to ease their work and make it more efficient.

(Evans, 1986, p. 100)

From the point of view of the research project, it was our hope that as Pauline and Joan became more proficient as computer users, their existing and substantial expertise as educators would again assume prime importance in relation to their handling of yet another potentially powerful and flexible teaching resource.

Teacher Training: Previous Experience and Available Resources

On several occasions Pauline and Joan had taken groups of children to the University to work with computers as part of field-testing exercises of software designed by a University team of developers. They had found this an interesting and enjoyable experience. In the setting of their own classrooms, however, they were less enthusiastic: 'That was at the University. But in school I didn't want to be bothered with MAPE tape or BLU File. Cassettes are too much bother' (Joan).

The use of these required some rudimentary training that amounted to no more than switching on and running a program from disc by pressing SHIFT/BREAK. Since few of the usual 'housekeeping' skills had been covered the teachers were not equipped to manage the system or handle day-to-day problems. Furthermore, the kind of software being tested was limited in its scope and application to drill-and-practice activities which had not led to any understanding of the potential of the computer as a learning tool. Pauline had responsibility for the school library and in that capacity had attended a short course on using the computer for library management. But she had had neither time nor opportunity to put what she had learned into practice. What became evident to the researchers as time progressed was that without opportunity for regular practice of skills, Pauline and Joan soon forgot what they had learned. Frequent hands-on experience supported by on-the-spot technical backup was to become an essential ingredient of any successful training programme.

School Resources

When the project began, the school had minimal computer resources. Efforts had been made to stimulate interest in computing among the staff, one teacher (Mrs. Silver) having taken responsibility for computing across the curriculum. But her duties also included an oversight of school science and the latter was considered a higher priority activity at the time the researchers arrived at Broadwood Primary School. Less computing had been attempted than Mrs. Silver would have liked. The situation was not helped by the fact that only one computer was available, together with a modest collection of software.

When the researchers arrived at school only moderate use had been made of the computer across the curriculum and across age groups. Some effort had been made to create a systematic record of the computer programs that were available in so far as Mrs. Silver had worked through the documentation of each program and had written a short description or specification of what a particular program was about and for what age or ability grouping it was suited. Some examples of these descriptions are given below.

Granny's Garden – 4Mat
The average 7 year old can complete this adventure game, which increases in difficulty as one progresses. Occasional hints from the teacher would perhaps be helpful. Children are spirited away to a magical land – the Kingdom of the Mountains. The King and Queen have been imprisoned in a secret cave by a witch and their children have been imprisoned in four strange locations. To complete the adventure the missing children must be found. (Proved to be very popular with two teachers working with 1st and 2nd year juniors).

Sheepdog – Ladybird Longman
Aimed at children 5–9 yrs. and can relate to the language and number curriculum. Two workcards within the pack. The program simulates putting sheep into a pen, with various options available. Orders are given to the sheepdog Bonza by use of the arrow keys or keys for the compass points. (Used by three infant classes).

Basic Number Help A and B – Ladybird Longman
These programs are designed to support existing number work by giving help in the form of animated graphics when requested, or when an error is made; and also to offer practice in using the variety of language related to number work. A. Addition and subtraction of numbers up to 10, or up to 20, using a number line. Three work cards are provided. B. Addition and subtraction involving hundreds, tens and units. A work card provided enables the children to solve problems practically, copying what is on the screen, with counters. (Not terribly popular, the teachers preferred to teach this in other ways).

Of all the programs available, by far the most popular were those on MAPE TAPE 1 and BLU-FILE. 'Staff tended to use the short and easy-to-get-going programs – especially from the MAPE TAPE cassette pack' (Mrs. Silver). It was frequently necessary for Mrs. Silver to provide support for the rest of the staff as well as doing her own teaching. She transferred each program on to a separate tape cassette to make them easier to find and load. 'The staff were no wiser than the kids at that time! As soon as anything went wrong people didn't know what to do' (Mrs. Silver).

We do not intend to document every program in detail but it may prove useful to provide brief reference to the rest to give readers an overall picture of what was available at the time when the research project began. The collection was predominantly one of a drill-and-practice or adventure kind.

- Adventure games by Anita Straker. ECL, 'The Lost Frog' and 'Merlin's Castle'. Simple problem-solving activities. (Not used at all.)
- Primary Programs One. ECL, including 'Alphashoot', 'Pairs', 'Spelling', 'Cloze', 'Move' and 'Directions'. Simple word-study exercises including alphabet and spelling. Described as being 'content-free' but only in as much as the words or letters to be used in fixed exercises can be changed. (Not used at all.)
- Primary Programs Two. ECL, including 'Tens', 'Targets', 'Estim', 'Hangman', 'Hangit', 'Initial', 'Tenbott'.
- 'Vowels', 'Add/Sub', 'X Tables', 'House' and 'Cargo'. This is a mixture of number games and word-study exercises similar to those in the previous set. ('House' used extensively by three or four teachers with infant classes.)
- *Note Invaders*. Chalksoft. An introduction to music notation. (Not used.)
- *Terrible Tales*. Ladybird Longman. Adventure programs to stimulate creative writing within a rather rigid frame. (Some use with third- and fourth-year juniors including one of the teachers participating in the project.)
- *Primary Maths and Micros*. MEP, including 'Blocks', 'Size', 'Find Me', 'Tea Shop', 'Data Show', 'Maths Talk', 'Halving', 'Diagram', 'Patterns 1 and 2', 'Boiled Eggs' and 'Bounce', described as an excellent selection of mathematical games including a utility for sorting and displaying any eight items of data in a table, bar or pie chart. (Very little use.)
- *Bonzo*. Ladybird Longman. To develop and test the concept of size. (One of the field-tested programs, used by all infant classes.)
- Language packs 1 and 2, including 'Storytime', 'Wordplay', 'Tins', 'Tray and Create', 'Mallory', 'Eliza' and 'Tracks'. Activities for storywriting, conversation and problem-solving. (Not used at all.)
- *Flowers of Crystal*. 4Mat. An adventure simulation to promote creative project work. (Not used at all.)
- *Podd*. Acornsoft. Word study (verbs). (Used by infants.)
- *Locate*. ECL. A utility for storing, searching and presenting data in a variety of ways. (Not used at all.)
- *Hobby Package*. ECL. A datafile of census returns for use with *Locate*. (Not used at all.)
- *Micromap, Kingdom of Helior*. Ladybird Longman. Both programs had been used in pre-publication form as part of the programme of field-testing.
- MAPE tape 1. A collection of simple programs on tape. (Some programs used extensively.)
- MEP Blu File. (Some programs used extensively.)

The intention of Mrs. Silver's classification and documentation was that teachers who thought that they might like to use the computer could quickly discover whether the school possessed a program to suit their particular needs. The problem, of course, was that no facilities had been provided for training. It's one thing to have a computer and programs available; it's quite another to have a group of teachers sufficiently confident and competent to use the facility. The result was that the computer was used quite extensively by some members of staff and very little, if at all, by the rest.

At the outset of the study it had not occurred to us that our work with Pauline and Joan would have any significant impact on the general state of computer awareness outside of the two classrooms in which we were working. In this respect we were not a little naive for the research was to prove a turning point for several other members of staff at Broadwood Primary School. When the project ended there was a significantly greater demand for computer time throughout the school.

If at First You Don't Succeed . . .

It may seem odd to begin our account by describing a training programme that, in retrospect, was singularly unsuccessful. With hindsight, however, it proved to be one of the most important learning experiences that we gained from the total project. Whilst the exercise was a failure as far as Pauline and Joan were concerned, it was extraordinarily helpful to us in helping elucidate the necessary conditions by which teachers might come to acquire an array of basic skills and understandings without an overburdening weight of frustration and sense of failure. Perhaps the fundamental error we made was simply to forget just how difficult it had been for us, not too many years ago, to acquire our expertise following that initial 'gut feeling' that a mastery of information technology might hold the key to a wide variety of educational developments. In those days, we recall, there were not the benefits of a range of software from which to choose. As Fiddy (1981) observes: 'Initially the enthusiasts experimented. We wrote for ourselves, learning what the systems would do and for what they might be used in school. If the programs worked, our classes and schools used them. It was new, exciting, obsessive, fascinating, creative, and wonderful in many ways, but exceedingly inefficient'.

But it was not just inefficient; it was incredibly difficult. The group that Fiddy describes was a dedicated band of enthusiasts who happened also to be teachers. After several years as a competent computer user, one tends to forget the difficult times and the frustrations, remembering instead the exhilarations and the triumphs. In brief, our expectations of the speed at which Pauline and Joan would assimilate large quantities of computer knowledge were grossly optimistic. The initial training programme we devised for them derived from the premiss that we should not dictate which programs they were to use. On the contrary, if we were to provide a comprehensive overview of what could be done using a variety of program types, then they would be able to make the choices for themselves.

We began by teaching Pauline and Joan how to manage the computer, how to set it up, load programs, format discs and make backup copies. Some of this, of course, was already familiar to them although their previous experience had been primarily with programs on cassettes. Various program types were demonstrated – a wordprocessor, database, drill-and-practice and simulation. These were followed by offprints of accounts written by teachers elsewhere telling how these particular programs had been used in their classrooms. Our hope was that such real-life examples would enable Pauline and Joan to see for themselves where a particular program type might be integrated into their existing schemes of work.

Having completed this initial introduction to the programs in three half-day sessions during the first three weeks of the 1987 Spring Term, Pauline and Joan were encouraged to introduce a new computer application of their own choice in Week 4 and a second in Week 10 with detailed and specific help being given by us whenever they expressed an interest to introduce a specific software package.

By the first week in March, it was clear that the training programme was not working satisfactorily. Basically, the problem was that in trying to cater for what we had perceived to be the teachers' needs, we had seriously underestimated their difficulties in coming to terms with the new technology.

From our perspective it seemed that for some reason few of our suggestions for activities had been taken up and that Pauline and Joan were still using two drill-and-practice programs on a regular basis that had been field-tested some time ago by our University colleagues. On the rare occasions that the teachers did try out any of our suggestions, we felt that the computer was there as an addition to, rather than an integral part of, their overall lesson plans. It was almost as though Pauline and Joan felt that they had better get the computer out because the researchers were there. It would be easy, of course, to argue that the teachers were in some way at fault in not wanting to take up our ideas. The truth of the matter was that we, the researchers, had got it wrong. In retrospect, perhaps, Pauline and Joan had already begun to integrate some computer use into their schemes of work. Although the programs they used were rather crude, they both agreed that their curriculum plans had been formulated with those programs in mind some time prior to the introduction of our training programme. That notwithstanding, our concern at the time was that we had failed to convince them that the computer could become part of their overall view rather than some troublesome appendage. The question was – how could we change their perspectives?

At the beginning of March 1987, a significant event occurred at a meeting with Belgian and French colleagues who were conducting parallel projects to ours in their respective countries. The French group provided us with details of a precisely structured training programme which was more sharply focused and directive in nature than our approach at Broadwood Primary. In their Paris school, regular weekly meetings were scheduled, starting from first principles and leading to more and more advanced uses and applications. At that point in time the French team seemed happy with the way the training was going although their teacher had not yet plucked up courage to introduce the computer actually to teach a lesson. The French researchers' problem seemed to be one of building up the teacher's confidence in her ability to cope when, in her view, some of the pupils knew more about the computer than she did. This observation was corroborated at roughly the same time in our own fieldnotes when Joan commented: 'I think you need to know the programs better than the children so when they come up with problems then, you know, if they're stuck, you can help them'.

Meeting Teacher Needs: The Revised Training Programme

We decided to follow the example of our French colleagues at once and to plan a more carefully sequenced and structured approach that provided regular opportunities for

Pauline and Joan to 'play' and 'experiment' with the computer away from the pressures of school and classroom.

Provision of Further Support

In addition, we decided to encourage both teachers to make use of Jane, our part-time researcher-observer as if she were a parent/helper. To this point in the project, Jane had been actively engaged in the C.O.M.I.C. interactional analysis recording in both classrooms. She was to do whatever they directed, but only as and when instructed. Our intention here was to encourage Pauline and Joan to think about planning for the use of the computer in their respective classrooms without having to cope with the additional burden of its minute-to-minute supervision. This arrangement was to prove particularly beneficial when we introduced work with a database. As Joan reminisced: 'I don't think either of us could have coped without.'

Initially, the addition of 'parent/helper' support was intended as a temporary expedient. It proved to be so successful, however, that the strategy was continued until the completion of the project in December 1987, the amount of actual support being systematically withdrawn as Pauline and Joan grew in confidence and expertise and the researcher-observers (now two in number) concentrated more on their work with the C.O.M.I.C. interaction analyses.

A regular weekly training programme was initiated, Mrs. Black, the headteacher, arranging for supply cover every Wednesday afternoon. Pauline and Joan came to the University and were joined there by Jane, the researcher-observer, who had had no previous computer experience or training. Their broadly similar levels of computer knowledge and their sharing of learning experiences during the Wednesday afternoon sessions helped cement closer relationships between observer and observed:

> Certainly we didn't feel any strain with Jane being there. I think we both got on very well with her and she got on well with the children which wasn't particularly easy for her with the groups we had at the time. They just accepted her, and she wasn't obtrusive and yet she was positive with them. We certainly never felt 'Oh God here she comes again!' you know, which we do with some people coming in.
>
> (Pauline)

Our decision to take a more direct, active role in the progress of the project from this point onwards raises questions not touched upon in the outline of research methodology in Chapter 3.

In so far as we were now committing ourselves and our observer/teacher helpers to initiating, along with the teachers, interventions into the functioning of the [classrooms] and to examining the effects of such interventions (Halsey, 1972) we were engaging in a form of action research. We deliberately use the phrase 'a form of action research' for it was not our intention to pursue a methodology that was to incorporate the ideas and expectations of all those involved in a collaborative arrangement in which all participants were to be symmetrical . . . and the roles of teacher, learner and researcher [were to be] available to all participants (Holly and Whitehead, 1986). This clearly could not be the case since, as we said earlier (page 35), 'initial technical knowledge and backup had to come from the research team'. That notwithstanding, we sought a facilitators' role that could provide a sounding-board against which our [teacher-] practitioners could eventually try out ideas and learn more about the reasons for their own actions (Carr and Kemmis, 1986).

Why did the Teachers Appear not to Take up Researchers' Suggestions?

The friendship and collegiality that had developed between Pauline, Joan and Jane set us wondering again about the first term of the project and why it was that things had been so slow to get off the ground. We broached the question in August 1987 by discussing the issue in some detail:

D.B.	When the project started what did you think about the computer as an additional classroom resource?

Pauline	Although we'd used it no one seemed to be very sure of it. I was quite willing to use it, and have done, but at very much face value. But when I wanted more than that there was never anyone there to help as you've done this year. No one that you could say 'well what am I doing wrong?' And I found that quite frustrating. Just to be able to ring you up, or you were in fairly frequently, to be able to say 'look, what am I doing, I know it's stupid but what am I doing?' That was very helpful.

D.B.	You've heard me mention already that I felt at that time the computer was being used as something tacked on at the end. I didn't feel that it was viewed as a central part. . . .

Pauline	It wasn't integral to the actual teaching. It was used really as a teaching aid.

D.B.	So were you at that time really a bit sceptical about whether the computer was all it was cracked up to be in the classroom?

Pauline	Yes, partly because of the software that was available as well, it was limited, but I think the thing I've been most interested in is the use of it as a wordprocessor. I think that most of the software we've used is quite limited in a way, you've got to think of a use, to use it in more than one way.

Joan	I thought it was something we needed to use in the classroom because the computer is such a part and parcel of the environment. I felt it was important for the children to use the computer in the classroom. But I felt that I didn't like the drill-and-practice type programs, and it was more a matter of finding programs that I felt would work with the things which I wanted to do. You know, which I was hoping I was going to get some help with.

D.B.	At that time when it started, did you think that it might, in the end, turn out to be something very valuable to use in school, or did you still feel – well when they've gone we'll get back to normal?

Pauline	No, I never felt like that. I always felt that it had great potential, and I suppose I was irritated by the fact that I didn't know anything about it to use that potential. I think it's necessary nowadays to understand the computer. It is probably more necessary for these children than it is for me, I could probably muddle along without really knowing much. But they might need to know, a good many of them will need to know how to use the computer.

Clearly the two teachers appeared willing to participate, but how willing? Would they have chosen to participate?

D.B.	In the beginning were you keen to take part, or did you feel pushed into it?

Joan	We felt it was convenient that we two did it because we tended to work on joint projects and the children were the right sort of age. I felt it would be quite stimulating so I was quite happy to take part.

Pauline It's a little difficult to answer that because it was a little bit of both. Yes we were very interested but we were a little bit unsure about what we were letting ourselves in for.

D.B. Would you say a part of the process was that we had to convince you that what we were going to do was going to lead to something worthwhile?

Pauline Yes. We didn't just want it to be an intrusion into our time unless there was going to be something from it.

The informal interrogation of Pauline and Joan was to throw into clear focus what we, and indeed, our French and Belgian colleagues, had forgotten: the fundamental problem of coming to terms with the computer, the hardware, jargon, unfriendly screen messages, incomprehensible manuals, poor documentation and inadequate software. We were to be reminded of frustrating hours dealing with loading errors, inadequate instructions and unexpected breakdowns together with software that failed to match up with our expectations because of our inaccurate and misguided conception of how computers worked.

Pauline I think the main thing is that it assumes too much knowledge, everything seems to assume too much knowledge. There was nothing that was so basic that we could understand it without referring to you. You really want to have to do it, to fight your way through that. . . . Lack of time is a major point because at the end of the day you've still got your ordinary preparation and marking. . . your own family to cope with. There just never seems to be the time to actually sit down and try new things.

D.B. I'm interested in the way you put that, 'you've still got your ordinary preparation', which indicates that the computer is perhaps being a bit separate from ...

Pauline Well no, even integrating it into things we do, you've still got to think about what you're going to do with anything else, but not everything is involved with the computer. You've still got to plan the day, mark the work. There never seems to be enough time really.

The unrealistic expectations that people hold about how computers and their software work is a serious problem deserving greater consideration than we can afford to give at this juncture. Some brief comment, however, is appropriate.

In order to become an efficient computer user it is necessary to have an appropriate mental image of how a particular program is working. This need not be technical; but it must be structured and logical. Probably the greatest advance in this respect is the user-friendly interface provided by the WIMPS (Windows, Icons, Mouse and Pointer) environment of the Apple Macintosh, the GEM desktop and Microsoft Windows where the screen display is designed to resemble the desktop with its folders, documents, wastebasket etc. Unfortunately these things are generally beyond the scope of the BBC model B computer, and were therefore not available to the teachers at the time.

D.B. When I started the training sessions did you understand what I was talking about?

Pauline At times yes, it was afterwards we tended to forget things but usually between the three of us we would manage to remember things. At the time it did seem fairly easy, but the more we did the harder it became. Sometimes you would show us things and you would do them too quickly so it was difficult to follow and we couldn't remember how you achieved it.

D.B.	Could you remember what I had said afterwards?
Joan	Not often. Pauline and I used to talk it out together, some people would remember some bits and other people would remember others. It would all come together as a joint venture.
D.B.	Did it make sense to you at the time?
Joan	Yes, but they seemed to go so quickly. Sometimes you did things, I didn't know what you'd done to make it do them.
D.B.	In the beginning did you feel confident that you could try things out in school?
Joan	Some things that I'd become happy with, but when things started to go wrong and I'd forgotten things, I'd perhaps start it off and I'd forget something I needed to know and the manual didn't seem to provide the information, that was frustrating. If you approach it with a group of children, and you think you've got it together and you find you haven't, it just sort of falls flat.
D.B.	Did you find the time to read the articles I gave you, did they help at all?
Pauline	Yes I did. It was interesting at the time to read about what some other teachers had tried, but I can't remember what they were about now.
Joan	Yes I read them but I don't think I absorbed it too well.
D.B.	At the beginning of the project what was the main barrier or obstacle that would prevent you from using the computer?
Pauline	It was to do with getting it organised really. Having another thing to cope with in the classroom.
Joan	It was probably more to do with my rigid timetabling attitudes really because I would use the computer at set times and didn't feel willing to use it at other times. During those times it was getting it out and loading it and coping with organising the children on the computer and organising the rest of the group. In the normal classroom environment you've got a constant stream of children round you with their work, and the computer is just another demanding feature in the corner.
D.B.	Has that got easier?
Joan	Yes it has. When things didn't work properly.
D.B.	Did you ever think of packing it in altogether?
Pauline	Oh no!
Joan	Oh no, no I don't think that thought ever crossed my mind.
D.B.	When thinking about the work for the next day or the next week how important was the computer in your thoughts by the end of the Spring Term? And now?
Joan	Yes, by that stage it was quite important.
D.B.	If you compare that with the beginning of January, would you say that your thoughts, your attitude towards it had changed?
Pauline	Well at the beginning it did come in, especially with things like Micromap [one of the programs they had field-tested], because it fitted in with other things we'd got planned. I'm sure that the computer has become a more central part of our thinking about our teaching. It would be very difficult to imagine now not to be using the computer, to imagine it not being there.
Joan	Yes, because there didn't seem to be enough time to do things that you would have liked to have done.
D.B.	Can you identify a time this year when any significant change occurred for you with regard to using the computer, where perhaps you felt 'ah! now I'm making some progress'?
Pauline	I think it was when we started coming to the University every week. You used to show us something and then leave us to try it for ourselves. It was nice to be away from everything with time to experiment.
Joan	I thought when we were coming for the training, the every week thing, that really helped. I did an assembly at the end of the Spring Term, and I did that about how we used the computer. That was quite interesting. It was good the way the children talked about it in front of the rest of the school.

The revised and more directive training programme was put into effect in the second week of March. Both teachers said that they felt the need for more time alone at the computer to experiment and get used to it and its ways. We began with a tutorial on 'basic housekeeping' – setting up the system, formatting discs, copying programs and making backups. All simple procedures, but it seemed to be useful as Pauline and Joan began to attempt simple operations for themselves back in school. This was followed by sessions on INFORM, a database, WORDWISE, a wordprocessor, EDFAX, a teletext emulator, and AMX SUPER ART, a paintbox package using a mouse. The choice of software was designed to encourage exploratory, experimental and reflexive behaviour by allowing the children to solve problems and express ideas in new ways.

D.B.   How different did you find the new training programme?

Joan   Very much so because it gave us time to play about with the things. You would often show us things and then go off and do something else. We'd come up to a difficulty and then we'd talk it through and work it out for ourselves. We found it better, coming together. We don't really seem to have the time to do that in school because even if you sit down to do it say one lunchtime, there are so many interruptions.

Pauline   Yes it was much better, in fact it was much more relaxed. It was much better to be away from the school, away from interruptions.

D.B.   Do you think that having Jane there made it even better?

Joan   Yes I think it did.

D.B.   What were the major constraints for you at this time, what things made it difficult for you?

Joan   At that time we only had the school computer and one from the University. Of course sometimes other teachers wanted to use the school computer. Certainly towards the end of that term both of us were wanting to use it quite a bit. I think that was about the time when we had students in the school, so the school one tended to be used a bit more.

D.B.   Perhaps we should say that an important thing generally which encourages you to use the computer whenever it is appropriate is for it to be there in the room, handy.

Joan   Yes, it would be nice to have it there actually in the area. We could do with a computer in every area really.

An Introduction to a Database

During March the two teachers planned to take about 25 children away to a local authority field centre for a week. Their plans included a study of the village churchyard and the gravestones within it.

As a part of our more aggressive training programme we showed them how a database (INFORM) could be used to enhance the graveyard study. We even visited the graveyard ourselves to collect sample data. We then formulated a suitable set of fields to be used and constructed a convenient coding sheet for the children to use. These were desperate tactics, but we wanted to make it easy for Pauline and Joan to use the computer without any major modification to their existing plans. Our discussion of INFORM included suggestions as to how the data collection might be organised to prevent duplication of records.

On the day in question the children began to work in the churchyard making rubbings of gravestones, drawing pictures of the church and completing a three-page worksheet. Halfway through the session they were all called together, each to be given a coding sheet. As we hadn't been there earlier to listen to any briefing it all seemed a bit hurried, and when we talked to several children as they worked they didn't seem to realise that the activity was connected with the computer at all. Subsequent discussions with Pauline and Joan gave us a better idea of the way in which the children had been prepared. Those talks, moreover, indicated that while the teachers had a feeling that the activity might be useful, they hadn't sufficient experience to understand quite what the advantages might be.

D.B.	Were you happy to accept my suggestions about using the database?
Joan	Yes.
D.B.	You didn't do it just because I said come on you can do this?
Joan	Well it couldn't have been easier really, you did it all for us.
D.B.	Did you discuss the computer with the children before they went to the churchyard, had they been briefed about the coding sheet before going there?
Joan	Well actually before they did the rubbings they had a worksheet to work on about the graveyard. We talked about it, I'm sure we did, before we went out. But they hadn't really taken it in, the meaning of various things. Even when I used it again later we had similar difficulties, but we probably didn't leave enough time for gathering that data on the day.
Pauline	We discussed the worksheet and the database program the evening before in the school room of the field centre. They found it difficult to imagine how we could use it in the computer.
D.B.	At that time did you really understand what the children would get out of using the database?
Pauline	I thought it would be a useful means of collecting information and it would have numerous applications.
Joan	No, I think they got more out of it than I thought they would.
D.B.	Do you think that they understood its purpose at the time?
Joan	At the time, no.

Many children had difficulty with the fields. They couldn't remember what some of them meant, e.g. SPOUSE, STATUS, BORN etc. and it was necessary for Pauline, Joan and other helpers to check constantly that the children were not completely stuck.

Using the Database – A Turning Point?

An extract in the fieldnotes of Jane, the researcher-observer, describes the activity of entering the data and the obvious enjoyment of the pupils involved:

Friday 6th March 1987

Joan set up the INFORM program and chose three 'computer capable' children (Melanie, Sandeep and Jason) to continue with the graveyard survey. Melanie and Jason in turn keyed in their own data while the other two acted as reader and checker. We calculated the dates of birth when they were missing. Sandeep wasn't on the field course, so he keyed in the data which had been collected by a child in class 8.

It took one and a half hours to enter 26 records. These three children seemed to enjoy doing this rather mindless task. They said that they weren't bored but they thought that asking the computer questions later would be the best part.

Jane's perceptions and recordings of the above events were given to Joan for comment.

Joan   You must bear in mind that those three children were among the brightest in the group.

D.B.   Were these three the only children to get anything out of it?

Joan   No, but the comments at the end about asking questions of the data were likely to occur with those three children rather than some of the others who were not particularly imaginative, requiring much prompting.

Jane's fieldnote records continue:

Monday 9th March 1987

Joan set up the computer ready to start. We had already decided that two of last week's children (Melanie and Jason) would act as teachers of one new child. I suggested that two of the 'target children' (Gregory and Sarah), who had both been on the field trip, be shown how to key in their data. Melanie and Jason explained how to do it and Gregory keyed in his data with great confidence. The reader spelt out difficult names, and the checker worked out dates of birth. Sandeep and Gregory then acted as teachers while Sarah keyed in her data. This system is working well. Melanie and Jason talked about the sort of questions they would like to ask the computer:

1. Which was the most popular surname?
2. What Christian names were most popular? Are these the same today?
3. Which is the oldest grave?
4. Sandeep would like to find out if any First World War dead are buried there.

Clearly, some children were enjoying using INFORM even before the records were complete. Jane's fieldnote records describe work in Pauline's class and then go on to reveal something of the feelings of the two teachers at this point in the research programme.

Tuesday 10th March 1987.

. . . the children enjoyed working at the computer, one said he likes practising on the keyboard, another said it was good fun putting in information you've collected yourself. . . .

Various circumstances are combining to make Pauline and Joan feel that the computer project is 'just one more thing to have to think about'.

Once again, the researcher-observer's records were given to Pauline and Joan in order that they should have the opportunity to 'tell-it-as-it-was' from their perspectives.

Joan   I think perhaps we went through a few times like that, and I'm sure that a lot of the problem was to do with coping with such a difficult group. Both of us had pretty difficult groups, and this really didn't help. I think we felt we weren't giving as much as we possibly could have done to the project. I think this is a factor which must be borne in mind. It's a pity really because more could have been got out of the project with other children.

Pauline   Many factors contributed to this feeling, the mid-year low, the pressure of having a difficult group and the feeling that we weren't doing ourselves or the project justice, as it was becoming increasingly difficult to interest the group, particularly the 'leavers'. Also I felt that you were becoming impatient of the slowness at which the project was taking off.

D.B.   Did the children's reaction to entering the data and asking questions surprise you?

Joan   Yes.

D.B.   Were you aware of the enthusiasm on the part of the children?

Joan   No, and in point of fact some of the children who came up with the questions were not those children I would have predicted. They were other children. For instance

Carl's response, he really enjoyed it. I couldn't remember all the commands for example, and he became the expert who quite liked to help me out with my difficulties.

D.B.   Did this influence or alter your view of the possible value of INFORM?

Joan   I'm sure it must have done.

D.B.   So, who told the children about asking the computer questions?

Joan   Before we actually started I seem to recall that I told the children about it, to explain. I have a feeling, but I can't remember whether we talked about gathering the data before we went to Quorn or not. Certainly at some stage I talked to the whole group about how we'd gathered all the data and how we were going to put it on the computer and ask questions.

Pauline They needed much prompting. We had a group session to begin with but their interest waned very soon.

D.B.   Can you recall actually giving several examples of the kinds of questions they might ask?

Joan   I think I did. Certainly at a later stage, when we'd got all the information keyed in they had their rough books and they had to formulate three questions to try out. When we actually came to ask the questions we realised that we were quite constrained by the commands. So a lot of the questions the children had thought about were difficult to ask the computer.

Interrogating the Database

The first the researchers knew that Pauline and Joan had actually got their pupils to interrogate the database was when they put up an interesting display of computer printouts, together with some rubbings and samples of children's writing about their work with INFORM. Some described the screen display, some the collection of data; others outlined the task of defining the fields and yet others said something about the actual operations involved in entering raw data.

D.B.   What interested me about their work was that it was accurate, and seemed to indicate that they really understood what they had been doing. Am I right?

Joan   Yes certainly I didn't write them. It was definitely their own work. In that situation I would obviously read it through and check spellings and punctuation, but no, it was their own work.

We could barely disguise our surprise at the relative sophistication of the children's descriptions and comments. It seemed to us at this stage that the children were more familiar with INFORM than their teachers. However, Pauline didn't quite see it that way:

Pauline It was more of a combined effort when we used the program, i.e 'the blind leading the blind'. Obviously initially the children knew nothing.

D.B.   Did the children's reaction to using the database and the way your assembly came together, I know you were very anxious about it beforehand. Did you feel that you were finally getting somewhere?

Joan   Yes I was pleased with the assembly, and actually we had the computer in the hall, and some of the children demonstrated what they had done.

D.B.   Did you get any comments from any of your colleagues about that?

Joan   Yes, that probably was the turning point when they realised that after sort of pulling our hair out at various stages we were actually doing something, and a lot of children stopped and looked at the work.

D.B.   Getting back to the writing, obviously they were briefed about what you wanted them to do. . . ?

Joan   What I usually do is map out the various areas that I want covered for an assembly and ask for volunteers to do the different bits. Children volunteered for areas they had been concerned with.

D.B.   The technical details about actually using the database, how did they learn those? Did you demonstrate to everybody as a class or did you do it individually?

Joan   I think I did it as a class. I demonstrated that to the whole class.

D.B.   Did the children know more about it than you did at that time?

Joan   No, I was just about ahead of them at that stage.

D.B.   Am I right in thinking then that probably, from your point of view, and perhaps for the children, that activity using INFORM with the subsequent display and the assembly was a milestone, an important event in the process so far?

Joan   Yes because certainly the assembly was purely about using the computer to work on the field course data. The children felt involved and gained something from it. They could see that it had a valuable use.

Pauline   The work and the display drew many comments from a variety of sources; other staff, parents and visitors, but perhaps more pleasing, from other children in the school. Obviously this was gratifying and it did mark a major milestone in the project to date. We both felt more at ease with the computer and felt more able to ad lib in a crisis. The effort now seemed much more worthwhile.

Testing the Children

A prime focus of our interest in the pupils a Broadwood Primary School was the ways in which they might change in their attitudes and behaviours in response to the new stimuli introduced into their classrooms. Specifically we sought to identify a small number of boys and girls in each classroom whose self-concepts of ability were significantly at variance with their views of themselves as computer users. What we were looking for were those pupils who, for some reason, had positive self-images as learners but low or negative views of themselves in relation to the computer. The children in both classrooms were vertically grouped, consisting of third- and fourth-year pupils. Because our research project was to span two academic years, we chose to concentrate on the younger age group in order to maintain continuity of testings and observations throughout the period of the study.

A number of quantitative measures were used to monitor the progress of those children selected for 'intensive' observation. Areas of interest included academic self-image (Barker-Lunn, 1970), achievement striving (Holmes, 1971), choice-status within peer groups (Gronlund, 1959), group structure (Proctor and Loomis, 1951) and self-concept of ability when working with computers (Kilpatrick and Cantril, 1965). Profile measures were to be obtained on three occasions: at the beginning, half way through and at the end of the twelve-month observation period. (In order to retain the full complement of target children (i.e. both third- and fourth-year children) the profile measures were administered on two occasions only, in January and in May 1987.)

When identified, 'target' children were to be encouraged by their teachers who would 'tailor make' experiences for each child, placing them in friendly, compatible work groups, for example, or giving extra turns or longer exposures to the computer as and when it was possible to do so unobtrusively. Target children's behaviour, both as individuals and as members of groups, was documented by means of various qualitative observations, informal interviews and discussions and by means of a quantitative technique (C.O.M.I.C.), specifically designed by the researchers to record behaviour at the computer.

Throughout the period of the study the research team (two part-time research assistants with additional support from the University) worked alongside Pauline and Joan, interacting with them and their pupils as true participant observers attempting always to portray the on-going events of the classrooms as they were perceived by the principal participants themselves. Sue and Jane, the research assistants, were experienced primary school teachers in their own right though this did not mean that their perceptions of classroom events were necessarily congruent with the ways that Pauline and Joan saw things around them. It is important and indeed very revealing to take account of Sue's and Jane's fieldnotes as crucial and legitimate data in our descriptions of the on-going events at Broadwood Primary School.

The Role of Headteacher and Parents

Support from Above and Beyond

It goes without saying that it is impossible to undertake an extended study in a school without the full support and cooperation of the headteacher and the school governors.

Initial discussions with the headteacher revealed that she was very happy to cooperate provided that the project work itself was likely to result in positive benefits for the teachers and children involved and for the school in general. At the beginning of the research there was no parent–teacher association attached to the school; the usual link with parents was through regular notes and newsletters sent home with the children. The governing body was informed of our intentions by the headteacher herself, who undertook to keep them informed at regular intervals. Reports of developments and progress as the project developed were all recorded in the minutes of governors' meetings. It was felt that links with parents could be strengthened. Moreover, there was a need to pave the way for Pauline and Joan to be able to recruit parent/helpers from time to time, and there was a great need for parents to understand that the work the children were doing with the computer was beneficial in an educational sense rather than just an 'excuse to play games'.

Organising a Parents' Evening

A parents' evening was scheduled for September 1987 where the parents could try out for themselves the very programs being used by their children. For this purpose we installed a further ten computers which were situated in or near to the places where the children would normally be working. The evening began with an introduction to the project and a description of the ways in which the teachers and children were being encouraged to use the computer. The walls of the school hall were covered with examples of the children's work to illustrate the idea that the computer was being used as a tool to enable them to explore and manipulate ideas in new and exciting ways. The response from the parents was even more remarkable than we had anticipated. Not only did many express surprise at the quality of the children's work, but many agreed that they had not previously realised the educational potential of the computer in the classroom. Parents took the opportunity to try some of the programs for themselves, becoming visibly more enthusiastic as the evening developed. As if this were not reward enough for the hard work that had gone into the project so far, some parents were quick to notice that, at that time, the school only had one computer of its own. The one question which stands out most in our minds on that evening went something like: 'Is there an educational reason for having just one computer in the school, or it is just a lack of money?'

Interestingly, the question of acquiring further computers for the school had recently arisen at a staff meeting and the view had been expressed that the ideal situation would be to have one computer permanently installed in each class area. Consequently it was not necessary for us to answer the parent's question since the teachers themselves already had their answer prepared. What we had not anticipated was that a sufficient number of parents felt strongly enough about this issue to press for the formation of a parent–teacher association which could undertake to raise funds for the purchase of more computers and software. This they did with the full blessing of the headteacher and her staff. The association is functioning well having raised enough money to buy two more computers and a printer by the end of that school term.

6
HORSES FOR COURSES
Different Programs for
Different Purposes: A Chronicle of Events

Spring Term 1987

Observations began on Monday, the 12th of January 1987 when Jane, our research assistant, visited the school for the first time. We had hoped to begin earlier at the start of the new school year in September but there had been a delay in Brussels over the details of the budget and we were reluctant to employ a research assistant before funding was finalised. What follows in this chapter is the chronicle of events as seen at the time by Jane, Sue (our second research assistant who joined us in June), the two teachers and ourselves.

The programs introduced into Pauline's and Joan's classrooms are described. Their intention, scope and practical details are examined and a brief appraisal is made of the cognitive and interactional skills that potential users need to acquire or to develop in order to use them effectively. We then turn to the retrospective accounts of teachers and the fieldnotes of Jane and Sue by way of piecing together a picture of where they saw themselves at the end of their collaborative experience. We, as researchers, venture a tentative on-going explanation of the processes involved.

Our account begins with Jane's initial visit to the school to administer the first battery of pupil measures. The children, she discovered, were already using a drill-and-practice program in connection with a topic on Eskimos. Although we were not anxious to encourage the use of drill-and-practice programs as such, it is important to begin with Jane's description of the work in order to help set the context within which subsequent computer work was to take place. What is more, Jane's description of how she began her integration into the classroom as someone who sat in and heard children read, serves as a good example for potential participant–observers. It proved to be more important for the project than we realised at the time for it was only later when we decided to modify the roles of the two research assistants to behave as parent/helpers that we realised how valuable Jane's speedy and successful integration into Broadwood School had been.

On her first day Jane notes:

> I met the headteacher and was taken on a guided tour of this well-organised, immaculately clean open-plan school. The two groups of children taking part in the study are based in adjacent working areas at one end of the school building. The children are used to visitors and my presence was almost unnoticed. After meeting Pauline and Joan and their classes, I spent the rest of my visit getting to know some of the children. As the computers were not being used at this time, listening to children read provided the opportunity for chatting to individual children while observing the rest of the class (excellent cover!).

By January 20th all except 5 of the 48 children had been tested. They were divided into four groups of ten or eleven and taken in turn into one of the 'quiet' rooms adjoining their work area. Jane continues:

> Lou Cohen and I together tested the first small group of children in case any unforeseen problems arose. The only slight query resulted from the test which asked the children to write 1 or 0 next to all of their classmates' names depending on whether they thought that they tried more or less hard than they themselves. It was suggested that they decide one way or the other even though the difference was very slight. They appeared to be satisfied with this forced choice and accordingly assigned 1 or 0 to everyone on the class list. I tested the three remaining groups myself. . . . It wasn't surprising that in such a well disciplined school, the children were on their best behaviour and the tests were completed with minimum fuss. The general opinion was that filling in the booklets had been good fun.

The following day gave Jane the opportunity to observe some children using the computer for the first time. Other pupils missed the opportunity.

> The group was time-tabled to use the computer all morning. However, their teacher was late because of heavy traffic and she explained that she hadn't had time to organise this activity.
>
> Three children in the other group (two girls and a boy), used one computer for half an hour before break and about forty minutes after. They were using a program called 'The Explorer', part of the Ladybird-Longman package called 'Other Worlds'.

'Other Worlds' is a suite of programs providing a means whereby children and teachers can together create worlds, learning from and about them as they work. For example, the authors provide a few ideas:

1. A person visiting a place for the first time.
2. A tree living in a threatened rain forest.
3. A Roman centurion stationed on Hadrian's Wall and so on.

The package contains two separate programs. 'The Explorer' emphasises the physical environment:

> You are transported to another place and by interaction with the program simultaneously create and interpret what you discover. . . .
>
> The explorer's role is to observe carefully; match observation with previous knowledge and information and interpret the unfamiliar, strange and dangerous. The explorer is an intruder, and his priorities are to survive and observe.
>
> (Teacher's handbook, p. 7)

'The Inhabitant', by contrast, concentrates upon the social fabric of a world:

'From this point of view a world is far less mysterious. The inhabitant is at home. Again the prompts and questions from the program indicate areas for consideration. The inhabitant's role is to explain to an interested visitor fundamental aspects of his society and interpret them for this stranger'

(Teacher's handbook, p. 7).

These programs provide a wealth of opportunities for invention, explanation, empathy, discovery, language development, expression and problem-solving. In addition, the authors emphasise the importance of children moving away from the computer into other activities which may involve the library, drama, artwork, modelling and even visits. The text in both programs is designed to suit a reading age of approximately 8.5 years, although the authors claim success with infants and other groups with higher or lower reading ages.

Jane's account continues:

> They had already decided who they were called and where they were going. During the seventy minutes' observation they worked their way through the rest of the program. I was fascinated by the way they reached consensus over their choices, and how they shared out turns at operating the computer. ... They didn't take turns at operating the computer in any strict order. When they felt that someone had been left out for a while, they agreed that it was time for that person to have 'a go' now. Overall it seemed to work out fairly.
>
> Two queries arose during the operation. One was, 'Can we obliterate a whole page from the screen?' They decided that they couldn't do this, and carried on. The other was, 'Why did the computer suddenly stop and bleep after printing about two and a half lines of their description?' They didn't know the answer to this either but decided not to go and ask their teacher. Instead, they carried on with the next screen page. I was surprised at how many skills were being practised here. They included a variety of social skills, creative thinking, decision-making, various language skills and manual dexterity.

By the last week in January we had formulated some questions for Jane to raise, informally, in conversation with Pauline and Joan. These, and the replies they elicited, are given summarised below.

Question 1   Have the two participating teachers studied the handbooks for the 'Other Worlds' programs?

Answer   Pauline and Joan had read the teachers' handbooks and referred to them whenever a problem occurred. Apparently neither teacher used the handbooks as a source of inspiration for the further development of activities. 'Once you've read one you've read them all, particularly the Ladybird handbooks. The children's handbooks are much more useful.'

Question 2   How does 'Other Worlds' fit in with the teachers' overall plans for the topic?

Answer   One teacher thought it followed on quite well after the class study of Eskimos. She also thought that 'Other Worlds' would be useful in the summer when she plans to introduce local studies.

Question 3   Why can't the computer be out all the time? Pauline and Joan now have a computer on loan from the University. It is solely for the use of these two classes and is conveniently housed on a trolley in a room adjacent to the teaching area. In addition to this, the teachers are scheduled to have the school computer for a morning each during the week.

Answer   Both teachers could see no reason why the University computer should not be in use in their areas most of the time. Their reasons for not doing this so far were that they either didn't remember to get it out, hadn't the time to set it up or were worried about its security if left unattended.

> When asked whether two computers could be used in the area at the same time, one teacher said that it hadn't occurred to her to do so, but that she could see no reason why this shouldn't be done in future.

At this early stage in the project, it seemed to us that Pauline and Joan viewed using the computer as something of an afterthought, that is, if there was time to think about it after planning and initiating the 'real work'.

Question 5 What is the usual pattern of computer use throughout the week/year in the whole school?

Answer Mrs. Silver, the teacher in charge of resources in the school, was invited to answer this question. The school computer timetable indicates six out of fifteen blocks of time when the computer isn't scheduled for use at all:

> The school computer is used far less now than when it first arrived. Why is this? (J.W.)
> One reason is that there are now four classes housed in mobile classrooms. The effort of wheeling the computer outside and lifting it up the steps to these classrooms is daunting to say the least. The deputy head plans to take a computer to his mobile classroom for long blocks of time, in order to use the 'Flowers of Crystal' program next term.

The resources teacher is in charge of an infant class. She finds that another factor limiting computer use is that an adult must be present with the infants using it. She has trained two parents to help her but obviously they can't be there all the time.

Jane continues:

> The question of computer use throughout the whole school was put to the teachers participating in the project. As far as they could tell, there had been a marked decline in its use. They thought this could be due to the difficulty of finding relevant programs and so the school's software collection had been exhausted causing interest to wane.

Referring back to the list of software available in the school (see Chapter 5), readers will recall that it was rather limited in scope, being mainly drill and practice and simulation. Indeed, the most commonly used programs had been those which were easiest to get up and running. The consequence of this was that the more open-ended and versatile programs had hardly, if ever, been used. It is not surprising that interest had waned. It was our hope that, by introducing and encouraging the use of more open-ended and versatile programs, we could revive the waning enthusiasm by extending the teachers' view of what was possible.

Having come to the end of the first round of testing, Jane was able to concentrate more on observing the children's behaviour when using the computer:

> During that week the two remaining children completed the tests. A new boy joined class 1 in the previous week but he would need a little time to get used to his new school. He will be tested the next time round.
> I observed Donna and Teresa (Class 8) using the computer. They made quick decisions and worked through the whole of 'The Explorer' in thirty-five minutes (according to the teachers). On Wednesday I observed Gregory and Robert (class 9). . . . Their responses were not very adventurous. They chose to go to the Arctic, saw polar bears and whales and heard ice cracking. [The class topic had recently been about Eskimos.]. . . Their choice of clothes was a little more daring. Keeping in mind the wetness and low temperature, they decided to wear woolly hats under diving helmets, track suits under big wetsuits and three pairs of socks inside wellingtons.

During this first month of the research, we suspect that Pauline and Joan found Jane's frequent observations of their pupils somewhat puzzling. It's not uncommon, in our experience, that teachers sometimes think researchers are only interested in highly active or troublesome children. An 'aside' from Joan to Jane concerning pupils Gregory and Robert is recorded in her diary: 'Their teacher commented that it was unfortunate that I was observing two quiet little boys. I pointed out to her that whatever went on in the classroom was of interest to me'.

Jane Tries 'Systematic Observation' for the First Time

It was now the first week of February and the project was into its second month. The first round of tests was completed and the special target children identified and made known to the teachers. Jane had spent some hours working with small groups and with individual children and was accepted in and around the school just like any of the other parents or helpers. Now was the time to start using C.O.M.I.C., the systematic observation schedule which we had devised to record the proportion of time children spent on various tasks when using the computer (see Appendix I for a detailed description).

When I arrived at 9.30 the computer wasn't in the teaching area. The teacher was handing the children's workbooks back and discussing their merits. After the class had settled down to maths practice, the University computer was brought out. The teacher plugged it in and set it up ready for use. . . . Two boys and a girl were chosen to work on 'Explorer'. It is interesting to note that this period is time-tabled for project work and also to use the school computer. Two computers could have been in use in the area at this time. The teacher commented that with this particular class, she hasn't been able to cover all the work she had planned and that topic work has gone by the board to some extent.

I sat with the group (Ben, Brian and Sonia) and filled in the first C.O.M.I.C. tally sheet. I had memorised the twelve categories and found that ten second intervals gave just enough time for recording and occasionally making a brief note. The children reached consensus fairly amicably to begin with but Sonia began to feel left out and dissatisfied. . . .

The last three minutes on Sonia's tally sheet reflected her increasing disenchantment. She started to watch the other two boys in action and to daydream. When I asked her whom she would like to work with, she replied: 'With Sarah-Jane, she's my friend.'

After break Ben commented to someone else in the class that: 'We've already been on this for half an hour!'

Clearly, he was beginning to feel that they had been long enough on the task and was anxious to finish it. He discovered that he was making many more notes than the other two and concentrated a great deal of effort on copying the summaries from the screen. I asked the group why they were writing notes down. Ben replied: 'We have to show everybody in the class when everybody has had a go. We're going to write a story about it.'

A more usual answer to this question was: 'I dunno'.

This group had an interesting operational mode. They discussed their responses and keyed them in almost simultaneously. They often keyed in a response together i.e. Sonia keyed in two or three letters, Ben keyed in one letter, Brian added a few more, and so on.

On the following day the teacher chose three more children to work at the computer (Carl, Andrew and Andrea), while the rest were engaged in a variety of other work activities. She asked if they recalled which country they were to explore. They remembered 'The Arctic'. The class had recently been studying Eskimos.

Andrea was easily distracted throughout the observation period. She got off her chair, scratched her leg, ate little sweets from her pocket, turned round whenever she heard her teacher's voice raised, smiled frequently at me and fiddled in her pocket with some cards. In spite of all these distractions she joined in the discussions, took her turn at operating the keyboard and made notes. Although the group said that they were taking turns at operating the keyboard and holding the handbook, it appeared to me that Carl, in the middle, was getting the lion's share. He took the task quite seriously to begin with. He said: 'We don't want to waste time. We don't want to spend too long.'

When asked why, he said that he had lots of other things to do. This may be related to the fact that Mrs. Brown frequently reminds the class not to waste time and that they have spent far too long on certain tasks.

Andrew had a much more light-hearted approach. He said: 'Let's make it comical', and proceeded to make absurd suggestions. He wanted to enjoy himself.

The group was having difficulty with certain spellings. The teacher intervened. She asked who was the best speller in the group, to which the unanimous reply was 'Andrea!' She suggested that Andrea change places with Carl and sit in the middle to operate the keyboard. The new arrangement made little difference. Later Mrs. Brown reminded Andrew disapprovingly: 'Andrew, you are always seeing the silly side of things. This is a serious learning task. Use your brains.'

During the first three weeks of the project both classes had been using 'Other Worlds' as a follow-up to previous topic work. Class 8 had been working on 'Dinosaurs and Monsters' and Class 9 on 'The Arctic'. Throughout this time groups of two or three children had been taking turns at working their way through the package. This would continue until everyone had had a turn. Class 9 had been instructed to explore the Arctic, although it was by no means certain at that time what would happen to notes made by the children. While the computer group was in action the rest of the class was engaged in other activities not connected with the topic. The computer still seemed to be in use as an additional extra rather than an integral part of the overall plan. Only one computer was ever in use in the area at a time. It seemed more desirable to Jane that two computers be used as much as possible in order that the children have their turn as soon as possible: 'So far they have been taking turns over a three week period and they still haven't finished' (J.W.). By the following week the teacher had decided to provide additional turns for those whom she felt hadn't done very well the first time. She chose Wayne, Timothy and Richard for the first group. Previously she had rated Timothy as one of the least academically able, least popular and least able on the computer. He had also been rated as one of the least popular members of his class. Jane describes the activity at the computer:

Tim didn't help the situation by wanting to put in his own version of the story or press RETURN before the others were ready. He found it very difficult to cooperate.

When the first summary came up on the screen Richard and Wayne began to take notes.

'I'm not going to bloody write that!' said Tim. I suggested that he needn't write all of it – just the important words. He was happy with this suggestion and made a list of things to take on the expedition. He found the prospect of writing a lot of notes quite daunting. His attention wandered to the window and out towards a distant hill. It was a glorious sunny morning.

'Have you ever been up that hill?' he asked me.

'Do you think it's further away than it looks?'

Tim spent most of the time looking round the room, gazing out of the window, trying to read the screen, watching the other two, trying to share the reference book and trying to use the keyboard when he wasn't supposed to. When asked later whether he would like a chance to use the computer all by himself his eyes sparkled,

'Yes I would!'

I suspect that he would be quite good if given the chance. When asked whom he would choose to work with he chose Conrad. He is rated as one of the most popular in the class but according to his teacher: 'For the wrong reasons. Conrad is a bully.'

After the break Wayne failed to return to the computer. The others said he was sulking.

Class 8 and 9 Go on a Field Trip

Pauline and Joan had planned to take a group of thirty children to Quorn Hall, a Leicestershire residential study centre, for a week towards the end of February. An important part of their local-studies programme was to gather information from the gravestones in Quorn churchyard.

By this time it was the general feeling of the research team that Pauline and Joan had been rather slow in taking up suggestions about how the computer might be used in their work (see Chapter 5 for a detailed analysis of this problem). Because the children were to collect data from the gravestones we thought it a good opportunity to introduce the database as a tool with such a concrete example of its possible use so close to hand. Some preliminary data were hurriedly collected from the churchyard and a small datafile compiled to serve as an example for the teachers. This was then used as the basis of a training session at the University to help Pauline and Joan see how the database might enhance the work they had already planned. Everything was done to make the task easy for them, even to the extent of designing and printing multiple coding sheets for the children to use when collecting the information in the churchyard. We chose INFORM as the database program because it is relatively comprehensive and easy for children to use.

INFORM is a BASIC program designed to facilitate the interrogation of fixed-length record datafiles using the BBC microcomputer equipped with a disc drive. The program was developed to facilitate datafile interrogation through:

1. access to many different files using a single-user program;
2. the possibility of a wide variety of searches as specified by the user;
3. the user's own choice of which information is to be output; and
4. the use of a simple procedure allowing searches on files to be carried out by children in the classroom,

thus encouraging them to think about information, its storage, retrieval and uses.

The maximum record length is 225 characters and the maximum number of fields is 24. Datafiles may also be created or edited using 'Wordwise', a wordprocessor for the BBC computer. The program provides a comprehensive range of commands and utilities including:

DESCRIBE (describe field)
FIND (specify a search)
GO (commences search)
GROUP (group frequency distribution)
HELP (list of commands)
INDEX (load/use index file)
NEWFILE (select file to be interrogated)

LIST (list a selected record)
OUTPUT/PRINT (select output to screen or printer)
SORT (sort output in numerical or alphabetical order)
STAT (statistical summary)
USER (to use user options or routines)

During file interrogation the following tests are permitted using single-key entry:

1. Greater than
2. Less than
3. Equal to
4. Not equal to
5. Contains
6. Does not contain
7. Starts with

Jane accompanied Pauline and Joan and the children on their trip to Quorn and so was able to maintain her role as participant observer and parent/helper. This is how she describes their common experience in the graveyard:

The children and teachers walked from Quorn Hall to Quorn Parish churchyard on a sunny but cold and frosty morning. They had two sheets of data to collect:

1. provided solely by the teachers which asked for

   a. the oldest gravestone
   b. the youngest person buried
   c. the oldest person buried
   d. details of Thomas Finn's grave
   e. records of memorials

and

2. the datasheet suggested by the research team which was set out in a form which would simplify data collection and make it easier for the children to build up a databank.

The children set out collecting the first sheet of information with enthusiasm. They picked up clues from each other. A flurry of excitement in one corner of the churchyard attracted the attention of a few others. They spread out all over the churchyard, most of them completing the sheet in half an hour.

When the teachers thought that most of the children had finished the first data sheet they called them together and gave them their second assignment which was to complete a rubbing or a drawing of something in the churchyard.

By the time this was done there were about twenty minutes left in which to complete the second data sheet. Fingers and feet were beginning to feel cold and numb. The sun hadn't reached some parts of the churchyard and frost was still thick on the grass.

This was definitely not the best time to begin the marathon task of collecting data for a data base!

I had already asked the teachers to explain the second datasheet to the children (terms like *spouse*, *sex* and *mason* needed clarification) and had pointed out that the children would need to be organised into small groups and assigned to various areas in the churchyard in order to avoid duplicating information. I assumed that trained teachers had understood these basic principles of organising children to undertake such a task. Unfortunately this was not the case. They were about to be despatched haphazardly when a timely reminder from me prompted the teachers to send them off in groups and to ask them to each record information from different gravestones.

I went off to help one small group. They sensibly allocated themselves one gravestone each. They decided among themselves what was meant by SEX and SPOUSE. One little girl needed FORENAME and SURNAME reclarifying. MASON had to be explained to all of them. A recurring question was: 'How do I find out when he was born?'

I explained that if the year of death was known and the age of the person who died, it was a simple 'take away' sum. It was suggested that those calculations could be done later in the classroom.

Clearly it would have been a good idea to discuss these problems before the visit. I felt that a little more forward planning was needed.

Pauline had picked up a chest infection whilst on the field trip. As a result she was unable to return to school the following week. Her class was looked after by a supply teacher for the week and so no computer work was possible.

Jane took this opportunity to persuade Joan to use the two computers in her area, thus getting twice the amount of computer work done. Jane was to get the children started on entering their data.

Three children used the 'Other Worlds' program while three others worked with me on setting up the INFORM database. Joan chose three able children, Sandeep, Jason and Melanie, to work with me. We entered the fieldnames and descriptions and then set about entering our data. Melanie and Jason each entered their own data in turn while the other two acted as reader and checker. We calculated the dates of birth where they were missing. Sandeep wasn't on the Quorn Hall trip so he keyed in data which had been collected by a boy in class 8. (Joan is deciding whether the class 8 children should be invited to key in their own data. My feeling is that they should.) It took us one and a half hours to enter twenty-six records. These three children seemed to enjoy doing this rather mindless task. They said that they weren't bored but they thought that asking the computer questions later would be the best part.

On the following Monday Joan set up the computer ready to start. We had already decided that two of last week's children (Melanie and Jason) would act as teachers of one new child. I suggested that two of the 'target' children (Gregory and Sarah who had both been to Quorn) be shown how to enter their own data. Melanie and Jason explained how to do it and Gregory keyed in his own data with great confidence. The reader spelt out difficult names and the checker worked out the dates of birth.

Sandeep and Gregory then acted as teachers while Sarah keyed in her data. This system is working well. Melanie and Jason talked about the sort of questions they would like to ask the computer:

1. Which was the most popular surname?
2. Which Christian names were the most popular? Are these the same today?
3. Which is the oldest grave?

Sandeep would like to find out if any First World War dead are buried at Quorn.

Jane Tries to Stimulate some Forward Planning

There had been some previous indication from Pauline and Joan that they found their present pupils somewhat less motivated and more troublesome than children in previous years. This seemed to be particularly true of the older members of these two vertically grouped third- and fourth-year classes. Following the rather limited success with the database so far, we encouraged Jane to try to get Pauline and Joan to think about work for the Summer Term and to attempt to integrate several other kinds of programs into their schemes of work. The topic of local studies seemed to lend itself to the use of not only the database but also a wordprocessor and a teletext emulator. Joan's response provided further evidence of the teachers' feelings towards the children and gave us the first substantive example of the different definitions of the situation constructed by the teachers on the one hand and the participant-observer on the other. Clearly the teachers had known the children for considerably longer than Jane and therefore, one might argue, should have known the children better. Some of their knowledge was, of course, 'hearsay' since the children had not been with Pauline and Joan throughout their primary school career, but the pupils' behaviour in the churchyard and their subsequent performance in using the database seemed to be somewhat at odds with labels such as 'disruptive', 'troublesome' and 'unmotivated'.

This is how Jane saw the situation:

> I discussed with Joan the idea of planning a local studies project for the summer term, using some other programs, spreading the work across the curriculum. She liked the idea but said it would be very difficult for her to teach in this way. She commented that the two classes: 'Are just not interested in anything. Last year's group found the churchyard much more interesting.' Yet the children set about the churchyard search with enthusiasm, and they are enjoying compiling the database and some are already formulating questions to ask. Is this a prime example of a self-fulfilling prophecy at work? Pauline and Joan have already made up their minds that this year's children are nowhere near as capable as last year's. Because of this they don't try to stimulate them with interesting ideas in case there is little response.

Still the children did not seem to be getting a great deal of 'hands on' time with the computer; for some it was much less than for others. Over the last seven-week period, each child in Joan's class had had one turn on 'The Explorer' for 45 minutes to two hours. These figures refer to use of the University computer only. To this point in the project little use had been made of the school computer even when it was available. Joan agreed to keep a record of use of both computers as well as the degree of teacher involvement in these activities.

A Very Useful Management Strategy

Children's experiences with the computer over this period were much the same in both classrooms. The same strategy was adopted whereby two more experienced children tutored a third. The distinctive roles of reader, checker and keyboard operator were adopted with great success. As a classroom strategy for managing the computer as a scarce resource, this arrangement proved to be extremely successful in many subsequent computer-based activities throughout the project.

The Datafile is Complete

The datafile was finally completed on the 16th March. Much to everyone's surprise it contained 170 complete records. However, despite the fact that both Pauline and Joan had Jane available to help with the computer and ready to do whatever they suggested whilst they got on with other things, there seemed to be a degree of tension. Pauline was preparing an 'assembly', an event involving many children and one that generally seems stressful to the teacher responsible. Meanwhile, 'The Inhabitant' was still the most commonly used program. Jane continues:

> Pauline and Joan didn't seem too pleased to see me. The children were restless, perhaps the Spring weather and the headteacher's continued illness were contributory factors. Pauline and Joan were complaining that they didn't know whether they were coming or going. Pauline is concerned that her assembly for Wednesday isn't 'coming together' and she will have to rehearse it on Tuesday.

Having said all that, the two teachers had not abandoned the computer. In fact they had taken another important step by introducing the use of the printer to some of the children. As a result, Jane was greeted enthusiastically by one child who wanted to show her what she had done:

> As soon as I arrived this morning, Sonia came jumping up to tell me that she had written a story on the printer. She showed me the story in her book which had been corrected ready to print out. Two boys were working on their stories this morning. It seems to be working well.

On the following day Jane still found the teachers to be a little tense, although they were managing to keep the work with the computer going despite their feelings about being under pressure. Jane arranged to spend some time observing two of the target children using the computer.

> When I arrived this morning Pauline was busy mounting pictures and keeping an eye on her class at the same time. Joan's class was in the hall. Pauline was feeling concerned about her assembly presentation for the next day so I offered to help with the mounting. Two of Pauline's class were using the printer.
>
> Joan's class arrived back and I set up the school computer ready to begin 'The Inhabitant'. I asked if I could observe the target children, so Joan chose Robert and Gregory. She instructed them to imagine that they were one of the people who lived at Beaumanor Hall (one of the historic places visited when on the field trip) and to refer to information in their folders in order to decide who to be. They looked at a sketch of various servants at Beaumanor Hall and an 1861 census of people in Woodhouse and decided to be a butler.
>
> 'The Inhabitant' was really designed to prompt children to visit an imaginary place and some of the questions were not appropriate for a butler in 1861. However, the children responded as sensibly as they could.
>
> I completed tally sheets for both Robert and Gregory.
>
> They were confused over the section of the program which asks 'How long is your day?' They keyed in 14 hours. The next questions asks 'Divide the day into work, rest and leisure.' Because rest is included they thought of 24 hours and the computer rejected this. They couldn't figure out why.
>
> Sarah (the other target child in the group), explained that they had to divide fourteen hours into work, rest and leisure.
>
> Apparently this had confused some of the other children. Robert and Gregory enjoyed most of all thinking up a menu for their next meal. Robert said, 'I would fill myself with that food if I could. . . .'
>
> I was interested to note that Gregory applied today's unemployment situation to the butler in 1861. In answer to their question 'Will you be doing the same job a year from now?' He said, 'No, I'll probably have lost my job.'

By March 20th the teachers' enthusiasm was becoming more evident, so much so that Joan reported to Jane that she and Pauline were 'now fighting over the computers'. Clearly they were beginning to feel much more confident and interested. By this time Joan was interrogating the database. When she organised a school assembly based upon the work done with the database it was a roaring success both with the children and the rest of the staff. This is hardly the work of dissaffected and unmotivated children. (For a more detailed account of this, see Chapter 5.) The teachers themselves saw this as a significant event in the year:

D.B.	Am I right in thinking then that probably, from your point of view, and perhaps for the children, that activity using INFORM with the subsequent display and the assembly was a milestone, an important event in the process so far?
Joan	Yes, because certainly the assembly was purely about using the computer to work on the field-course data. The children felt involved and gained something from it. They could see that it had a valuable use.
Pauline	The work and the display drew many comments from a variety of sources; other staff, parents and visitors, but perhaps more pleasing, from other children in the school. Obviously this was gratifying and it did mark a major milestone in the project to date. We both felt more at ease with the computer and felt more able to ad lib in a crisis. The effort now seemed much more worthwhile.

Although the children's work with the database had been the central part of the assembly, the display of children's work had been supplemented by some other exciting creations using a simple newspaper-editor program called 'Front Page'. The major attraction of this program is its simplicity. Indeed, it is so simple that Pauline and Joan had to be shown it only once for them to be bubbling with ideas of how they could put it to use in many different areas of the curriculum.

'Front Page' is a simple BASIC program which allows children to create the content of a newspaper without having to be concerned with designing the layout. Simple prompts are provided at all stages. The user is taken through a set sequence of operations to produce the title, date, price, headline, text (justified in both left and right margins), a picture and finally an advertisement. An opportunity to edit the text is provided before the finished product is printed on a dot matrix printer.

We Try to Cash in on the New-Found Enthusiasm

Following Joan's assembly there had been a considerable increase in interest from other teachers in the school and Mrs. Silver, the head of resources, asked Derek Blease if he would be willing to demonstrate the printer to the staff at a lunchtime training session.

Jane was away for a few days that week and Joan didn't use the computer at all during that time. Pauline's class had been using 'Front Page'. They drew their own pictures in the space provided. The computer drawing is very limited and unsatisfactory; the weakest aspect of 'Front Page'. We had a training session on Wednesday afternoon and, in anticipation of the planned local-studies project for next term, Derek Blease introduced 'Edfax', a teletext emulator.

'Edfax' is a program which allows for the creation of teletext-type pages of information on the screen just like 'CEEFAX' and 'ORACLE' broadcast by the BBC and Independent Television. Instead of being broadcast, however, they are stored on a single floppy disc. These pages can then be accessed at random, just like the real thing. It is possible to include both text and block graphics in any individual page using a variety of colours and other visual effects like double-height text, flashing images and hidden detail. Initially the procedures for creating pages are not easy to master.

Pauline, Joan and Jane worked their way through the handbook in an afternoon training session at the University. Two possible uses for 'Edfax' in the local-studies project were suggested:

1. To present the children's work in text and in pictures.
2. To compile a reference programme for the children to use. The researchers would help to put this together; the teachers would decide what to include.

Derek Blease visited the Leicestershire Records Office and the local-studies department in the Loughborough Library to assess what local information was available. Jane made an appointment for Pauline and Joan to meet the local-studies librarian on the last Friday of the Easter holiday. Since Pauline already had a computer of her own at home, we suggested that Joan took the University computer home in the Easter holiday so that she could practice with 'Edfax'.

Summer Term 1987

The summer term began with our anticipation of better things to come. We hoped that we had sown enough interesting ideas so that our two teachers would be really enthusiastic to include the computer as an integral part of their planning and activities. To Jane's dismay, things were not as we had hoped for:

- This was the first week of term after the Easter holiday.
- Pauline and Joan didn't keep their appointments with the local-studies librarian.
- Pauline said that she was away.
- Neither had they thought about reference material for putting on to 'Edfax'.

There is no doubt that both Pauline and Joan get very tired by the end of the term, and teaching in a primary school can be particularly taxing during the winter months. However, this could not have been the only reason why the appointment had not been kept nor the material for 'Edfax' planned. We suggested earlier that according to their teachers' perceptions of them, the pupils were rather difficult to motivate and tended to be badly behaved, needing a constant firm hand. It would be quite unfair to suggest that this was just a figment of the teachers' imaginations. We had all experienced incidents in the classroom and elsewhere with some of the children which served forcibly to reinforce this view. Nevertheless, we felt that there was a distinct possibility that the teachers' expectations served finally to reinforce this sort of behaviour rather than to eliminate it. Jane pursued the idea further:

> Pauline is very dissatisfied with her class of children this year and she often says so. The following account illustrates this:
>
> The Head of Resources was talking in the staffroom of a superb project on 'The Edwardians' which she had seen at another school in the area. She described the pictures, models and writing in great detail. Pauline responded, 'Yes but they are *proper* children in that class aren't they?'
>
> I think she has given herself a perfect excuse for not planning interesting projects for her

class. She says that she has to concentrate on '*the basics*' and her class are so slow that she hasn't time for anything else.

Despite the fact that both classes had been working for more than a term with 'The Inhabitant', there was evidence to suggest that it had not achieved full integration into the scheme of things nor into the way that teachers and children thought and felt about their work. The following incident illustrates the point:

> I was observing Maurice and Stephen in Joan's class. The rest of the class were to have a spelling test. I asked if these two boys could continue with the computing. Stephen was very concerned that he was missing his spelling test. I pointed out that he had spent a lot of time on spelling that morning. He and Maurice had been making changes on the 'Inhabitant' program which involved correcting various spelling mistakes. The spelling test contained several words which the children would hardly ever want to use, whereas the spellings they had corrected in their computer work were entirely relevant to their experience.

This is an apt illustration of the way in which the computer was still regarded by the teachers as something 'extra' to the curriculum; it was not surprising that the children also reflected this viewpoint.

A new 'Local-Studies' Project Begins

On the Wednesday morning of the first week in May, Jane went with Joan and her class on their first visit to Thorpe Acre, a small village on the outskirts of Loughborough. Their brief was to look out for any buildings which had been built before 1960. They visited Thorpe Acre church and collected some information from the gravestones. As Joan put it: 'I'll give them some time to collect information for *your* database'. In Joan's view, it seemed, the computer database was 'an additional extra' to the Thorpe Acre local-studies project!

While this was going on, the research team was planning to introduce yet another computer-based resource to enable pupils and teachers to explore the world of computer graphics. Our initial objective was to provide a means whereby simple line drawings could be created which could be easily infilled with colour or tone. Not wanting something as geometrically precise as LOGO, however, we opted for a straightforward computer art package called 'AMX Super Art'. This choice also allowed us to introduce the 'mouse' as a more user-friendly alternative to the keyboard for moving the cursor around the screen and for creating the many effects made possible by the program. The mouse is increasingly becoming the preferred means of communication with computers in industry and commerce, not as a replacement for the keyboard, but as a versatile addition to it. This would be good enough reason for its introduction into school, but it actually makes computing more fun too! Since Jane was also a novice we once again included her in the training session:

> We were introduced to the 'AMX Mouse' this week. I found it quite difficult to control the line drawings. I need to practice hand/eye coordination, also we probably need to use the mouse on a rubber mat. I'm sure the children will enjoy using this when it is set up and working well.

'AMX Super Art' is a program which allows the user to create diagrams, pictures and text of various sizes and styles on the screen, and ultimately print on to paper. This is largely achieved by movement of the mouse, a hand-controlled device which moves the pointer on the screen as it is moved across the table. Various tools or modes are provided which can be used to create effects like lines, circles, ellipses and boxes. The thickness of the lines can be varied, including a spray mode which gives the effect of a paint spray. Backgrounds can be filled with a range of colours and a variety of patterns or textures. The text can be placed anywhere on the screen.

Ultimately we hoped that the children would be able to progress from creating simple patterns and shapes to more complex pictures where text and graphics would be fully integrated so as to represent ideas as a whole rather than as picture with captions or brief, written comment. In this respect, our hopes were not fully realised in the time available although some of the children's artwork far exceeded our expectations in terms of complexity, creativity and sheer manual dexterity. More of this later.

Jane continues with a description of some work which bears an uncanny likeness to the Quorn Graveyard study of the previous term:

This morning I went with Pauline's class to visit Thorpe Acre. We went to the church first of all and the children seemed to find it quite interesting. Points of interest were:

The £1 coin left as payment for leaflets
the two fonts – ancient and modern
the eagle on the lectern – a bird of 'prey'
the kneelers beautifully cross-stitched in bright colours
the grids and cover in the floor
the elaborately embroidered alter cloth worth £2,500
the old and new bits of the church.

We went from the church to the church hall where a display of photographs shows the progressive stages of adding new wings to the church. A photograph of the old organ aroused some speculation: 'It's a fireplace', 'No it's one of those pianos with sticks that move up and down'. 'Don't be daft it's an organ!'
The class was then divided into three groups and dispatched to different activities:

a) to gather information from the gravestones
b) to do some rubbings
c) to sketch the church

We then went down to the old cottage in the village and the children sat on the grassy bank and sketched it in about ten minutes. Next we walked round to see the old wrought iron gate which belonged to the Grange. It has been left standing by the 'Maltings' pub.

Suddenly Pauline revealed something which took Jane quite by surprise. Had we underestimated the effect of our presence in the school since January?

As we were walking along together Pauline volunteered the information that she and Joan had (at last) visited the local studies library (Loughborough) and had borrowed some old photographs, books and photocopies of newspaper cuttings about Thorpe Acre. They found that the local studies materials were very disorganised, even so the information salvaged was worth collecting. During lunch time I sorted the gravestone material collected by Joan's class, ready for putting into the data base.

That afternoon both classes were on the field for town-sports trials. Jane decided to try out the 'AMX Mouse': 'It's working better than last week but I still lack coordination. It might be interesting to see what the children make of it'.

We all Visit our Belgian and French Colleagues

Towards the end of May we arranged to take Pauline, Joan and Jane to Liège for three days to meet the Belgian and French researchers and teachers who were involved in the two projects parallel to our own. We hoped that the visit would help them see the relevance of our project and give them a feel for its European dimension. Because the visit was also a normal part of the coordination procedure of the three projects, Lou Cohen and Derek Blease had to participate in a number of meetings, leaving Jane and the two teachers to spend some time together and to visit Belgian primary schools including the one involved in the project. This was the first time that teachers from any of the experimental schools in the three countries had met. It provided a unique opportunity to compare experiences, methods and problems. Jane also found it useful because it gave her a chance to get to know Pauline and Joan in a different social context. She was anxious to find out more about what they really thought about working on the project.

> While Lou and Derek were engaged in presenting our research so far to the Belgians and the French, I went with Pauline and Joan for a 'tout a pied' round new and old Liège. This gave me a chance to get to know them socially and to ask them informally what they felt about the research. This situation was not always possible in school.
>
> 'Front Page' has been a great hit because of its ability to produce an interesting result in a simple way. The graphics facility is hopeless. The children's own illustrations are much more satisfactory.
>
> Pauline and Joan are not very keen on 'Other Worlds', 'The Explorer' and 'The Inhabitant'. They would prefer more open-ended packages.
>
> 'Edfax' hasn't been introduced yet. Pauline and Joan don't feel comfortable with it themselves at this point in time. 'AMX Art' hasn't been introduced either, for the same reason. Both of these programs will probably be left until the autumn term.

The school visits were of great interest. First of all, Pauline, Joan and Jane visited the participating Belgian school at Crisnée, situated in a small rural community some miles out of Liège. Like many schools in Britain these days, the children were bussed into school each day. The second school visited was at Ciplay, where the team was able to see 'LOGO' in action for the first time. Our visit to Crisnée was seen as a major event by our hosts. The whole school participated in a welcoming reception which started with a school assembly. Here is what Jane wrote in her diary:

Crisnée

> On our arrival at the school we were greeted by Madame Montoulet who talked to us about the school. Next we went to assembly and were entertained by the whole school including two of the children who performed a mime for us to music of their favourite pop stars. Over coffee, Madame Montoulet talked further about the school in its local and national context.

Computing in the School

Before the project began, the primary school was given a computer donated by the bank which handles the school's financial affairs. Apart from this, computer services had not yet reached the school. At the headmistress's nomination, two teachers (a man and a woman), each in charge of a fifth-year class (ages 10–11), agreed to take part in the study.

Jeanine has been teaching for 28 years at primary school, the last five years at this age level. She runs her class in a rather traditional way and admits to a certain fear of change. When it came to computers, she was a complete novice. The fact that her own children are students in the subject has not diminished her anxiety about everything to do with computers.

Jules has been a teacher for 22 years and has taught fifth-year classes for 16 years. He has already taken part in several computer workshops. He has established a useful contact with a teacher from another town, and their pupils exchange letters and produce a small periodical review. At home he already has a microcomputer and has already followed a training course in programming in BASIC. Nevertheless, before this project he had never used a computer with his pupils in the classroom.

Jane continues:

We then divided into two groups to visit the two classrooms of the teachers involved in the Belgian project. The children had been using a wordprocessor to write a story and they were examining their computer printout in order to arrange it in paragraphs (Jules' class). We went on to the computer room where the children were using a variety of different programs.

Ciplay

The children using 'LOGO' in the school had come by bus from a neighbouring school to use the computer facilities. There were fourteen children using eight terminals with three teachers on hand to help with problems. Pauline and Joan felt that they would prefer this kind of arrangement.

The children had been instructed to create a picture which included a circle somewhere in the design. I hadn't seen 'LOGO' at all and was fascinated to understand how the turtle is instructed to move so many paces at specified angles in order to create the design. The children are also learning some simple programming rules.

Overall the visit to Liège was very successful. Pauline, Joan and Jane gained valuable insights into the ways in which the Belgian school worked and into the kinds of problems experienced by their Belgian colleagues when trying to come to terms with computers in their classrooms. We returned to England with a new spirit of participation and cooperation to be joined by a new member of the team, Sue, who joined us on June 4th and was to work in school with Jane alongside Pauline, Joan and the children. Like Jane, Sue was an experienced primary school teacher but a complete novice as far as using computers was concerned. It was important that we integrate Sue into the classroom as quickly as possible and that we involve her in the training sessions as a full participating member. Jane first of all introduced her to systematic observation using C.O.M.I.C.:

Sue started to work on the project today. I talked to her about the systematic observation. She watched me for five minutes and went off to observe Diva using 'Front Page'. Diva chatted to Sue off and on for the first few minutes and then settled down to the task in hand. Diva is very sociable and likes extra attention. She was the first one to chat to me when I arrived.

I joined Anne for half an hour to explore some of the mysteries of the concept keyboard. We were making quite good progress when my lift home arrived. Sue was getting on well with C.O.M.I.C.

Sue had never been involved in a research project of this kind and so it is not surprising that she felt some apprehension:

Entering school in a different capacity from a teacher made me reflect on factors involving my new role. How could I cause the least stress to the teacher whilst carrying out my observations? How could I be useful to the teacher or the research when waiting to observe? In what way could I extend my own computer knowledge to help the teacher and the research project?

During the week Joan seemed to be under considerable stress which was compounded by two computer faults. I had to rely on her for information when Jane was not present and was very conscious of a lack of knowledge. I wished I could be more useful. I contented myself with a humorous approach to diffuse situations, drawing from my own teaching experience. I felt much more comfortable when I had acquainted myself with 'Front Page' and 'The Inhabitant'. Computer faults were another matter, the motto being, 'Send for Derek to explain!'

However, all noble thoughts had flown on my first visit, after a tortuous journey in the rain. Had I made an impractical move? This problem was resolved by working out a rough weekly attendance pattern with Jane. Some work could be completed at home. Jane's support and understanding was invaluable and gave me confidence.

By the 10th of June Sue was settling in to use C.O.M.I.C. to observe children using 'Front Page'. As Jane commented:

Sue was in school on Monday and again this morning. She appears to enjoy C.O.M.I.C. but wishes that she could note more of the children's comments as she goes along.

Pauline's class has begun a second round of 'Front Page' reports. They were asked to be reporters at the scene of demolition of old properties in Thorpe Acre. I observed three children today. Teresa is the first child I have observed so far who has shown complete self-assurance at the computer. Pauline rates her as one of the most academically able, computer competent and motivated children in the class, yet Teresa rates herself as average in these categories.

Sue continues:

My first attempt at observing was with 'Front Page'. This was straightforward recording once my subject had calmed down and established procedure. I waded through three sheets with her, but by the end felt in my stride. My first time observing 'The Inhabitant', with two subjects, proved harder. This was because there were so many interesting exchanges about the program which I wanted to record that I almost forgot the clock. The teacher in me wanted to extend the children's comments and I was not acquainted with the program so I kept glancing at the screen to see what was happening next. I began to work out a procedure to make notes when clockwatching, whilst remaining straightfaced at even the most hilarious comments. I thought 'Front Page' an excellent introduction to using the printer. It is really encouraging children to think about punctuation, spelling and presentation. Later I discovered that 'The Inhabitant' was not being used as originally intended, but from an historical perspective. A more open-ended program could prove invaluable in thinking out and imagining many situations. . . . Initially, actually being required to think seemed to produce consciously ridiculous comments from the children.

However, when they went back to alter their work, more coherent results were produced. They really needed a checklist to remind them of areas to be altered and to take notes of their original comments to assist with their alterations. So much time was wasted in repeatedly running through the menu and summary. By the end of the week I had adjusted to school routine and was beginning to formulate a method of working after acquainting myself with programs. However, I was conscious of seeking ways to better utilise my time and of filling gaps in computer knowledge.

At this particular time, more than at any other, computer faults seemed to be bugging both teachers and researchers. It was not so much that the equipment was becoming unreliable, but that the operators were now beginning to try more adventurous things, seeking to apply the new experiences and triumphs of previous weeks.

They were beginning to show a greater degree of independence and this inevitably led to a higher incidence of snags. This was a time when swift and sensitive support was needed most. The worst thing that could happen would be for them to become reluctant to ask for help whenever things were not right. Jane noted the beginning of the problems on June 12th:

> Joan complained that her printer had ripped up a mass of paper and that the disc drive kept going wrong. The printer Pauline was using suddenly refused to produce a second copy when f5 was pressed. Also, when she first loaded the disc it wouldn't operate. They both agreed that without 'Derek to the rescue' they wouldn't know how to solve these technical hitches. What will happen when this backup service is removed after Christmas?
>
> The neighbouring class has been using 'INFORM' to compile a data base about the houses in Newtown Linford, eg. style, building materials, date etc. A Loughborough teaching practice student has been in charge of this. He commented on the difficulty of getting children of that age (7–8 yrs old) to formulate questions. Many are still only able to deal with one concept as a time.

By the following Monday Sue also noted how technical hitches were interfering with the work:

> At the beginning of the week Pauline and Joan were feeling particularly jaded and frustrated as the work they had prepared for the computer experienced long delays because of computer faults and various circumstances. The summoning of Derek sorted out Joan's problem, and I was able to proceed observing children using 'INFORM' to enter their data.

Jane provides a little more technical detail and suggests some sound advice for us all:

> We had some minor problems today which were easily solved with Derek's help. Neither Pauline nor I could load with 'Front Page' or 'The Inhabitant' discs into one of the disc drives. Derek suggested removing the disc and replacing it or jiggling it about – it worked!
>
> Joan had tried to set up 'INFORM'. She used the school master disc and came up against a problem she couldn't solve. Derek formatted a new data base disc for us and we used the University master disc. Problem solved.
>
> We tried using 'AMX Super Art' but couldn't get it to print out. We hadn't created a file space for our drawing first of all – simple solution. Pauline wonders what will happen when we can't call in expert help. This points to a major difficulty facing the busy primary school teacher. Can she take time to sort out hiccups on the computer when twenty-five other children need attention? She needs to be prepared to spend a lot of time on her own – at home or after school – getting to know these computer idiosyncrasies and finding out how to solve them.

By mid-June Sue was really coming to grips with how the children might be organised to enter their data when using 'INFORM':

> Joan was using the more computer-confident children to pass on procedure information to others. Three children (eventually) were working on the computer, one operating the keyboard, one checking and making calculations and the third reading out the information. They all had a turn at each job before one left and a newcomer was absorbed into the procedure, starting on keyboard.
>
> Some observations were very short when the children concerned listened and reacted to each other and understood the procedure (eg. Robert and Melanie). Observations lengthened when the child was unsure of any procedure (eg. Andrea), instructions were not clear from

checkers (eg. Andrew and Gregory), or when the child would not listen to instructions and argued (eg. Sandeep).

Inserting the data gave them good practice in making calculations like from two given dates or from one date and one age for example.

Jane did explain the database to me but I did not absorb it fully. However it did enable me to put the observations into perspective.

On June 25th Jane noted that Joan had really taken on board the idea of interrogating the database. Children were encouraged to think about their questions before sitting at the computer:

Joan surprised me by saying that she was going to use *two* computers in her area after break. She introduced 'how to interrogate the data base' to her group (very competently indeed – even I could understand it). The children were sent away to formulate questions in their rough books. Four of them went on to interrogate 'INFORM' and four worked with me on the 'AMX Art' program.

Stephen produced an excellent picture with 'AMX Art' and Joan asked him to leave it on the screen for the new third years to see. They visited the area in the afternoon and Joan drew their attention to the screen and told them it was 'one of the goodies in store for them next term'.

Sue Meets 'AMX Super Art' for the First Time

Up to this point very little work had been done using this program. There had been a number of initial technical problems to solve but the program itself is a little complicated, requiring the teacher to sit down with it for a while and experiment with the variety of effects and tools available. Sue took to the program with great enthusiasm, quickly seeing its shortcomings. Ultimately she made a very significant impact on the project by creating an environment in which teachers and children could quickly and efficiently achieve excellent results with this program. This is how she describes her first encounter:

As Pauline was planning to use 'AMX Super Art', Jane showed me the program and we ran through it in the lunch hour. I found it fascinating and Jane kindly suggested that I work with Pauline in the afternoon. I guided one child through the program before making an observation, but we encountered some problems with tool selection and printing. Eventually we managed to print but I realised that I did not know enough about the various functions. Pauline wished she had time to 'fiddle'. Therefore, whilst the children were at games, I went through the handbook, noting down any simple procedures which the children could use. The next morning I began to run through those procedures with Krishna. We experimented with the line tool, useful for making triangles, with the gridlock for pattern making (Krishna noted that we had tried to draw with black on black). I thought that eventually Pauline's time may be saved if I tried and tested various parts.

This time it was Sue who most needed some technical support as she started to become more adventurous and independent. It was very satisfying to see how, for all of them, their expertise as teachers was overriding their reluctance and apprehension about the technology. They were all attempting things which were educationally sound even though their level of technical competence was not yet great enough to suggest simple solutions. Meanwhile problems continued to occur. By this time it was the last week of the school year and frustration levels were high. Everyone was looking forward to the holiday, a time when we could check all the equipment and iron out any recurring problems in preparation for the new term in September. Up to this point it had always been a standing joke that things would never go wrong when Derek Blease tried them even when everyone else was having problems. Usually it was something they had forgotten to do or a feature that they didn't fully understand. However, when this was not the case they revelled in the knowledge that Derek was not infallible. This is how Sue recorded that final week:

This week we have been plagued with delays caused by ailing computers. 'Front Page' would not load until the computer had been switched off for at least an hour. 'AMX Art' loaded correctly, but half way through a picture would suddenly stop working properly and question marks appeared when the paint roller and the ellipses were selected. We had double-checked the procedure but could find no logical explanation for this. By the end of the week, when trying to load 'Front Page', the basic label was being deleted and there were strange symbols appearing on the screen. Needless to say, frustration levels were high. Surely there must be a fault on the computer? At first the fault seemed to be that the disc drive was not plugged in properly. However, when Derek tried to use 'AMX Art' he encountered strange problems too, much to our delight, and finally admitted that there must be a computer fault. It is easy to see how teachers can become disenchanted with using computers if technical problems cannot be rectified immediately.

When using 'Front Page' I completed an editing session for the first time and was surprised by the length of time taken to complete the task properly so that children understood their mistakes and made their own corrections. Jane commented that Joan felt it necessary to correct children's mistakes for them, but this does not use 'Front Page' to its full advantage. Children could be encouraged to go through their work line by line, noting down any mistakes, and having these checked by their teacher before correcting them on the screen. Once these mistakes had been eliminated, the teacher could concentrate on explaining grammar and punctuation.

With 'AMX Art', I feel confident when using the tool modes with their possible variations, and have been trying to build on that knowledge by looking at the options file. I have half-worked out this procedure by discussion with Jane reading the handbook and making my own notes. It had been frustrating that the computer problems prevented the use of the programs with the children, but maybe it is a good thing that this has been postponed until next term as Pauline is not acquainted with the program. Any problems should be solved by then.

Jane and I discussed the dangers of becoming so confident and competent that the teachers would not bother to carry out or try out the programs for themselves. We agreed that by becoming competent we could provide a backup service, but only as and when needed. There is a definite need to restrain enthusiasm and be backward in coming forward.

I completed the observations with 'INFORM' where the children were entering data. No general information was given by any of the children to new users, just an instruction for the first task, but new users soon understood procedure by the time they became checkers. I think we could learn a lesson from this as sometimes we make explanations too complex and difficult to absorb. Usually the teacher was contacted for help with different procedures if a mistake was made. Only one child (Joanne) asked about how the information was processed. The children did not seem to find the procedure of recording information as threatening as an 'The Inhabitant' or even 'Front Page', probably because there were other children there telling them exactly what to do or whom they could ask. Even Diva did not panic. Actually making these observations became hectic because of their brevity. Any comments were kept to a minimum.

Throughout this week Jane and I had deliberately kept any pressure off the teachers. Pauline felt guilty at not starting anything new and felt distracted by having a sick child at home. I reassured her by praising her work so far and tried to ensure that the new programs would be ready for use next term when she was refreshed. I took my lead from Joan who seemed keen to complete her 'INFORM' information. She enjoyed demonstrating how to prepare the disc to me, showing me how the previous one on Quorn had been developed. This type of material seems to fit in with her teaching style. It will be interesting to note her response to the more open-ended 'AMX Art' program. She likes to feel that she is in control and responds well when her opinion or help is requested.

So, by next term, computer faults should be rectified and new material should assimilated. Heaven help me with 'Edfax'. Here's to next term!

Autumn Term 1987

During the long summer vacation we had very little contact with the two teachers. Pauline spent a large part of the time camping in France with her family, and Joan – while taking a shorter holiday abroad – occupied her summer working at home for most of the time. The break gave us opportunity to come to terms with some of the technical problems encountered towards the end of the Summer Term, especially with 'AMX Super Art' which had been plagued with difficulties. Of these, the most frustrating of all was the reluctance of the pointer to respond quickly and consistently when the mouse was moved across the table. We had tried several alternative surfaces to see if it was just a case of a slippery table. In the end, the problem was solved by moving the AMX chip into a different slot on the BBC computer's circuit board. To be fair to the manufacturers, the installation instructions do mention that problems may be encountered if this chip is installed in the wrong slot, but without getting too technical, the installation procedure is beyond the scope of the average user involving, as it does, the removal of the computer's outer casing and the keyboard as well as moving one or two other chips around. Whilst this may prove fun for enthusiasts it certainly points to the need for readily available technical support for most busy teachers who simply want to get on and use the technology without having to get bogged down with the mysteries of its internal workings.

The major activity planned for the new term was a study of the Vikings; a collaborative venture between the two classes. Much of the initial stimulus for the children was to be obtained from reference books and stories. The highlight of the whole project however was to be a day trip to York to visit the Jorvic Centre. Pauline and Joan had been preparing for this project for some time, collecting materials and ideas. We therefore took the opportunity of encouraging them to include thoughts about how the computer might be integrated into the fabric of this project, a sort of amalgamation of the ancient and historic with the modern and high-tech. Further developing our view that the most valuable and versatile computer programs are the open-ended tools, we suggested three programs in particular that might be considered, a wordprocessor rather than 'Front Page' which was proving to be rather limiting, 'Edfax', a teletext emulator, and of course 'AMX Super Art' for the designs, pictures and illustrations. Once again, our intention was to provide means whereby teachers and children could extend and develop ways of expressing their ideas.

Introducing the Wordprocessor

One can develop many skills by encouraging children to use a wordprocessor. These skills enable children to develop and broaden the scope of their writing without replacing more conventional methods of working. We had introduced 'Front Page' as a simple and attractive way into wordprocessing. Although outstandingly successful, it lacked the sophisticated text-handling facilities of the real thing. At the beginning of the project we had suggested that Pauline and Joan tried 'Wordwise', a powerful wordprocessor designed especially for the BBC computer. This is indeed a very good product, but it proved a little too sophisticated for their needs at the time. An alternative was to introduce a simpler wordprocessor called 'Writer', based on 'Wordwise', but designed specially for children. This is what Pauline said about it:

> From the outset of the computer project I had been using 'Wordwise' with the children, albeit in a very amateurish way. From a personal point of view this was a slow business as I had neither the expertise nor the necessary keyboard skills myself. Consequently I was not as sure of my ground as I would liked to have been. However, we did make some headway and had produced work and captions for display. Our main problem was in remembering all the commands. So when we saw 'Writer' we were very excited at the prospect of using it.

'Writer' is a wordprocessor designed especially for children. Text is presented on the screen in double-height characters in conventional 'what you see is what you get' format. In other words, the text layout on the screen is identical to that which is printed on to the paper without the use of embedded control characters. The program provides conventional editing facilities such as 'search and replace', 'move', 'copy' and 'delete'. In addition to this, blocks of text can be highlighted in different colours on the screen. Output to the printer can be set to a variety of font sizes including doubt-height and expanded characters. Facilities are included to enable input from a concept keyboard.

Sue begins her diary by describing her reaction to the introduction of 'Writer':

> We were introduced to 'Writer' to be used with the children as soon as possible in readiness for the imminent trip to York. I was surprised at how easy this was to understand and use. There were very few variables to take into consideration before I felt sufficiently confident to try the program with the children. The handbook was easy to follow and well presented. I liked the way in which the authors had attempted to make the program foolproof, for example, work was not wasted if the printer was off.
>
> The children were surprised at how quickly they could start the program and were very impressed with the results. Instructions were soon understood but care had to be taken when editing that the text was examined systematically. The boys were prone to rush through their work, ignoring their mistakes. By the third child we had worked out sufficient presentation points to achieve a good result. The whole procedure lasted approximately ten minutes per child and could become self-correcting, making less and less demands on teacher time.
>
> Pauline and Joan were enthusiastic about the results. Pauline thought it ideal for presenting displays and Joan thought it lent itself to presenting poetry. Both are much more vital this term.

We had decided that it was about time we involved parents a little more in our project. A date was therefore fixed in the third week of the term when we could hold a parents' evening. The theme was to be 'Computers in the Classroom'. We decided that rather than just tell parents about the project it would be a nice idea to show them what their children had done and to provide them with opportunities to try the programs for themselves. Although one might have expected that the bulk of the preparation would fall upon the shoulders of the research team, that did not turn out to be the case. As with all parents' meetings in school there is always great pressure on staff to make the school look as attractive as possible with the best examples of the children's work displayed about the building. Attractive wall displays are the norm at Broadwood Primary but extra effort always went into the activity before a parents' meeting. Our venue was no exception. Because it was to be about using computers, there was a greater than normal demand for computer time during the week leading up to the chosen date. This meant that normal computer work was somewhat interrupted, but since any increase in computer-based activity was to be encouraged, Jane and Sue quickly found other things to do in preparation for work later in the term as well as assisting in the preparation of special display items. Here is Sue's account of how events leading up to the computer evening led to Pauline and Joan taking more responsibility for decisions about the computers and their use:

> The week began with a dilemma as examples of work from 'AMX Super Art' and 'Writer' were needed for the following week's Parents' Computer Workshop. With time limited, and Pauline and Joan organising project work, it was decided that Jane and I would work out how to use the programs and introduce them to the children. We could not work on 'Edfax' as the information disc was elsewhere, so we decided to postpone this until after the Parents' Workshop. 'Writer' proved easy to introduce as Pauline had some work on Owls which lent itself well to the program. To incorporate the class's new children (remember that these were both third and fourth year vertically grouped classes), we used one previous term's child to demonstrate while the new child observed and dictated notes. Joan used the 'Owl and the Pussycat' poem to introduce 'Writer' to her children. Pauline took up a suggestion from Derek to arrange the text into the shape of an owl.
>
> If the children made a lot of mistakes from typing, the editing section was used fairly comprehensively, but if mistakes were few the potential for the editing section was lost. Therefore in the future some experimentation with arranging and rearranging text is needed. It took me some time to appreciate this.
>
> 'AMX Super Art' worked to perfection since Derek's alterations. Jane and I refreshed our memories on procedure and realised how tedious it was wading through the handbook.

Jane noted a similar point in her diary:

> Sue and I spent the morning refreshing our memories on 'AMX Art'. We found we couldn't recall how to clear the picture file, and couldn't quickly find instructions about this in the handbook. We concluded that the handbook is too detailed and complex for primary teachers to refer to in the classroom situation. A simplified version would be more useful. We decided which aspects of the program to introduce to the children to begin with. As they become familiar with the procedures we will introduce text and other features. Finally we successfully cleared the picture file.

Sue continues:

> A more visual handbook, aimed at starting off with primary children could have been a great asset. There could easily have been examples of the effects of the basic modes, even a display section for future effects on the disc would have been useful. Short cuts would have helped too, like what to do when the disc was full, clearing the screen on an open file or clearing space on the disc. Teachers do not always have the time to create another drawing disc.
>
> I tried various ways of introducing the program from printing out after each mode group (spray mode, line and fill mode, box and frame mode and ellipse mode), to starting from a picture after a quick demonstration of modes and discussion about which would be useful for the picture. The more hesitant and systematic children gained from the former, whilst the more confident gained from the latter. However, the more confident children sometimes became over-confident and did not absorb information as well as their more systematic

companions. Whereas Bryan and Peter were so anxious to produce a result, rushing from one mode to another without watching the effect they were creating, filling every available space, Krishna and Lindsey took much more notice of the overall effect and produced a much more balanced picture. Krishna knew what she was going to draw and only needed advice about how to use the tools to draw a sun. Lindsey did not know what to draw, so I suggested a house and garden and suggested the tools she might use. Bryan and Peter needed a lot of verbal prompts to think about their actions. However, Bryan did begin to listen to how he could achieve the effect of a billowing sail on his Viking boat and carried this over to a painting session afterwards, producing a very accurate sail using circles and lines. Only when Bryan was out of the way did Peter concentrate.

Here was an interesting example of what we had been hoping to see. Rather than the computer replacing more conventional classroom activity, it enhanced and developed it. Instead of transferring an already developed idea from paper to computer, Bryan actually used the computer as a tool to explore ideas and relationships. He used its quick and convenient facilities to work out how a problem could be solved and then transferred the solution to his work using paper and paint. Is this one facet of what we mean by integration?

Finally came the week of the parents' evening and a consequent increase in preparations:

> On Tuesday morning there was a hive of activity. Both computers were raring to go. Even allowing for the computer evening and the desire to display work, there seemed to be a renewed energy in the school with lots of work being planned. During the rest of the week 'Front Page' and 'Writer' were being incorporated into the fabric of the class's day. As a consequence I started to receive more instructions from Pauline and Joan.
>
> Both teachers took over their role when using 'Writer' with the children. Pauline took over the editing sessions from me and encountered the same problems, eg. pressing RETURN incorrectly and messing up the text, putting the cursor in the wrong place and then panicking at the result. Having made the mistakes myself I could quickly help her. Joan decided to work out how to save work on disc and enlisted my help. We referred to the handbook, worked through it stage by stage and it worked first time. Suitably impressed, Pauline tried but received the message 'Disc faulty/unformatted'. However this proved to be a minor fault requiring that we check the startup conditions to ensure that the program was set for a single disc drive. The next morning Joan asked me to work through the sets of discs to ensure that they were all set for the correct disc drive. Sure enough, the fault was on the master disc and was quickly put right. Great deductive work and team work. If one of us has a problem, she would call to the others and we all chip in with our little bits of knowledge. Joan was elated by her success and rushed off to tell Linda (an auxiliary-helper) how she could make effective workcards.

The Parents' Computer Evening: Triumph and Frustration

We do not intend to describe this event in depth here since this has already been detailed in Chapter 5. It is important, however, to emphasise our purpose in organising the parents' evening because it bears a direct relationship to subsequent events. Our prime objective was to inform parents about new work going on in the school. There was, and still is, much suspicion about the use of computers in school, many people equating computers with playing games. It was important to legitimise the use of computers at Broadwood Primary by showing parents that they were being used for serious activities which had important educational applications.

Readers will recall from Chapter 5 that the evening proved to be very successful and elicited many compliments and offers of help to raise funds for the purchase of more hardware and software. Our second objective was less overt in that it was concerned with finding a small number of interested parents who might be persuaded, in the course of time, to assume the parent/helper roles then occupied by Jane and Sue. After all, it is one thing to use experienced teachers as parent/helpers, but quite another to use real parents. In actual fact, we were not only anxious to find out how well things would proceed with real parent volunteers, but we also felt a growing unease about how Pauline and Joan were going to cope once our project was over and our classroom support withdrawn. We had to be thinking for some weeks about how our teachers could prepare parents to take over the support role in as gradual and natural a way as possible.

The question of continuing technical support was another issue altogether. No one would deny that formal provision for technical support within the county was, and still is, woefully inadequate. It is not a question of won't, but one of severely under-resourced and over-stretched central provision of resources and personnel. The idea of 'on-the-spot' technical support was out of the question. Sue describes her feelings after the experience of meeting the parents:

> Much interest was aroused amongst both parents and staff at the computer evening. Some parents were loath to leave it. One mother tried to draw a dog on 'AMX Super Art' but began to see shapes in the patterns she was creating with the line mode. Her dog ultimately became a windsurfer. She had been afraid to touch the computer until encouraged.
>
> A few parents volunteered to come into school.
>
> Personally, I found it useful to set the project in context. It made me realise how much I had learnt in a short time, and how my confidence had increased when using the computer. That feeling of panic is history and I am more willing to work out any problems.
>
> So far so good. We could be excused for thinking that we might have acquired conscripts. In fact I had spoken to two parents in particular, Heather and Valerie, whose children were in a lower class. They seemed quite interested and so as Jane had been away for a few days, thus missing the workshop, I spoke to her on the telephone suggesting that she might like to work with them during the following week.

By the following Monday, however, they seemed to have had second thoughts. Sue comments:

> The week began with a misunderstanding about how soon the parents who had expressed an interest in computers were to be involved as parent/helpers. I think the thought of this had discouraged one parent immediately. The other parent was absorbed in 'Writer', completing some work for Ann (another teacher) with a lower class, but seemed eager to learn at her own pace. I think, however, that it will be some time before a parent/helper becomes a reality. The problem was that both parents were interested in the lower school.

This account seems to suggest that perhaps we were a little too optimistic about their willingness to join us. When Jane returned she discovered that the two parents were apprehensive about working with the older children.

> On arriving back I chatted to Derek on the phone and he said that a very interesting new development had resulted from the parents' evening. I understood him to say that two parents currently working with Ann were to take over the role of Sue and I as parent helpers and that we would observe and record our observations. When I arrived in school this morning the reality proved to be rather different. First of all I talked to Joan, who was very surprised to

think that Valerie and Heather would be working in her area. Ann confirmed that Valerie and Heather would continue to work with her. In fact Heather was having second thoughts about coming in at all. She is very keen to learn about computers but feels that she couldn't work with the children and certainly not with eleven year olds. She isn't coming this Thursday but says she will come the following week. If she does we will try to reassure her and give her lots of time on her own to feel familiar and confident.

Valerie was already working in room A on her own with 'Writer'. She has fed material into computers in her previous job and feels confident with them. She typed in a story and made corrections. She found the handbook easy to follow and soon mastered the basic ground rules. I suggested that she select 'continue writing' and check the text carefully, a procedure we use with the children. When she printed her text she was surprised that the printout was in a narrow paragraph and that gaps appeared where she had not intended them to be. We worked out a solution to this problem together.

1. we hadn't checked the startup conditions. Double height had been selected which automatically prints in a narrow paragraph down the middle of the page if set on 20 characters.
2. 66 lines is the normal condition, then a space is left before the next 66 lines. This explained the gaps.

Valerie left feeling that she had enjoyed her morning and was looking forward to coming again on Thursday. She confided in me that Heather is feeling 'anti-school' at the moment, and that's why she doesn't want to come this week.

Clearly the parents' reasons for not wanting to joint the project were complex. The last thing we wanted to do was to put them off completely. After all, they were getting involved with the younger children and as their confidence increased and their own children moved up through the school, it was to be hoped that they would want to continue to do the same. Perhaps they were potential recruits for the future, an asset to the school for some years to come.

In the meanwhile Sue and Jane set about preparing for the Viking Project. The trip to York was going to produce large quantities of information of all kinds and they felt that they must be fully prepared to help Pauline and Joan use the computers to their best advantage in handling and presenting the burgeoning data they were likely to acquire. Sue had noted that the integration of 'AMX Super Art' was taking rather a long time:

'AMX Super Art' does not seem to have become part of the classroom organisation like 'Front Page' or 'Writer'. Probably this is because Pauline and Joan are not completely au fait with it. It could be used to more advantage during project work. I have not started any observations on it as I have been phasing Pauline and Joan into the program whilst the children are using it.

At this point Jane and I discussed strategy. With the York trip imminent, it was felt that 'Edfax' might be of some use. The procedure, even to make a start seemed complex so we decided to persevere with it for the rest of the week. Neither Pauline, Joan, Jane nor I could see an immediate use for the program but hoped all would be revealed as we waded through it. Jane and I felt that if we learnt it piecemeal we could easily forget it. Only when we understood it fully could we hope to introduce it to the children.

'Edfax' was probably the most complex and difficult program for the teachers and observers to master, particularly because they couldn't define a proper use for it for themselves. It's axiomatic that difficulties are easier to overcome when one knows where one is going and what one is trying to achieve. This was one of the most important things we learnt throughout the project. If one can help teachers define a use for a program for themselves they will move heaven and earth to achieve it. However, we had not yet reached this stage, and our feeling was that Sue, Jane and the two teachers were experimenting with 'Edfax' just because we had asked them to.

But with the frustrations come the triumphs as well – the times when things begin to go right:

> Working through the text examples was relatively simple and linear graphics was easier than expected. We created a boxed page with flashing features and even tried the 'Reveal' feature. After saving the page, we tried to recall it but then we realised we had not created an Index page. Creating the Index page using different backgrounds proved a useful exercise in recalling previously tried techniques. Again we tried to recall our boxed page but were unable to test the 'Reveal' feature until we were tuned into 'Display'. Oh the excitement when it worked!

Following this minor triumph Sue and Jane began to think about what they could show the children. This led to their first realisation of what the teachers might do with the program:

> By now we decided to build up our pages to include small pictures, using the 'Define Pixels' routine. Jane was much better at reading off the relevant squares than I was, but both of us grasped the principles and discussed basic shapes we could use with the children. Having completed a man, and having a 'Sports' file I drew a boat and a sail and mast. We had problems with the mast due to difficulties with spacing, but we could find no guidelines in the handbook. Exhausted, we left this problem for next week. It may be useful for Pauline and Joan to create three or four headings relevant to their project and store interesting pieces of work, information and pictures.

It is interesting to note that Derek Blease had actually made these suggestions some weeks earlier, and had gone so far as to create a demonstration disc for teachers and parents to see at the parents' computer evening. It serves to show how much more effective it is to provide first-hand experience than simply to tell people about one's own ideas. We had already learnt this lesson in our training sessions when Derek Blease had left Jane and the teachers to their own devices after introducing a new program. What they were able to learn and assimilate through sharing their individual pieces of incomplete knowledge was quite remarkable. Jane's account confirms this:

> We continued practising with 'Edfax'. Yesterday we created a page 200 containing sports results with a hidden score. Today we created page 100 as our main menu and were able to display our page 200 to see whether the 'Reveal' function worked. We were pleased that it did. We started to find out about the graphics and began to create a picture on page 302. We decided to use coloured pencils on the graphics paper and began to translate to the screen by the 'Define Pixels' method. We guessed that the children would probably cope more easily with this method. We are keeping an open mind however, until we have tried the 'Lower Case' method. I translated from the graph paper and gave Sue instructions as to what to key in. We found it quite complicated at this point in time and we wonder how the children will cope. We may be pleasantly surprised!
>
> One thing we didn't take account of is the apparent impossibility of having two colours within the same set of six pixels. I'm sure we will understand how to deal with this as we progress. By three o'clock we were feeling quite punch-drunk and decided to save our picture so far and add more to it next week.

It was now the end of September, and the following Monday brought more frustration, so much so that Jane and Sue abandoned 'Edfax' for a while. Sue reports:

'Edfax' was abandoned in frustration when we could not change from colour to colour in a limited space for our picture. Using 'Hold Graphics' we changed colour along straight lines but the moment we wanted to change from one character to another in a different colour we encountered deletion and colour problems. We tried many variables but could not fully understand the procedure for achieving different colours in the same picture. The instructions may have well been in another language! We (Jane and I) have devoted some considerable time to acquiring a basic working knowledge of the program but I wonder how far busy teachers would come to terms with it, especially as there is not an immediate incentive.

'AMX Art' continues to be at the experimental level as most children need a lot of support when using it, so that the tools can be used to their best advantage. Some of the children are thinking how they can use it for their project. This hinges on how successfully the children can operate the mouse. One major problem was that the children wanted to fill in every available space (eg. Julie) with all the different types of pattern. However, this provided an opportunity to discuss positive/negative shapes, construction of shapes and tonal effects.

The computer continues to be very much part of the classroom with 'Front Page'. It is just another classroom area. Observations are changing slightly, in that Pauline and Joan are leaving the children for short sessions when editing to see if they can recognise their own mistakes, then talking them through corrections they cannot find. One slight problem has been the editing procedure which differs from 'Writer'. The teacher has to check that the children are using the correct procedure. It would be ideal if certain procedures were standardised in software. Another problem has been that certain children (Wayne and Anthony for example), use up the space very quickly and it must be very frustrating to have to cut a story short. Is there any way of checking this before starting? Then, a useful exercise in condensing short stories could be implemented. Working in pairs seems to be giving more hesitant children like Wayne more confidence. He was unsure of the keyboard and progress was painfully slow on his own but with Lindsey's help he became much more efficient and began to relax. Hopefully this pairing could be implemented with 'AMX Super Art', once the children have gained sufficient knowledge.

The difficulties with 'Edfax', coupled with the definite triumphs with 'Front Page' and 'Writer' led Jane to wondering whether it would be better to concentrate on the easier programs for a while:

We think that after the York visit we may have to record events using more familiar programs ie., 'AMX Art', 'Front Page' and 'Writer'. Later on we will attempt some computer pages with 'Edfax'. . . . We would be all right using text in different colours with different backgrounds using 'Flash', 'Conceal' and 'Double height' but the *graphics* – not yet. We haven't yet understood all the basic ground rules. I don't think we have understood the influential positioning of the control and graphics characters. Probably when the last two or three bits of the jig-saw have slotted into place, the whole will become crystal clear. Here's hoping.

The trip to York was arranged for Tuesday, October 6th. On the Monday, preparations of all kinds were in hand, including work on the computers. Sue set about working with some children using 'AMX Super Art' while Jane observed the children's activity. Sue writes:

The week began with Pauline wanting to use 'AMX Super Art' to produce cover designs for folders about the Viking project. She had experimented the previous Friday with a quick learning child who had produced an effective head and shoulders. There was a problem when this was first printed as spaces were left producing a separated image effect. This occurred when using other programs and needs investigation. However Pauline wanted to try the children working in pairs with me observing. Initially this seemed to work but when the child working on the computer encountered problems, the child helping did not know enough to be of practical assistance. Therefore Jane took over the observation whilst I helped the children. It was apparent that this program was proving more difficult to phase into the classroom than we had thought previously.

Some children, like Fiona, could assimilate the information very quickly and use modes appropriately. Others, like Mark, were the complete opposite. He was desperate to produce a good result but could not control the pencil mode. Thus, I had to think up a way he could use the other modes to draw a Viking ship. He needed a lot of verbal and physical prompts to complete the picture. All this would consume much of the teacher's time.

Pauline was very conscious of this and asked me to demonstrate the procedure to a group of four children. This was the maximum that could view the screen comfortably. To prevent them from being bored, each had a turn with a particular mode. Again, some grasped the procedure quicker than others. This explanation process took one hour. There would be no way the teacher could devote this amount of time to one group. She could explain one part, then let them experiment whilst she went to another group, but many of the children want to produce a picture and become impatient very quickly. Perhaps a simple guide to modes could be written down for them to work from reminding them of such procedures as using the mouse button with the line, box, frame and ellipse modes. This would remind them which modes they should be concentrating on and to disregard others.

After the introduction to a small group, Jane started to take them singly to produce a picture. When observing with C.O.M.I.C., both Jane and I found that we could have used a new category of using the mouse and screen simultaneously. We coded this behaviour under category 2.

Jane goes on to describe the same session:

I completed three systematic observations of Sue showing three children how to use AMX Art. Pauline came across occasionally to see what was happening. Sue demonstrated what each mode will do and the children practised before going on to draw and print out their pictures. They catch on quickly as a rule. Some are more adept at controlling the pencil mode than others. Mark found this difficult but Sue showed him how to make more use of the square and the circle modes so he was much happier.

It's early days yet. When the children have spent much more time on the program I'm sure they will see all kinds of combinations and possibilities.

Derek replaced the printer ribbon so our pictures were greatly improved. The Print × 2 picture came out elongated with alternate blank lines on the first copy. Subsequent copies were OK. We have no idea why this happened. Pauline said exactly the same thing happened on Friday.

The Trip to the Jorvik Centre and the York Railway Museum

Jane sums up the day:

Prior to the trip, quiz-type worksheets were distributed to the children for completion at the Railway Museum and York Minster. The emphasis at the Jorvik Centre, however, was on the sheer enjoyment of the audio-visual presentation itself.

As school outings go, this was very successful. Apart from the expected minor mishaps such as losing Sue and her group while we all went to eat our tea in the Railway museum, three children being sick on the bus, almost losing a child's duffle bag, someone punching somebody else in the privates on the way home and singing rude songs, it was a very enjoyable day. Little unexpected deviations from the planned programme enlivened the proceedings. We had to wait half an hour to enter the Jorvik Museum and two buskers, probably music students practising in the precinct, entertained the children royally. The children were fascinated and the time passed quickly.

We arrived in the vicinity of the Railway Museum far too early so we trekked back into the city to have a closer look at York Minster which we had previously seen in the distance from the city wall.

We ate our lunch sitting or standing in the park in the drizzling rain while passers-by glanced pityingly in our direction. By mid-afternoon the sun came out in time for our single-file sortie along the city walls and a quick gallop over Lendle Bridge to admire the recently renovated Rose window of the Minster. The children were rather tired by the time we reached the Railway Museum. By the time my group had boarded two or three trains, viewed the model railway, bought a few platform tickets and entered the museum shop they were bushed. The girls sat down on the inviting carpet at one side of the shop, got out their purchases from the Jorvik museum and decided what was to be given to which member of the family when they got home. They were clearly on sit-down strike!

It will be most interesting to read the children's interpretation of the day's events.

By the Thursday things were getting back to normal in the two classrooms except for the fact that Joan was unwell. Jane got on with some more systematic observation:

Joan was away sick today. Very unusual for her. I began by observing Louise using 'Writer' to type up a very long story. She approached the keyboard with great delicacy and slowly and deliberately plugged away at her mammoth task. After an hour Pauline suggested that we edit the work so far and save it to be continued later.

The printer was playing up again. Pauline was printing out 'Front Page'. The borders were peculiar and we had extra spacing – similar to the 'AMX Super Art' printout last week. Pauline commented on how frustrating it is when things go wrong and we don't know why. Too much for the busy teacher to cope with.

Sue introduced a group of four children to the Art program before lunch. Pauline said she felt it was going to take far too long otherwise for children to have a turn. They all want to record their York experience straight away.

I worked with Lalit in the afternoon and he produced a superb Viking longship. We followed the printout procedure and instead of Lalit's picture we got Mark's which was the previous one. Again, we didn't understand why. We lost Lalit's picture which was a shame as it was very effective.

By the following Tuesday teachers and observers thought they had worked out for themselves what the problem had been. Once again, as they were getting more confident as computer users, they were beginning to try more complex things. In this case it seemed to be a question of opening and closing the appropriate files at the right time. What is significant about this is that they did not seek our help, but pooled their expertise to solve the problem for themselves. Pauline, Joan, Jane and Sue had been working together for long enough now to be able to share their fears, misunderstandings and insights in a perfectly natural and positive way. Sue had already identified a need for easier instructions for the art program. Now Pauline saw the need as Jane describes:

Pauline said she would welcome a simplified list of instructions for using 'AMX Super Art', so Sue and I spent some time working on this. We intended to produce workcards for the children as well as instructions for the teachers. We finished writing the instructions and decided to try them. I operated the computer on Sue's instructions. All was well until I tried to print my picture – 'ERROR – DISC READ ONLY' came on the screen. Then we got printouts of the FILE list. We couldn't understand this at all. We lost the picture, followed the same procedures again exactly, and all was well.

The same puzzling thing happened this afternoon when I tried to print out Matthew's picture. Again, we finally lost the picture. On trying again all was well. WHY? – we didn't understand. Is it that the disc isn't in the drive properly, and when we replace it and try again the problem disappears?

Clearly the problem was not solved, so Sue set about creating a set of easy-to-follow instructions for setting up and running the program:

I wrote down step-by-step instructions for opening a file and clearing the screen and Jane then worked with Matthew on his picture. However, she could not print out as 'ERROR – DISC READ ONLY' appeared. The picture was lost. Again, after re-starting, it worked. Is there some faulty connection in the disc drive or printer? I did not dwell on the reason but decided to include a secondary check in the instructions. Pauline (and Joan) had indicated that some simple step-by-step instructions would be appreciated. Joan had followed our progress with interest but seemed to be waiting until we had found a satisfactory introduction process. She is happier with programs like INFORM, whilst Pauline is more craft-oriented. Thus, I wrote a series of instructions for the teacher under headings:- starting off; selection procedure; initial checking procedure; drawing session; opening an existing file; creating a file; printing procedure. I gave a copy to Pauline and Joan, asking them to work through it giving their written comments. Then I thought why not take a complete novice through the instructions? I asked Debbie the headteacher, if she would oblige at an appropriate time.

Because of the difficulty of introduction to the children, I suggested to Pauline that a series of work cards might prove invaluable. She was very enthusiastic, so I stayed at home the next day to try and work this out, taking 'Writer' with me. I envisaged these would range from mode selection to mode experimentation. The teacher would be released for some time but could check that each card had been completed. A major stumbling block is the translation of their ideas into appropriate modes.

When working out a format for the work cards it was obvious that lengthy written explanations were out. Therefore, I used scan charts for a quick reference card showing simple examples of what each mode would do, and for a discovering modes card which gave both step-by-step instructions for achieving simple results and graded exercises for each mode plus things for children to find out and observe. I discarded the basic information card as it was too wordy and boring. I then broke it up into simple headings with diagrams and simple, logical sentences. It was apparent that the best program for drawing up the cards was not 'Writer' but 'AMX Super Art' itself. This helped me tackle the problem of encouraging the children to think in terms of modes when drawing a picture. What about a series of picture cards, eg. house, tree, face from which the children have to find out the different mode used and try to copy the picture? Thus, I had the following for Jane, Pauline and Joan to try out and comment upon:-

Basic information card
Quick reference card
Discovering modes (Cards 1–4)
Picture interpretation cards.

During the same week Sue gained some insights into Ian's learning difficulties with 'Front Page':

I observed 'Front Page' with Ian, who was being assisted by Gregory. It was interesting that his learning difficulties were apparent through this observation. I had noted down category 2 for using the keyboard but, at the same time, he was talking himself through the task, asking Gregory questions, arguing with Gregory's answers, making puns on words and glancing at the screen. During the editing session he saw only two out of nine mistakes and kept racing the cursor to the end of the work each time he had found a mistake. After giving him time to find his own mistakes Joan had to talk him through the rest. The editing session could be used to help him think more systematically. I mentioned my observations to Joan who noted them down. Apparently, she had been wondering about the best way of approaching his parents at a forthcoming parents evening. A potentially capable child, his progress was plagued by his diverse mind and lack of concentration. Having encountered exactly the same problem with my eldest daughter, I made suggestions to Joan who noted them down.

As the week progressed more and more success was observed with 'Super Art'. There were some good pictures and printouts. Sue continued working on her set of simple instructions for the teachers and work cards for the children, so that, hopefully, they could quickly become independent of the researchers.

Joan Announces that she is Ready to use 'Edfax'

Tuesday, October 20th was the day when Joan, quite unexpectedly, declared that she was ready to use 'Edfax'. Until this time nobody realised that she had even thought about it. It meant that Jane and Sue had to do some quick thinking. Here is Sue's account of the day:

> The week started with a surprise, Joan announced that she was ready to start using 'Edfax' and asked for our help. As we were not tuned into the program, we paled at the thought! Joan explained that she had completed a basic introduction on Monday and had created page 100. Joan and Pauline had worked out between them that the content would be about the visit to York. How we were to introduce it to the children was not discussed enough with Joan. Jane and I were in at the deep end! So, we referred to the handbook and went through basic graphic and text procedure with Leah and Sarah, mainly to refresh our memories. Fortunately, most of the information came flooding back and then we were able to show the children how to code their work. Using a page layout with which we were familiar, Jane was able to help them set out their first page in the morning. When storing the page there was a problem with cycle pages but the three of us worked it out together. Jane was very proud of herself that afternoon when she started simple graphics. Leah and Sarah had drawn out the shape of a mask on the 'Edfax' sheet and Jane showed them how to translate this onto the screen. She said they picked out the shapes fairly quickly. Both Jane and I were conscious of the amount of time taken in explanation and introductory techniques. How would the teacher cope in a normal classroom situation? Any introduction took a lot of time and thought.

Jane took the opportunity to discuss with Pauline how she felt about the computer:

> She feels that things are really taking off and is anxious to keep them going after we have finished the project. She would very much like to keep the University computer until the end of the school year. The school computer is being used nearly all the time now. I asked her if she thought this was due to us using the computers in our own area. She thinks this has been very influential. A very positive pay-off from the project!

Sue noted:

> If it was a surprise that 'Edfax' had been started, it was no surprise who had started it. Joan enjoys essentially logical programs and likes to share what she has achieved. On the other hand, Pauline is very enthusiastic with creative programs like 'AMX Art', which was why I left Jane with 'Edfax', at a relevant point. We were going to swap over that afternoon but Jane had become hooked on 'Edfax' and wanted to test the graphics.
>
> Pauline wanted to continue with basic introduction procedure of 'Super Art' to groups of four. This time my group comprised Krishna, Bryan, Scott and Suzanne. I worked with the procedure I had used on the workcards. There were no problems using the mouse. To hasten proceedings, after the initial introduction session I asked the children to draw their picture on paper first, then asked them to think about their use of modes. Krishna completed her Viking Village very quickly using this method. For a while there was good interaction between Scott and Bryan with constructive suggestions being made. However, this declined when Bryan could not achieve the effect he wanted. Curves were the main problem. It would have been very useful if the program contained curves, as only a limited effect can be achieved by using

the ellipse and then rubbing out. Suzanne learnt from Bryan's mistakes and completed her picture very quickly. Pauline commented that the children had finished sooner, so I discussed ways of encouraging them to translate their pictures into modes.

Jane expressed the need for the children to experiment for themselves:

> After my very successful day last week using the Art program with Pauline's children, they tried it themselves and although results were not quite as good, they were quite effective. It is important that the children have time to experiment on their own at this stage as well as working under supervision.

Jane was soon to find that Joan's enthusiasm for 'Edfax' was preventing others from using it.

> I wanted to finish 'Edfax' to check on a few points but Joan had commandeered it. She is really keen to find out all about it at present. She talked to the class about planning 'Edfax' work. She explained the various options for text and simple pictures. They looked at the sample disc yesterday. Today she talked to them about the various possibilities for 'Edfax' – colours, different text, flash, reveal etc. and asked them to plan some work with this in mind.

Pauline commented that she too felt she had reached the stage at which she would have liked to have started the project! Both Pauline and Joan wondered how they would cope in January when both computers and additional help were no longer available.

The children were beginning to produce some interesting results with 'Edfax', but as Jane notes in late October, they still needed a lot of support.

> Joan was ready to begin 'Edfax' when I arrived this morning. I worked with Leah and Emma, and by the end of the day we had created a page of text using double height, background, different colours and flash. They are now planning a Viking helmet on graph paper, so tomorrow we hope to create a picture. We all agreed today that we have no idea how the regular primary teacher would cope with introducing 'Edfax' in a busy classroom situation – unless she had spent a lot of time previously getting to know it inside out.
>
> By the end of the next day we had almost completed three pages of 'Edfax'. We'd made a start on drawing the Viking helmet. The children hadn't made allowances for enough command spaces when planning their drawing so they had to go back to the drawing board. We still haven't properly understood what the Hold Gaphics function does. We can do a row of graphics in different colours joining on to each other but we still come unstuck when we try to draw a similar thing in a picture. Something hasn't quite clicked yet. I'm sure it will.

Finally Jane considers her role as a researcher. The programs now in use are complex, requiring much investment of time and energy on the part of the teachers. Both she and Sue, Jane feels, are taking too active a role in making decisions and teaching the children. There is a sense in which the project is becoming too much action and not enough research. This level of on-the-spot support could never be provided by a local authority. Even a resident teacher/information-technology expert could not easily deliver such sustained assistance.

> I reminded myself this week that our original brief as researchers was to play the role of 'parent/helpers'. Ideally we would like Pauline and Joan to take the initiative while we observe how they cope. This isn't happening right now. Sue and I have become the 'experts' with 'Super Art' and 'Edfax' and we are taking the initiative in teaching the children. Because these programs are more complex than the others we have used so far and because of the busy classroom situation, we have been forced to change our roles.

Having said this, it would be wrong to suggest that the process of integration had not come some considerable way since the start of the project. 'Other Worlds', 'Front Page' and 'Writer' were well under way and 'INFORM' had made a considerable impact on the teachers' ways of thinking about information. 'Super Art' and 'Edfax' were really in a different league. Nevertheless, both Pauline and Joan were thinking about the potentialities of those two programs, even though they were not yet able to fully operationalise their thoughts.

The last week of October brought a welcome half term break during which enthusiasm for the two programs didn't wane in the slightest. Sue set about working with 'Super Art' while Jane worked with 'Edfax'. A definite pattern was emerging. Sue notes that they stepped in quickly when Pauline and Joan had to attend a meeting:

> There was a slight hiccup at the beginning of the week as Pauline and Joan had forgotten an appointment, so Jane and I pitched in to help. Pauline was anxious for more children to complete pictures on 'Super Art' and Joan was eager to continue with 'Edfax'. Again Jane worked with 'Edfax' and I with 'Super Art'. I think we must be hooked on the programs!
>
> I worked with pairs of children, Wayne and James, then Christopher and Scott. The initial introduction sessions took one hour with the former but much less with the latter as their table had been facing the computer that morning. Quickness in completing a picture depends on retention and control. For example, James completed a Viking Longship very quickly whereas Wayne had some difficulty controlling the pencil. Actually moving the mouse does not present too many problems until a fine level of control is needed; then Scott needed some slight physical prompts to move the mouse. To work from a picture seems to help the children translate the drawing into appropriate moves and to provoke discussion about difficult points of art and design like perspective. Scott was working from a picture of a Viking village which was drawn in perspective. By using the line mode he was able to explore the effect of various angles, mistakes being easily rectified. He found this enthralling as I did. I had to stop myself from taking over. Scott achieved a fairly complicated result which would have been difficult to reproduce with a pencil and ruler. It was a pity the print out was not coloured, as the patterns he used tended to merge when printed in black and white, but he gained a great deal from the exercise.
>
> On the other hand, Christopher was over enthusiastic when drawing his Viking Warrior and he frequently forgot procedure. Here the work cards would have proved invaluable. It was not until Thursday that I completed the first part of the Discovering Modes work card, which I discussed with Joan, suggesting that, when completed, it would be useful for her more inexperienced children to try out. Really I could do with a day at the University so that I could complete the work cards as soon as possible. I had cut the reference work card to size and was ready to laminate. Derek arranged a time for the following Thursday.

Jane describes her experiences:

> Leah and Sarah completed their picture with a great deal of help. We had one 'problem line' on the screen. It remains empty and we don't know why. It has taken such a long time to complete the picture that we have decided to leave it for now and let someone else have a turn.
>
> We are learning the best way to introduce the program. A little practice first on a spare disc is a good idea – using the 'strip guide' as a starting point.
>
> Everything must be planned on the graph paper very carefully remembering to leave enough blank columns to accommodate the commands. We still haven't properly understood what the 'Hold Graphics' feature does.
>
> Helen and Carla have made a start planning a page of text and a border.

Jane and Sue kept each other informed of their progress or problems with 'Edfax' and 'Super Art' respectively. While Mrs. Black, the headteacher, was in Joan's area on the Thursday afternoon she was watching the children using 'Writer' for their poems. She was very keen to use this herself and had asked Joan for a demonstration that morning. So far Debbie (Mrs. Black) had avoided any 'hands on' involvement in the work of the project apart from agreeing to act as guinea pig for Sue's work cards. She often observed to Derek Blease that she was a complete novice where the computer was concerned and that she wanted him to teach her how to use it. He had resisted this suggestion since he was convinced that her curiosity would eventually overcome her apprehension to the extent that she would ask Pauline or Joan for help. It seemed to be much more satisfactory for them to come to feel that they were sufficiently experienced to be able to teach Mrs. Black themselves. Derek restricted his involvement to helping Jane and Sue so that they could, in turn, help Pauline and Joan.

During the following week Sue spent some time with 'Edfax'. Joan decided to adopt the technique found to be so successful with 'INFORM' where more experienced children instructed the others in small groups:

> 'Edfax' and 'AMX Art' were used by Joan and Pauline respectively this week. With Jane absent, Joan used two experienced children to instruct two new comers. The children seemed to absorb the basic information quickly and were soon ready to set up their own page. As long as Joan was careful with the tasks and instructions she set them, the children worked on their own very well. They have an incentive because they can use the basic information at once to produce their own page. With the teacher, much information has to be stored for future reference which makes gaining a working knowledge of the program tedious. Joan was able to correct most problems encountered, only asking my help when she could not type information within a border. Fortunately I remembered where this was in the handbook and quickly referred her to it. A quick checklist for rectifying problems would be very useful as it is very time consuming to wade through the handbook when teaching a class full of children.
>
> I continued to introduce groups of children to 'Super Art'. When I arrived on Wednesday, Michelle and Donna were working on a Viking Village. They needed help fixing the position of the first house, but then referred back to their original picture and worked out the directions of the lines and some of the angles themselves. Choosing appropriate patterns proved a problem as they did not want all the houses to merge together. So, I decided to include a printout of the Pattern Box on the quick reference workcard so that the children could make their selections from this.
>
> With the work cards I also included a diagram of the mouse to refresh their memory when nobody was working with them. I managed to finish the quick reference card and prepare four sections of the Discovering Modes work card. Only Frame, Box and Ellipse modes remain. Hopefully, the first part can be used by Joan's children whilst the Quick Reference card can be used by Pauline's children when drawing their own pictures. My ego was given a boost by Sonia:-
>
> Sonia: 'How long have you been using a computer Miss?'
> Me: 'Oh not long Sonia.'
> Sonia: 'Not long? But you know everything!'
>
> I must be a good actor!

We were now approaching the time when the project would soon come to an end and we were anxious that everyone involved should write some retrospective accounts of their feelings and experiences about each of the programs whilst they were still fresh in their minds.

A set of guidelines was prepared so that the various accounts would be as comparable as possible. Teachers and researchers were asked not to discuss their accounts with one another. This exercise took up some of the participants' valuable time, as Sue discovered during the week commencing November 17th:

> Jane and I were beginning to reach a natural break in 'Edfax' and 'Super Art' when Pauline and Joan would be able to swap over programs. Tying up the loose ends took us until Thursday. We postponed the changeover until the following week as Pauline and Joan were preoccupied with the reports to be prepared for Derek and Louis. Joan did mention that this would be a good testing time for the work cards.
>
> With only three of Pauline's children to complete 'Super Art' pictures, I decided to introduce the work cards. Louise had progressed through an introductory session, and was ready to draw her picture. I explained to her how to use the Quick Reference Work Card. To use it as an aid with which to draw her picture needed constant verbal prompts from me. Maybe she would have been more confident if she had a friend with her. This seemed to make a difference when Leanne and John tackled the Discovering Modes card. They helped each other read through the instructions and could have been left on their own. When drawing their pictures and using the Quick Reference card, they worked well together, with Leanne prompting John to use certain modes for his Viking Ship. John readily referred to the card, rather than ask me initially (eg. he picked his own shape for the sun when I was elsewhere). Both found the pattern box print out very useful and this was instigating discussions about tones. John and Leanne found using the work cards fun. Louise did not. It would be interesting to chart the differences with Joan's children.
>
> At the beginning of the week, Pauline was using 'Writer'. The children were typing in their poems about the fair. Most discussion was about arranging paragraphs and of punctuation. Systematic observations were made of Sonia, Jennie and Christopher. Typing time is ten to fifteen minutes but editing time has lessened and has become more pupil-orientated with Pauline giving fewer instructions. This takes no more time than if she was correcting a problem in a subject area.
>
> Towards the end of the week I felt that Pauline was running out of steam, especially after the meeting with Derek when she was trying to work out how to fit in both report writing for the researchers, for school, and, at the same time, start festive preparations. With 'Super Art' pictures completed plus various poems printed on 'Writer', she could hardly be expected to think of using 'Edfax'! So, I asked her if I could plot out the box, frame and ellipse modes for the 'discovering modes' work card. These I managed to complete. Whilst I was working on them, Mrs. Black came over to look. I showed her the finished ones and explained their use. I asked her when she would like to use them and she suggested the following Tuesday lunchtime. Meanwhile, Joan had been having trouble with 'Writer'. She could not load work that had been previously saved. Apparently, this had stemmed from the previous Thursday when the headteacher had tried to save some work. When I tried her disc in the computer I was using, the editing sections worked perfectly but she still could not load work, although it was stated the disc was full. This was one problem we had to refer to Derek.

As the end of November approached, thoughts moved on to preparations for Christmas. Pauline had the idea that every child should prepare his/her own Christmas card using the computer.

Sue's expertise was therefore in great demand:

> On Tuesday, Pauline was very eager to continue using 'Super Art' for making pictures for Christmas cards. Scott and Stuart had started working on a picture but had lost it as Pauline had not realised how to save it. I made a note to include this information on a work card. During the week there were many different compositions. Scott seemed to want to fill in every available space with objects, Sonia gave some thought to the size and position of her Christmas tree; Krishna thought out her composition and balanced her picture well. Mark kept his picture of a cracker very simple and won the admiration of his classmates. When I arrived on Thursday, Pauline had the class grouped around the computer. Lalit had started his picture

which was very small. Pauline was discussing the effectiveness of composition with them. She showed them many examples of their work and asked their opinions about the differences in effectiveness. Sonia commented that some were putting too much in. Teresa said that some were overdoing it with patterns. Pauline talked about the simplicity of pictures and thinking about the space to be used, using Lalit's picture as an example. She suggested planning out the picture in rough books and thinking about the modes to be used. I suggested that the paper should be roughly the same size as the screen. We both thought this would save a considerable amount of time. It was encouraging that whilst drawing their pictures for their Christmas cards, the children needed very few prompts.

I asked them to refer to the quick reference card first. Krishna and Fiona preferred to work alone; Scott needed a friend's support. There was considerable consultation between Scott and Stuart regarding the angles needed and the position of the lines for the Christmas tree. They ran into difficulty as they had worked up one side and down the other so the result was asymmetrical. However, it was so easy to explain how to correct this with the 'Super Art' program. It would have been very frustrating with a pencil. Scott needed four prompts connected with construction but none with modes or patterns as he would scan the quick reference card and/or consult Stuart. On the other hand, Dirshna knew exactly what modes to use and only consulted the work card for patterns. Her rendition was excellent. Sonia and Mark worked well together with Mark eagerly pointing out useful modes. Again the only prompts were for points of construction. Lalit reconstructed his picture of a snowman effectively. We discussed creating the illusion of distance by the strategic use of pattern. He added a humorous touch by drawing a smoke bubble from the snowman's pipe containing 'Happy Christmas'. I think we have almost reached the stage of total integration of the program in the classroom. Certainly this week I was able to distance myself from the children working on the computer. The quick reference work card seemed to be serving its purpose and I was able to complete part two of the Discovering Modes work card and, thanks to Mrs. Black, the first section of the Basic Information card. Overwhelmed by the prolific output of the children, I decided to use representative pictures for work cards.

Joan wanted to complete some Viking pictures so Pauline sorted out some repeats she had for me to photocopy. I kept copies of various Christmas card pictures.

Debbie (Mrs. Black) Tries her Hand with 'Super Art'

Debbie had a lunchtime session on 'Super Art' program lasting half an hour. She worked her way through the starting-off instructions I had printed out on 'Writer' previously. She was very apprehensive, asking which way up to insert the disc, and how to use the shift and break keys. I told her to think positive and to say 'I can and I will'. She took a deep breath and did just that! She needed some physical prompts to move the mouse and to move from the modes to the pattern box. It was interesting that her reaction to setting up the program and the difficulties she had were similar to those I had experienced myself. I had almost forgotten. She was invaluable in helping me make a more effective format for the Basic Information work card. In fact, I virtually re-wrote it! The difficult part over, she romped through the first part of the Discovering Modes card. Only spray mode needed clarifying so that she remembered to move from Spray to Nozzle to Pattern. She began to see shapes, 'Oh that's good for a tree', and looked for an appropriate mode to form the trunk. She was very interested in line mode and took some time to work out why the pattern had escaped from one shape. Debbie enjoyed this part of the session and set Tuesday lunchtime as a regular session.

It was Thursday and Jane and Sue were no nearer swapping over 'Edfax' and 'Super Art' with Joan and Pauline.

Jane had finished her outstanding 'Edfax' work, and 'Super Art' had reached a convenient point as it was not so time consuming. We did not want to exert undue pressure on Pauline and Joan, so Jane suggested trying out an experiment with basic linear graphics to introduce

'Edfax' to Pauline's children. This would not require Pauline to prepare anything but would probably whet her appetite when she saw the children working with the program. I had expected Debbie to be taking Joan's class that afternoon and hoped to use the Discovering Modes card 1 with a group of Joan's children. Mrs Black would be familiar with this and would have had some reinforcement. I suggested that she could use the program to illustrate the children's poems. She approved this idea but unfortunately she had to attend a meeting. However, I went ahead and chose four children (Robert, Leaha, Felicity and Erica) who had typed in their poems for the head. They worked their way through Discovering Modes card 1. I left a note for Joan in the hope that she could use these children to introduce the others to the card, as she had done with previous programs.

Jane was beginning to see some progress with 'Edfax' and managed to observe two of the 'target' children working on December 2nd.

When I arrived this morning, Robert and Gregory (two of our special observation children) were working at the computer. Erica and Michelle had shown them what to do the previous day. I asked Robert and Gregory if they had found the program easy and they said they had. The only problem had been when 'they tried to put coloured writing against the background and the background colour kept changing' (their words). They had a problem with a bit of the border because they couldn't find the right graphics character. When I arrived they were puzzled about why the border was flashing. They had forgotten to put FLASH off. Apart from these minor difficulties, these two have gained enormously in self-confidence since the project began. They completed a page and a half of text by morning break.

After break Julie completed her picture by adding a sentence 'This is York city wall'.

Then I talked with Robert, Gregory, Erica, Michelle and Lucy (Melanie was away) about their graphics design. We decided to see how much of their page was already occupied by text. I printed out:

(1) that columns have to be left empty for commands.
(2) that the picture must be planned by filling in the tiny squares on the graph paper.
(3) that 'fill background' is a useful function in picture making.
(4) leaving background empty is the only way to get 'black' in the picture.

Michelle and Lucy made a good start with their picture of a sword completed with *flashing* jewels and *congealed* blood.

Pauline was absent all the following week and so Sue decided to introduce the discovering-modes card to Joan's class:

I started to introduce the Discovering Modes card to Joan's class, using groups of four. The first group finished the second card in half an hour. The work card seemed to be giving them more time to experiment, so for example, Robert used spray mode with square nozzle to make a pattern from his initials. With another group, Sarah, Wayne, Emma and Julie, there was a similar response. They seemed to be responding to the suggestions on the work card.

Debbie came for a lunchtime session. She recapped by working through the completed part of the Basic Information card which she found very clear and straightforward. She completed Discovering Modes card 2. The only problem she had with this was with not making a box shape on the screen but a straight line. She went through the procedure for opening a file, testing and printing. She had an example of her work to take away. Next week we will move on to typing in and setting out a poem, probably with an illustration. Debbie was very keen to try this.

After Joan had commented that she would find the Basic Information card useful to acquaint herself with the program, I took the opportunity to plot it out. Starting off instructions were followed by the first check, then the completion of Discovering Modes cards 1 and 2. Next was the drawing session procedure (creating a file, second check) followed by printing and storing instructions.

To help teachers to think about mode use, I included three pictures for them to try by using the quick reference card as a guide. This would lead on to Drawing session cards 1–8, if they wanted further practice. I was aiming at teachers who were not particularly artistically inclined by giving them suggestions to build upon. I thought that Joan would find this particularly interesting.

By mid-December the Christmas preparations were really taking over to such an extent that regular observations of children using the computers were becoming quite difficult. In the end, the best thing for Jane and Sue to do was to join in with whatever Pauline and Joan wanted and to complete their own retrospective accounts of the computer activities. On December 15th Sue got involved in the production of more Christmas cards and found that her work cards were having a positive effect:

The first task was to help Pauline complete the Christmas cards using 'Super Art'. John, Leanne, Suzanne and Scott needed to finish their cards.

The children are working well with minimum adult assistance, especially if they are working in pairs. Leanne was able to discuss with Sonia how to construct her Christmas tree, and through the discussion, ideas flowed. Sonia was able to advise Leanne on which modes to use. They referred to the Quick Reference card for patterns.

John worked alone but discussed what he was doing with me. He was quite inexperienced, being new to the school, so I had to give him more prompts to think about mode use than I would have done with the others. He needed help with which part of his rather complicated picture of Santa and sleigh, to tackle first. As there was a lot of pencil work which was difficult to execute he needed prompts to persevere and make alterations. Suzanne, working alone, began with an idea of where to position her snowman which she constructed easily. She had more difficulty using the pencil to draw a tree and reverted to line mode. For the top of the tree I suggested she use small spray mode which she did with great effect.

Scott approached the computer very confidently. Clearing the screen for himself, and equipped with a scale drawing to help him, he was able to construct his own picture, only seeking my help to locate the Quick Reference card which he used to refer to patterns.

I continued constructing the work cards for 'Super Art', completing Basic Information cards 1 and 2. I printed out the necessary information for drawing session cards but cut them from 8 to 6 as Christmas preparations were diminishing time in the classroom.

In her lunchtime session Debbie worked through Basic Information cards 1 and 2. After a little effort, we created her own file. We had problems in that the original disc was full and Mrs Black made slight errors in procedure by taking her finger off Execute before she had reached Create. Once her file was created, I showed her how to type in a poem. She had only a few modes to deal with at any time and completed the poem quickly. She was thrilled when it printed out. I explained that she could go back to her file anytime and experiment with layout. The size of the text and printout seemed to suit her needs more than 'Writer'. If I have time I will demonstrate the different styles of text to her.

What do the Teachers and Researchers Think?
Some Retrospective Accounts

'Other Worlds'

The first programs to be introduced to Pauline and Joan were 'The Explorer' and 'The Inhabitant', both part of the 'Other Worlds' package produced by Ladybird-Longman. What is most evident here is that the teachers chose to use the programs in an interesting way, although somewhat out of context. The resulting problems were not entirely negative since they pointed to ways in which the package could have been rewritten to produce a more stimulating and certainly more versatile product. Unfortunately the group that produced these particular programs is no longer in operation. The two accounts which follow have many points in common; however, there are essential differences. For Joan, the programs were largely successful in meeting her objectives, with the exception of the improvement of the children's written style, but the question of the suitability of the programs never arose. For Jane, it was a case of inadequate preparation and insufficient knowledge and understanding of what the programs were designed to do on the part of the teachers using them. What we must remember is that both accounts are valid. Their high degree of concordance bears witness to that.

The differences reflect the particular orientations of 'teacher under pressure', on the one hand, and 'participant-observer' on the other. Here is part of Joan's account:

> My objective in using 'Other Worlds' was to encourage creative writing by stimulating a broader look at a subject through the questioning. The group I had at the time seemed rather limited in their creative writing and tended to be easily satisfied with their work. I hoped the program would lead the children into thinking more deeply about the subject.
>
> I initially used 'The Explorer' with my group in January, when I embarked on a mini-project on Eskimos. My group had been stimulated by three BBC drama programmes on Eskimos, which covered their way of life when they travelled to follow the hunting, both in summer and winter. We looked more deeply into their lifestyle and used 'The Explorer' as an outsider exploring this inhospitable place where they live. The program was easy to run and was split into several sections so that work could be saved and returned to later, although we tended to work this through in one session. The children worked in pairs or threes so that discussion was initiated and decisions made. At this stage we did not have a printer so that the final writing had to be copied in order to have a record of it. As I timetabled the use of the computer quite rigidly at this time it took quite a long time for all the children to use it. After a week's residential visit, which included studying life in Victorian times in a large house we visited in the vicinity, we used 'The Inhabitant' to formulate what life would have been like for the various people who lived in the house about 100 years ago. For this the children worked in pairs. Each pair chose to be a person who would have lived in the house, whether it was the owner, his wife or sister, or one of the many servants. Most children chose to be one of the servants and the program took them through their way of life, from growing up, their work, hobbies, money, food etc. Work was saved on disc and returned to at a later date. Some pairs worked through it quite quickly, but others seemed to take a long time. The children could work quite happily without too much teacher intervention, and it soon became just another group working in the classroom area. It took a long time for all children to work through the program (from March through to June) because there was insufficient computer time. At this stage both class groups involved in the project were working on 'Other Worlds', 'INFORM' and 'Front Page' all at once. We had one computer on loan exclusively for our use and the school computer available when not timetabled for other groups in the school. Another problem during the summer term seemed to be difficulties with the hardware. This proved particularly frustrating as one wasted a lot of time trying to get a program to work, while the children were getting restless and needed our attention. Because we were inexperienced, we tended to blame ourselves and think we were doing something wrong. It was a relief to discover that the disc or computer was malfunctioning. The children seemed to enjoy working on the program and most children worked very sensibly. It certainly initiated good discussion and thought about the class structure and life-style of people in a large country house 100 years ago and, I am sure, led to a better understanding of this period. When I joined discussions or looked at their summary, we wondered whether certain things were feasible, enhancing their knowledge and understanding. The group contained a number of

disruptive and rather silly children and some of these children chose to put in some silly statements, either without discussion with their partner, or deliberately. The program allows you to make changes, but a whole section of work had to be redone. This was fine if the facts put in were inappropriate, but proved tiresome if the children had made a few spelling mistakes or grammatical errors. For the less able children this wasted a lot of time. Whilst the program achieved what I had expected, and also gave the children a better understanding of Victorian life through their discussion, we found the final printout rather disappointing. Its style was stilted and ungainly, and so did not, in the end, assist written style in creative writing. Along with the difficulties of editing work, we came to the conclusion that the program only had limited possibilities. Pauline tended to use the program more freely, allowing the children to be more imaginative, rather than confining them to a particular place or time, as I did, and she felt it worked better. However, she also found the style stilted and editing small mistakes a problem.

Jane's Account of 'Other Worlds'

'Other Worlds' has been designed to help children expand their perception not only of fantasy worlds, but also of the world in which they live. 'The Explorer' emphasises the physical environment in which the intruder's priorities are to survive and observe, while 'The Inhabitant' concentrates on the social fabric of a world. The inhabitant is at home and it is his role to explain and interpret to an interested visitor fundamental aspects of his society.

The program writers admit that, 'attempting to capture all the answers and questions to life, the universe and everything in two program packages must fail in some respects'. My observations bear this out. In my view, the writers have failed to produce a series of prompts and questions sufficiently open-ended and appropriate for such a diverse range of situations. Their stated intentions probably could be achieved with much more careful wording of the programs. They have attempted to be too ambitious without testing and trying out the package in a much broader spectrum of 'other worlds'.

Using the programs

Both Pauline and Joan assured me that they had read and understood the Teacher's Handbook. How did they decide to use the programs? 'The Explorer' was used to follow-up two classroom projects. The first was about dinosaurs and monsters, the second was concerned with exploring the Arctic. In the case of 'The Inhabitant', both teachers asked their groups to imagine what it would have been like to live during the 1800s at Beaumanor Hall, a stately mansion in rural Leicestershire. As part of a previous school project the children had visited Quorn and Beaumanor Halls, collecting a variety of information on people and events in the past. Obviously, the successful use of 'Other Worlds' depended almost entirely on the teacher's careful preparation. The children needed to know a great deal about what the earth was like when monsters and dinosaurs existed, about social history in the 1800s and geographical conditions in polar regions, before they could successful exploit either program. The output from these programs was determined by the degree to which the children had been previously 'immersed' in whatever world they intended to explore or inhabit. Most primary school teachers need no reminder that when a particular topic is attempted the classroom area needs to be flooded with a wide variety of stimulating materials – books, photographs, pictures, artefacts, displays and so on. Children need ample opportunity to explore these materials, to write, draw, make, talk about, discuss with their teacher and other children. Relevant and informative visits are important in helping the children towards a meaningful understanding of 'other worlds' which are outside their actual experience.

I observed that this kind of preparation was limited. Consequently the computer output was mediocre. Notwithstanding these limitations, the children were very interested and engaged in their work at the computer. Having noted the importance of adequate exposure in a variety of ways to other worlds before using the computer programs, what of the limitations of the programs themselves?

The programs clearly engaged the interest and attention of children across the whole range of ability and aptitude. Despite the difficulties referred to above, most children were reasonably expansive and creative in their responses. Robert and Gregory decided to visit the Arctic wearing woolly hats under diving helmets, track suits underneath large wet suits and three pairs of socks inside wellingtons. Most of the others opted for conventional fur hats, coats and fur-lined boots.

No doubt the children were helped by the structure of the programs and the directness of the prompts they received. For children with writing difficulties, the final print-out of their interaction with the programs was a major achievement in their eyes. On the other hand, one suspects that the very structure of the prompts seriously delimits the potential creativeness of the brighter child. As a matter of fact, some of the prompts and questions were singularly inappropriate in certain situations. The children seemed unaware of this shortcoming and responded as sensibly as they could. For example:

PROMPT – please describe your vehicle.
ANSWER – this vehicle is big and it has four legs and a head and it is powered by its legs.

(This respondent deserves full marks for his/her ingenuity in trying to respond to a seemingly inane computer prompt.)

In the section on 'growing up' the word *people* would be better than folk. The latter sounds very quaint in certain situations.

Interaction with the programs resulted in some interesting learning experiences for particular pupils. For example, some children were clearly exercised with the question of historical time. In response to a prompt in 'The Inhabitant' which the teacher had applied to Beaumanor Hall in the 1800's, children's responses to do with travel were as follows:

You never make long journeys because you have to work. . .
(Walk?)
One vehicle used by your folk is a coach. . .
This vehicle is like a wagon and is powered by a horse. . .

Their responses to the working day showed that they had concluded that the working man worked long and hard with little time for recreation:

For 16 hours of each working day you are a laundry maid. . .
Leisure activities take up to 2 hours a day. . .

There were historical and geographical misunderstandings too, of course:

110 miles in lots of traffic. . .
1600 miles to Ireland. . .

The children, as a whole were unaware of the average life expectancy in the 1800s, judging it to be in excess of today's average, at 80 years or more.

There were also a number of examples of transposition of present day into the historical past (*with today's unemployment problems in mind*)

PROMPT – Will you be doing the same job a year from now?
ANSWER – No, I'll probably have lost my job.

(*with today's road safety problems in mind*)

PROMPT – What are some of the important things your young must learn?
ANSWER – It is important for young human folk to learn to play safe. (*sic*) They can also expect to spend 2 weeks learning how to cross the road. . .
You learned this at the side of the road. . .

(*with today's emphasis on physical fitness in mind*)

ANSWER – the cook would go jogging in her spare time.

General conclusions

The programs: Two shortcomings in the design of the programs were soon identified. In both programs an invitation to make changes in respect of an entry (even a single spelling mistake) results in a whole paragraph being wiped out. This irritated users, who often forgot their original input.

In the 'Inhabitant', there were numerous misunderstandings of the innocuous prompt –

How long is your day?
Divide your day into work, rest and leisure.

Many children appeared to interpret 'day' to mean the period from dawn to dusk rather than an interval of 24 hours. Thus when Joan and Susan (two of the more able children) divided their day into 12 hours work, 2 hours' rest and 2 hours' leisure (clearly 'rest' was not equated with sleep) the computer rejected their response because it did not add up to 24 hours. There was no explanation of how to correct the error.

The children: Not only did the children thoroughly enjoy the work involved in 'The Explorer' and 'The Inhabitant', it was quite apparent that they gained significantly in computer literacy. They became more proficient in using the keyboard and self-confidence increased with their growing mastery.

The teachers: For the teachers, two points seem to be pre-eminent. First, it is vital that they read and fully comprehend the intentions of the programs as set out in the handbooks. In this respect the final print-outs tell their own story. Secondly, with the educational intentions of the programs clearly understood, teachers need to prepare, and have at hand a variety of back-up and reference materials that can readily and immediately enrich the children's learning experiences as they occur.

'INFORM'

'INFORM', a general-purpose database, was the first full-scale program to be introduced after the project had started. It proved to be a major departure from the ways in which the computer had been used in the school in the past, being the first time that the teachers and children had experienced a genuinely 'content-free' tool.

It must be admitted that 'INFORM's' introduction was somewhat hurried by the need to 'cash in' on an activity which had already been planned. Furthermore, it was brought in at a time when the teachers had little time to experiment with it beforehand. Both the accounts of Joan and Jane reflect the shortage of time to understand 'INFORM' fully before it was used with the children, Joan even talking of problems of trying to teach the children whilst experimenting with 'live data'. For Jane, it was also a case of missed opportunities since the children's curiosity was not fully exploited by developing their wide variety of questions. For Joan the major problems seem to fall into two categories: first, a shortage of time; and, second, the fact that she and Pauline were not sufficiently experienced with this kind of activity to know just how much careful preparation was necessary. This is evident in Jane's comments about the lack of adequate organisation at the data-gathering stage in the churchyard.

By the end of the exercise however, with hindsight, Joan recognises the benefits of the children learning how to design the structure of their own datafiles. It is not surprising that mistakes were made. It was an extremely complex activity. What is certain is that overall the activity was most beneficial to children, teachers and researchers alike. Here is Joan's account:

'INFORM' is a program providing a database that children can use. My objectives in using the program were obviously to introduce the database idea and usage. I wanted the children to be able to type in simple data to form a database and to extend the study of a local graveyard by being able to interrogate the data collected by the children. I had seen this program demonstrated on an in-service course and could see it would give children an introduction to the skills required to use a database in the outside world (in the workplace, library etc.). On a residential field trip we were looking at interesting information from the graveyard in a worksheet format and through rubbings. We felt this program would extend our study, providing us with a fairly extensive record of the gravestones in the graveyard, from which interesting questions could be asked.

The program was a very minor part of our field trip, but it became a large part of the follow-up work back at school. Before visiting the graveyard the datasheets were explained to the children, showing them how to collect the data and mentioning what the fieldnames meant. However, when we were collecting the data, quite a few children had difficulties with the terms being used (eg. STATUS, etc.) and with just sorting out the information as they transferred it from the gravestone to their sheets.

When we returned to school I showed the collected data to the class (not all the children had been on the field trip), and explained how we had collected it and what the categories of information (fields) were. I explained that the information had to be put on to disc so that we could then ask questions about the information.

I chose three capable children to work with Jane in the role of parent/helper, to define the fields and to prepare the disc to accept the data. Jane and I had only had a brief look at how to use the program one lunchtime. We found the manual less than helpful, finding it difficult to understand and to find the information required when we had difficulties. Therefore we had to spend a lot of time learning how to use an unfamiliar program with the children and 'live' data. At the time I had a demanding and difficult class group so that it was very hard trying to divide my time between the bulk of the class and the effort of getting 'INFORM' started with the small group of children.

Once the disc had been prepared to take the data things went more smoothly. We devised a technique whereby one child would type in the data they had collected, another child would read out the data and a third would check what had been typed for accuracy and work out ages of deceased if any dates were available etc. One child would drop out as a new child came to type in their data, so that there were always two experienced children at the computer. The children seemed to enjoy this quite mundane task. Most children got an opportunity to type in data, as some of the graveyard information was collected by children from another class. Also the children from Pauline's group who went on the field trip typed in their data sheets in the same way. We had a total of 170 records when the data was all typed in. I gave a talk and demonstration to the whole class to show how we could 'interrogate the data'. The children thought of some simple questions and we used the code to find the relevant information. Then the children went to formulate their own questions – I got them to think of three each. They had to work out how they could ask their questions using the code we had to use. This proved quite difficult and so the questions the children eventually asked of the data were rather simple eg. 'How many men died over the age of 60?' 'How many people died under the age of 21?' We managed to get answers to our questions on the screen, but had recently acquired a printer and wanted them printed out. Once again, because the manual was difficult to interpret, getting this to happen was more a matter of trial and error. Pressure of time meant that we did not develop the questioning of the data as much as I would have liked. However, we used our learning experiences with this program to give an assembly to the whole school, demonstrating how we collected the data, defined the fields, typed in the data and interrogated it. We then put up a display of the work we had produced.

The following term I used the program again, in a similar way, to gather information from our local church at Thorpe Acre, as part of our study of how this once small hamlet had changed over the last hundred or so years to be a suburb of Loughborough. When preparing the disc, I used different children, but used one or two of my able children from last time as tutors. The children coped well with typing in their data using the same system as before. At the end of the summer term I had two computers out with both sets of data for more children to try out their questions. They enjoyed this, although, again, formulating their questions around the code was not an easy task, unless they were very simple.

Given the right situation, I am sure the program will be used again. Another group has already used it to collect data on houses – types of roof, walls etc. when they went on a field trip. I would think that its use would be improved if the fields had been chosen and the data sheets prepared by the children. It would have possibly avoided the difficulties we experienced in collecting the information. However, the program did achieve the objectives I expected in relation to database experience, collecting, typing in and interrogating data.

Jane's Account of the Use of 'INFORM'

The teachers

About six weeks into the project Derek organised an in-service introductory course on the use of 'INFORM' at the University. The main purpose of the meeting was to demonstrate 'INFORM' and explore its possible use in a forthcoming local studies project. The teachers and some of their children were about to stay at Quorn Hall, a local-studies centre, and it was thought that 'INFORM' could be a valuable tool for the organisation of local studies information that the children were to collect.

To this end, Derek provided the teachers with 'data-gathering' sheets (coding sheets) divided into nine fields. This was specifically designed to facilitate the children's data collection out in the field. Their task involved gathering information from the gravestones in Quorn churchyard. Having collected their data in the field, they would then be shown, back in the classroom, how to compile a database using 'INFORM'. Derek provided previously-collected data which the team used in their practice session.

The children were introduced briefly to the idea of information gathering before they left Quorn Hall. Meanings of the various fieldnames were explained to them, though not everyone seemed to understand their use. Needless to say, after a brisk ten minute walk down to the churchyard, and an hour spent collecting other information for their teachers, many children had forgotten the precise explanations. Fortunately there were plenty of adults on hand to offer further help. Terms like SPOUSE, SEX, and MASON needed more clarification. The field BORN was slightly problematic. A recurring question asked by the children was: 'How do I find out when he/she was born?' It was explained that if the gravestone was inscribed with the year of death and the age of the person who died, then a simple 'take-away' sum would provide the year of birth. It was suggested that these calculations be left until later to be completed in the classroom. In retrospect, it would have been a good idea to have discussed these points in greater detail before the visit.

I had previously agreed with the teachers that the children would need to be organised into small groups and assigned to different areas of the churchyard in order to avoid duplicating information. It seemed that this had not been properly understood and the children were despatched in a rather haphazard way to complete their assignments.

We felt somewhat disappointed that the teachers had not organised the data collection in a more systematic way. Surprisingly, however, there was not too much duplication. Back in the classroom I sifted through the data sheets and quickly eliminated all the unwanted information.

Derek concluded that better forward planning by the teachers would have resulted in a more efficient data-collection exercise. Some suggestions for the organisation of future data-collections include:-

(1) Provide a map of the 'field' divided into sections. (In the case of the churchyard it is already divided by paths and general layout). Send small groups of children to each

section (ideally with one adult to one or two groups) and allocate two or three different gravestones to each child to avoid duplicating the information collected.

(2) Explain the terms on the coding sheet more carefully ie. FORENAME, SURNAME, SPOUSE, SEX, MASON, etc.

(3) Talk about the relationship between date of birth, date of death and age at death, working out some examples, preferably from the children's own experience.

(4) Tell the children to concentrate on data collection when in the field and leave the calculations until they are back in the classroom.

Problems, difficulties and solutions

I was able to identify the following problem areas:-

(i)   Teachers' explanation and children's understanding
(ii) The time factor
(iii) Operating the computer
(iv) The handbook.

Teachers' explanations and children's understanding

Following the Quorn Hall visit, one of the teachers talked to her class about setting up the 'INFORM' datafile. She explained in simple terms the basic principles of data collection, creating a database and file interrogation. It is doubtful whether most of the children properly understood the teacher's explanation without simultaneous practical computer experience. Two week elapsed before some of the children had a turn at keying in their information.

The time factor

The time factor was another problem. With only one computer and three children working together, it took a fortnight to enter 170 records. This was almost three weeks after the children had collected their information in Quorn churchyard. Interest in interrogating the data was beginning to wane. Primary school children need more immediate feedback.

Operating the computer

After her explanatory talk the teacher chose three able children to work at the computer and delegated me to the role of parent/helper. The idea was that two of the children who had been initiated would stay at the computer and teach a new recruit. The system worked well. The two initiates acted as reader and checker while the novice keyed in the data.

The Handbook

On first sight the 'INFORM handbook' appears to be very complicated. Initially it isn't easy to find one's way round it. It grows easier as one becomes accustomed to the lay-out. It's packed full of information in fairly small print. The two teachers complained that 'it isn't explicit enough'. I also found that it wasn't easy to find the exact piece of information required when a problem occurred. This highlights another difficulty, namely that the teachers were not prepared to spend enough time reading the handbook and practising the program before working with the children. With a fairly complex program like 'INFORM' this preparation is vital. It is no use expecting to turn to the handbook in an emergency situation and being able to sort out a problem with ease and alacrity.

Primary school teachers need to thoroughly understand the program and instructions in order to use them in a simplified form with their children. Production of easy-to-follow instructions in big print on workcards would enable the children to work independently. In our particular situation it was fortunate that I was available to act as parent/helper.

The researcher's role in the introduction of 'INFORM' can be perceived under three headings:-

(1) fellow learner
(2) parent/helper and
(3) observer/recorder.

Fellow learner. The novelty of 'INFORM' led to some distinct advantages in personal relationships. Had I been an acknowledged expert there is little doubt the teachers would have found my presence somewhat intimidating. 'INFORM' was introduced early on in the project when the teachers had little computer self-confidence. Because we were all at the same level of relative ignorance a camaraderie was quickly established between the participants.

Parent/helper. From the very outset in the use of 'INFORM' it was agreed that my role would be that of parent/helper, rather than teacher/initiator of classroom activities. That is to say, I was to serve as a resource under the teachers' direction. In practice this worked out as follows:-

In the field I helped children to collect information from the gravestones and to complete their datasheets.

In the classroom I helped children to organise their data and feed it into the computer.

Observer/recorder. While fulfilling my roles as fellow learner and parent/helper I continued systematic observation and recording of interactions and events.

How the teachers handled the program

To this point in time, the teachers handled the program very well. Had they spent more time and effort on preparation and planning, the exercise would have been far more successful. For example:

(1) To begin with, the teachers should have become fully conversant with the manual instructions and the program itself.
(2) They should have spent more time preparing the children for the use of 'INFORM', i.e. ensuring that they understood what they were about to undertake by reference to past experience by working examples etc.
(3) They should have planned the field-work with greater care to ensure systematic data collection and avoid duplication.
(4) The children anticipated that the file-interrogation procedure would be the most exciting part after the rather routine feeding in of data and yet the teachers failed to develop this aspect. File-interrogation was very limited. It should have been developed much more. Only one class actually interrogated its data. Their teacher said that she would have liked to have done much more but didn't have the time. The children formulated some simple questions such as, 'How many women died over the age of eighty?' and 'How many children died less than one year old?' Yet when some of the children were inputting their own data they were suggesting a much wider range of possible questions such as, 'Were any 1st World War dead buried at Quorn?', 'What were the most popular Christian names in the 1800's and were they the same today?' Clearly, file interrogation could have tapped the children's inquisitive nature and evolved into a much more interesting exercise.

Skills and concepts which 'INFORM' seems best at developing

The first and obvious skills which 'INFORM' begins to develop may be grouped under the broad heading of *information retrieval*. The program fosters the children's awareness of the organisation of information in their daily lives, the alphabetical list of children in their class for example, the photographs and names of their teachers displayed in the entrance hall, Teletext, Ceefax, the list of their favourite football team, the dictionary, the telephone directory and so on. The children may be encouraged to suggest other collections of information to add to the list. From this they may be led on to collecting and organising their own information on topics of their choice. Hence, to data storage and retrieval.

The 'INFORM' enterprise requires children to exercise *care and accuracy* in searching for, recording, organising and transferring information to the computer database. The very nature of the program does not allow a 'slap-dash' approach. Children who normally adopt a cavalier attitude quickly realise that success depends on taking care. Keyboard skills, spelling, reading, interpersonal cooperation and communication continue to be practised.

Collecting information from Quorn churchyard fostered the children's *sense of history* by raising such questions as, 'Did all the children in this family die within a short space of time because of an epidemic?' 'Did the young men who died between 1914 and 1918 die in the 1st World War?' 'Have the surnames which people had in Quorn long ago survived to the present day?' Strictly speaking, the children should have been encouraged to formulate hypotheses and questions before structuring their datafile. Perhaps this would have been too ambitious a step for these particular children. This would be something to work towards in the future.

How well has the program been integrated into the teachers' repertoire of teaching resources?

The integration of 'INFORM' into the teachers' repertoire of resources depends on their willingness to arrive at an understanding of the program's wide range of possible uses. This in turn hinges on how imaginative the teachers are and how prepared they are to step aside from their established curriculum.

The teachers found Derek's suggested use of churchyard data interesting and they repeated a similar collection at Thorpe Acre churchyard in the summer term. So far however, they have not come up with their own original ideas. My assessment of the present situation is that if an obvious use for a database occurs in future classroom projects, then 'INFORM' will be used again. However, I doubt whether the teachers will try to include information retrieval in their everyday curriculum.

'Front Page'

Of all the programs that Derek Blease has introduced to teachers over the years, 'Front Page' has always produced the most positive initial response. Introducing it to Pauline and Joan was no exception. Up to this point, they had found it difficult to visualise for themselves how a new program might be used. Sometimes they would respond well to suggestions, but it usually took some days or even weeks of experimenting before spontaneous ideas emerged. This was not true of 'Front Page', and that is why its introduction was so satisfying.

Derek demonstrated the program only once, and even before he had finished both Pauline and Joan were suggesting what they might do with it and which skills the program might be used to develop. If any program was to become fully integrated into their repertoire it was this one, marking a great step in their development as computer users. Much of this is evident from the accounts of Pauline and Jane. Both reports emphasise the ease and simplicity of use and the children's reactions. The two teachers actually provided more resources and archive materials for this program than they had for 'Other Worlds'. Teaching children to use the program was much easier than it had been with 'INFORM'. Nevertheless Pauline and Joan adopted the group method used so successfully with 'INFORM' whereby two experienced children helped a third who was a newcomer. Here is Pauline's account:

My immediate response to being introduced to 'Front Page' was that it had endless possibilities. It seemed a very open ended piece of software. It gave great opportunities for interesting and exciting written work. I saw it as a means of improving the style of children's writing; the layout of the page means that there are some constraints placed upon them. This, I felt would make the writer think out and plan the work, leading to a concise, yet detailed piece of writing. The program was also a tool for leading the children away from their usual subjective style into a reportive style.

The program was first shown to us in March 1987. I hoped that the children would be similarly stimulated and interested. Having made some attempt at word processing using 'Wordwise' (which was proving rather difficult to monitor and to edit, requiring so much pre-knowledge and teacher intervention) the ease with which this new program, 'Front Page', could be used by a complete novice was very appealing. It also added a new dimension to reportive writing, in that the completed page has an instant visual impact which adds interest to even the most mediocre piece of work.

At the time that 'Front Page' appeared on our horizon, we had just returned from a week's residential visit to Quorn Hall where we had studied the local environment as part of the wider topic of 'Our Environment', undertaken that year. During our week away we had visited Beaumanor Hall, spending part of a day following the 'Murder – Mystery Trail'. The day began with a video of a supposed crime at the hall at the turn of the century. With the scene set, the children had to decipher clues, follow a trail and reach their conclusions as to the murderer. The children's imaginations were fired by this day and on their return to school they wrote an account of the murder of Lady Richfield. Then I suggested that it would be better if we could set the work out as a newspaper report. I decided that it would be appropriate to show the program to the class. After an initial discussion about the front page of a newspaper, its layout and requirements, we looked at the program. Together we discussed a suitable name for a newspaper of almost a century ago, a realistic price and a date. Collectively we decided on a headline and the format of the news. Finally we looked at our resources from the archives of Beaumanor Hall for a suitably authentic advertisement for the previous century.

This initial viewing of 'Front Page' by the whole class was most stimulating and generated much worthwhile discussion. At this point many children were anxious to get going for themselves. I decided that those who had completed a hand written account to my satisfaction could type it into the computer. Beginning with two fairly able children, one keyed in the work which was dictated by the other. In turn, this pair helped another child who was then able to monitor, and so on until the whole group had taken their turn. The actual program is quite self-explanatory, and after the initial period, my help was only really required to monitor the editing.

The fact that the children were able to help one another through the program was a great bonus for me; as I said earlier, this really is software that can be used by anyone. Perhaps our only real problem was to find enough time for me to sit with a child for long enough to make editing a worthwhile and educational experience. When Jane was in school she sometimes relieved me of this task; at other times editing went on at breaktime. It could be a job easily undertaken by an ancillary or parent/helper.

The children's reaction was one of great excitement and pleasure in seeing their work so displayed. Most children produced a creditable piece of work according to their ability. One of our main achievements was the article produced by a boy of ten with quite serious learning difficulties. It is hard to describe the sense of achievement that he obviously felt when, for once, perfectly executed work was put up on the wall display. His smile of pleasure said it all! As a group we decided that the computer picture would be too rudimentary and unrealistic, so we attempted to reproduce photograph-like pictures in pencil. The fact that they were to key in this work seemed to stimulate the class to greater efforts. Many of them benefited from actually seeing what others were doing, thus encouraging discussion and cooperative learning.

In the following term we turned our attention to a nearby district of Loughborough, the one-time village of Thorpe Acre which has since been absorbed into the town. A visit to the archives of the Local History Library produced some photographs of cottages, barns and a local Manor House which were demolished two decades previously. As a class we attempted to deduce from the photographs and old newspaper cuttings, the Thorpe Acre of the past. Following on from this research, I asked the children to imagine themselves as reporters on the day that the bulldozers moved in. This was particularly successful. Many children even used the medium of imaginary eye-witness accounts to convey the feelings of the residents.

'Front Page' allows children to create a polished piece of work that has great visual impact. Given that it arranges the layout of the page, nonetheless it doesn't become too prescriptive; it enables the child to develop the skill of looking at the page with an eye to its impact on the reader. As well as developing their keyboard skills, it also forces the user to think about the content of the work since space is not open-ended. Children of this age group quite often find it difficult to write concisely. With 'Front Page' they are encouraged to draw out the salient points of their writing and to blend them into a cohesive whole. So for me the program was a useful tool in improving written style.

Obviously then, such an effective and easy-to-use program has a multitude of applications. It appears to me that it could be drawn into almost every area of the curriculum, for a great variety of topics. I would like to be able to develop the newspaper theme further on to continuation pages which is possible once we obtain the software.

Although much shorter, Jane's account reiterates the same points in the program's favour, suggesting that 'Front Page' was well integrated:

Of all the programs tried and tested during the project, 'Front Page' has been the most successful. It was simple to use yet the end product was well presented and appealing. For a minimum effort the children were able to print out the front page of a newspaper complete with its name, price, date, main headlines, space for a picture and an advertisement. Even the least able child was able to obtain a highly satisfactory result; a page of his/her own creative writing set out in an interesting way rolled off the printer.

Top marks too must be given to the handbook. It is well set out in large print with easy-to-understand instructions. After an introductory talk, the children were able to use the handbook and work independently at the computer. This earned a 'big plus' from the busy teachers.

On the negative side, the one aspect on which 'Front Page' could be faulted was its limited graphics facility. It has an option for drawing a picture composed of lines, circles and boxes. The children found these drawings most unsatisfactory. They preferred to fill the empty space with their own more sophisticated illustrations. As a further alternative, black and white photographs would look effective. 'Front Page' has been used extensively by both classes and undoubtedly will continue to be included in the teachers' repertoire of resources long after the project is over.

'Writer'

Wordprocessing is a necessary and important skill to be acquired, being one of the most common uses for the computer in many offices. Despite fears that it might discourage conventional forms of writing, it has become a firm favourite in schools as a means to complementing traditional methods of creating and handling text. These two accounts of the use of 'Writer' serve to reinforce this view in that they concentrate on the advantages brought to the writing process of the computer's rapid and efficient editing facilities. Once again ease of use is emphasised by both Pauline and Sue, and although the activities they describe involve children writing in longhand first, they recognise the advantages of composition 'at the keyboard' as a positive future step. For Pauline it was an opportunity to develop work already begun using 'Wordwise', a program not designed specifically for children, and so the introduction of 'Writer' with its large type and easy-to-understand instructions, was very welcome:

In teaching the children how to wordprocess, I had hoped to fulfil a dual purpose. Firstly it would teach the actual keyboard skills that were necessary to write. I feel that this is a very valid task in this day and age when so many people require keyboard experience. Secondly, and even perhaps more importantly to me, was the opportunity for improving written work.

I've always been interested in this aspect of writing, using the draft method. However this can be a very laborious task, and many children, especially the less well motivated, can easily lose interest. It appeared that in 'Writer' there was an ideal solution to the problem. The added bonus of the program was that the young user would be able to self-correct many of the obvious mistakes. All of this would be considerably less tedious than rewriting by hand.

From the outset of the computer project I had been using 'Wordwise' with the children, albeit in a very amateurish way. From a personal point of view this was a slow business as I had neither the expertise nor the necessary keyboard skills myself. Consequently I was not as sure of my ground as I would have liked to have been. However, we had made some headway and had produced work and captions for display. Our main problem was in remembering all the commands of 'Wordwise'. So when Derek produced 'Writer' like a magician out of the proverbial hat, we were very excited at the prospect of using it. There were so many advantages over a conventional wordprocessor that were immediately obvious, one being that all text is displayed as double height. This is a great asset for younger children, and even more so for those with reading problems. Its visual display couldn't be clearer. Another major advantage lies in the ease with which the text can be edited. There are no complicated commands to memorise or use, the software automatically redistributes the text during editing.

We weren't expecting this program when it arrived, but I was immediately able to use it. The class had just completed a piece of writing on owls which used the four letters of the word 'OWLS' as the starting point of the lines of verse. Some of the work was required for display, so after a brief introductory session with a small group of children, we began to type in our text. Primarily I was more concerned with coming to terms with the software than with achieving perfection. However the first results looked very promising.

One of the first guinea pigs with 'Writer' was a boy who has serious learning difficulties. Mark managed to print out a piece of work that he was proud to put on display, his own writing being poorly formed and immature. All this was achieved with the minimum of teacher intervention. When we first began to use this program, I demonstrated it to a few children. Using the results of their efforts, I then involved the whole group. Together we explored some of its possibilities, a task which is easily done with a larger group, since the visual display is double height. Then various members of the group used the program to key in their work on owls. From here we decided that 'Writer' would be an ideal means of printing our Viking Sagas for our class book, since we could use the expanded type. In order to facilitate the typing, the children were paired, with one reading the text aloud. They were also able to aid each other with spelling and editing. This method of pairing worked well in most cases. The children had the work already written and I had already made some corrections, so their initial task was not too onerous. One major problem was with the editing. It takes a considerable time to go through a piece of text, discuss it with the child, and get them to make any necessary alterations, especially when they are still unfamiliar with both the keyboard and the program. Of course, while I was working with this one child, there were still the other twenty-six to monitor. Sometimes we were working with two computers in the area, both using different programs, while the rest of the class were busy with a variety of tasks. At times such as those (so normal in a primary classroom), it was extremely important to have the majority of the group engaged in tasks which didn't require too much of my attention. Of course, I was also fortunate to have Jane's assistance. As I became more familiar with the computer these problems didn't loom so large.

The reaction of the group to the program was very favourable. Almost all of the children gained immense satisfaction from the simple task of keying in their work. At the outset I had mistakenly assumed that they would find this tedious, neither had I anticipated fully their pleasure on seeing their work so neatly and perfectly executed. The fact that this was to be something unusual in that they would key it in to the computer, seemed to stimulate them in their work.

As more children became familiar with the program, I was able to withdraw into the background. Many of them are now able to use it virtually unaided, which is one of my ultimate aims. They still require assistance in saving work on a disc, but then we are still in the early stages. If the child is to become completely familiar with the program, to such an extent that they are able to be almost self-sufficient in its use, they will require considerable hands-on experience. This in itself is difficult to orchestrate, given the number of computers available to us.

Up to now we have used 'Writer' for just over three months, which isn't very long given the other demands on our time. However, I believe that many children have improved their keyboard skills, and to a certain degree, the standard of their writing, though hopefully this would have happened anyway. So, all in all, many of the class are now capable of loading the disc for themselves, and keying in text, having chosen their option from the menu. They now no longer see the computer as the means of playing games. We have probably made more progress than I hoped for in September.

Our use of 'Writer' has produced the desired results, and so by that yardstick has been effective. The initial stages were very easy to assimilate, and it is this ease of use that will make it a part of my future curriculum planning. Eventually I would expect some children to be able to key text directly into the computer, using its editing facilities before printing out. Hopefully this will be in the near future.

Sue notes how teacher-directed the editing sessions were in the early days and her observations of children actually working give some insights into why this was necessary. As the children became more confident and systematic in their use of the program it was possible for the teachers and helpers to withdraw somewhat, leaving the children to solve many of their own problems. Like 'Front Page', integration was well under way by the end of the project. There seems little doubt that 'Writer' will continue to enjoy very wide use throughout the school:

The use of this program was immediately obvious to everyone concerned. Pauline thought it ideal for presenting work for display, especially for the Viking project, whilst Joan thought it lent itself to presenting poetry effectively. Thus 'Writer' suited needs perfectly and had the added bonus of being very simple to use. The program was easy to understand with very few variables to take into consideration before introducing it to the children. The handbook was easy to follow and well presented. I liked the way in which attempts had been made to make the program fool-proof. There were indications of procedure to follow if a fault was encountered. The editing section would give the children the means to produce a good final result, thus encouraging them to correct their mistakes and to re-arrange their text. 'Writer' was in use very quickly by both teachers, especially for the Viking project. Different text variations were used. Pauline experimented with arranging the text into a shape (an owl) to illustrate her poem about owls. One experienced child was used to instruct an inexperienced child by dictating notes and giving instructions. This was very successful with very few children preferring to work alone. Typing sessions varied from ten to thirty minutes, depending on the length of the text and the cooperation of the pairs of children. Initially the editing session was much teacher directed, but eventually took no more time for the teacher than correcting a problem in a workbook. Both teachers could progress with the program as the need arose eg. when demand for the school computer was high. Joan was able to discover how to save work very quickly, everything being logically presented. We did encounter some minor problems eg. Pauline had a difficulty with the 'Save' procedure which proved to be an error in start-up conditions, whilst Joan could not load work previously saved on disc. But these problems did not interfere with the use of the program in the classroom. Together we could locate the root of the problem but needed some technical advice from Derek to resolve it.

Introduction to the children was no problem. The children were surprised at how quickly they could start the program and were impressed with the results. Although instructions were soon understood, care had to be taken during editing so that the text was examined systematically, as some rushed through their work ignoring mistakes. Once this procedure was established, and the children thought about and discussed their mistakes, the editing sessions became less teacher-oriented. It was invaluable for illustrating punctuation and grammatical details. If the children had made only a few mistakes, they did not benefit fully from the editing session. However, when typing in poetry they could experiment with arranging and re-arranging text. This was started but not fully explored because of the need to introduce other programs. 'Writer' fulfilled our expectations by giving an easily understood method of correcting work without distracting from the final result. I think it encouraged the children to learn from the mistakes they had made as they could see how improved their work was when correct; something they could not learn from a teacher's corrections with a red pen! It should be an invaluable aid for teaching grammar and punctuation. I expect that the displaying of poetry will develop by using increasingly complex arrangements of text. Such a simple effective program easily superseded Wordwise.

'AMX Super Art'

As we progressed through the project it seemed reasonable to introduce more complex and, therefore, more versatile computer tools to Pauline and Joan. 'AMX Super Art' promised to be an ideal tool with which children could explore the world of computer graphics and computer-aided design to add to the variety of ways in which they might express their ideas using the computer. Although a very powerful package, 'Super Art' is not blessed with a clear and easy-to-use handbook. Sue made mastery easier by the production of a series of work cards for teachers and children. Pauline describes her feelings of inadequacy when confronted by the complex program, feelings in stark contrast to those she experienced with 'Front Page' and 'Writer'. Subsequently, with Sue's and Jane's help, the children achieved far beyond anyone's expectations. The question arises as to whether this would have been possible without their assistance. At the same time, it points to the value of training parents to take on helper roles. Pauline writes:

When the mouse was first added to the computer in the Summer term of 1987, neither Joan nor I had a great deal of experience of the software. In fact our experience consisted of one afternoon training session at the University. We were both anxious to begin to create graphics, especially as we now had another printer in school. But the problem seemed to be where to begin. Our memories had been dimmed by the intervening weeks and there appeared to be rather a lot to assimilate. This was an important element at the beginning of the project. That is, we felt somewhat inadequate when confronted by these new pieces of equipment and software. However, these initial problems were to resolve themselves as we both became more confident with the computer.

In May 1987 I had hoped to produce graphics linked to the current work on Thorpe Acre. At first I thought that we could perhaps create pictures of the church or one of the thatched cottages in the village. Really, my expectations at this time were not too high as the pictures produced to date were fairly rudimentary. The mouse, however, was attached to our computer; it was another aspect of the computer work and another weapon in our armoury – if we could activate it! The results were potentially exciting, but at this stage the means of producing said results were fairly bewildering.

Initially I had hoped to integrate the program into our topic work. But in order to do this the children had to become conversant with the mouse. So, I began by demonstrating the possibilities of the program to the whole class. This was entirely an experimental session, with no one, including myself, entirely sure of what we were doing. However, at the end of the session we were more aware of the mouse's potential. Following on from this, various children experimented with it and produced some rather basic graphics. However, events overtook us and the end of term was upon us. At the start of the new term in September over half the children in the class had moved on to their secondary school, so the group now consisted of twelve children who were used to frequent computer access and fifteen who mostly had little experience. However, the group was a much more responsive one and I was determined that we get to grips with this piece of equipment.

So once more I demonstrated the mouse to the group to show its possibilities. By now Sue was working with us, so I asked her to monitor pairs of children in producing experimental pictures. Several children drew pictures or patterns using the various modes. This proved to be a minor success and on the days when Sue was not available we continued with our experiments. All the while we were learning from our mistakes, mostly by trial and error. There were moments of intense frustration, when having spent what seemed like hours creating a 'masterpiece' we couldn't obtain a printout, for whatever reason. At this early stage in the term I was fortunate in that a new boy had joined the class. Not only was he an able boy, but he was also familiar with the AMX Mouse. Initially he was a great asset in helping other members of the class to get to grips with the program. At the outset my main problem was the time that it took to create one picture when there were so many others eager to take their turn. Obviously this was inevitable when no one had great expertise, but it appeared imperative to structure the learning process more closely. We now decided that Sue should take groups of four children at a time for instruction sessions. Systematically they worked through all the modes available to them, experimenting with patterns and colours. In itself this was a fairly prolonged session, taking approximately an hour each time. When they came to draw individual graphics, I suggested that they confine themselves to something connected with our current Viking topic. A favourite example was the Viking warrior head of a ship.

From the outset of the term the majority of the class showed great enthusiasm. They were undaunted by their lack of knowledge or experience, and all were eager to have a try. As we introduced the small-group instruction sessions, the quality of the work improved. Many of the children quickly assimilated the necessary information and retained it well. They used the relevant modes to produce the desired shapes, deleting as necessary. They learnt to judge which colours or patterns to use, given that the final print-out would be in black and white only. By now their pictures were often relatively complex and were astonishingly effective.

Once the whole class had printed a Viking-related picture, we thought that the next use of the mouse could be to create our Christmas cards. This time I suggested that each child should plan a design whose size corresponded to that of the drawing window. So they worked out a plan on paper and pre-determined which modes they would use to get the final picture. Many children had the tendency to include too much in their design, the resulting print-out being somewhat indistinct. So I suggested, in a class session with the mouse, that the most effective designs were those which were fairly simple. This proved a success in that the end results were much more polished. An added bonus to pre-planning the design is that the time spent on the computer is less, a great advantage in the busy classroom.

The 'Super Art' package has become an integral part of our work, with every member of the group being familiar with its use. To have immediate success, the user needs to have good hand-eye coordination. Some find it quite difficult to relate the movement of the mouse to the picture on the screen. Equally, those children who are able to plan and to anticipate the finished outcome in black and white have the most success.

Our success with this program has gone far beyond my initial expectations. We have become conversant with the program in a relatively short space of time. I have been very impressed by the speed with which the children assimilate the basic principles. This must have been due to the fact that the children had the benefit of small-group tuition. This could also be achieved with a suitable parent/helper using the workcards produced by Sue.

In conclusion, although at first 'Super Art' seemed rather complicated, we found that this was not the case after frequent use. Once familiar with the various modes and the use of the mouse, it is relatively simple to use. Ultimately I would expect individual children to be able to use the mouse independently as an alternative method of illustrating their work when appropriate.

For Sue, the issues revolve around finding the best way to teach the children how to use the variety of effects offered by the program:

Initially AMX art was introduced experimentally, probably the main aim being to furnish the children with enough information to draw a picture. The program had instant visual appeal which motivated the children to use it. However despite its popularity, the program proved one of the most difficult to absorb into the classroom activities. Different strategies had to be employed to lessen the amount of time spent explaining the program, eg. the use of workcards. But it was well worth persevering with the program's introduction as the children began to explore facets of art and design which they would have found difficult with conventional art materials.

The first hurdle was that of technical problems, with mode selection and printing. After much frustrating discussion and trial and error we concluded that the problem was technical and not due to our lack of knowledge. When the chip had been moved to a different location, the program worked perfectly. An instant technical backup prevented us from becoming discouraged with the program. The next problem was the handbook which was tedious and not self-explanatory. Simplified instructions for complete novices were needed. The class teacher, with all her other commitments, did not have the time to sift through all the information and decide upon a method of introduction. Thus, as parent/helper, I took over this task, keeping the teachers involved at every stage. This did pose the problem of the parent/helper becoming more competent than the teacher, especially as parent/helper involvement in the program was prolonged because of the length of time taken in the introduction to the children. In the introduction, various modes were excluded (zoom, variations of text, scroll etc) and the remainder introduced in a certain order. The Options and Goodies files were excluded as was most of the Edit files.

Because of the initial problems, the introduction to the children was random and done singly. We tried introducing pairs of children to the program and then using one of that pair to instruct another pair of children, but there was a lot of information for the children to assimilate. We found that they could not function without some degree of adult support. Because an initial introduction took about an hour, the class teacher had to rely upon her parent/helper to complete that task. Thus, it was essential to find a method of breaking it down into manageable components for the teacher. After that initial introduction the children worked in pairs to produce a picture. Again they needed varying levels of verbal support, depending on their level of retention and their hand-eye co-ordination. They needed some assistance in translating their ideas into appropriate modes. All this was very time consuming.

Thus, by observing both children's and teachers' reactions I devised a series of workcards. To help with the initial introduction to the program, Discovering Modes 1 and 2 were devised. The modes were introduced in a certain order (pencil, rubber, text – but without variations, spray, line, fill, frame, box, ellipse). The Quick Reference card was for use when drawing a picture, to refresh the children's memories about the effects created with each mode, the positions of the buttons on the mouse and a black and white printout of the pattern box. These cards were drawn up on the 'Super Art' program itself.

Initially, the basic information wordcard for teachers, which was written on 'Writer' was far too wordy and did not flow. I decided to try it on the headteacher who was a complete novice, which helped enormously with effective wording and when to include a diagram. It was re-written on the 'Super Art' program and included helpful hints and tips if problems were encountered, eg. two checking procedures at the request of the teachers. The original wordcard increased to two, concluding with three simple pictures to recreate, to interest those logically but not particularly artistically inclined. This led to the Drawing Session cards, to assist picture construction with the other class. With the previous class, I had found that the children wanted to produce one of four items for their topic folder design which meant much repetition of instructions. I used examples of this work to devise some thought-provoking Drawing Session cards for use with Joan's class as she was involved with the same Viking project. Unfortunately I could not produce the cards as and when the need arose. I started introducing the Discovering Modes cards with Joan's class but really needed the Basic Information cards ready at the same time, for Joan's use. The Quick Reference Card was used by Pauline's class. Pauline had been very keen to try AMX Art and once the initial introduction was completed, used it to produce cover designs for a Viking project and for Christmas cards. I had expected the children to be more creative during the introduction to the modes, but they were eager to produce a picture as soon as possible which were always representational. One child tended to copy another's idea, which was why there were only four types of picture for the Viking project designs. The pattern box fascinated them and was greatly overused. Every available space had to be filled with something. This led Pauline to talk to the class about composition, discussing the use of size and detail, the creation of positive and negative shapes and tonal effects. She had plenty of examples to draw upon and could demonstrate how easily they could experiment on the screen and use the quick reference card to help them. To produce a picture the children had to think sequentially and remember rules. They had to concentrate and exercise a good level of hand–eye co-ordination when using pencil and small spray mode. If they had difficulty with this, the children indicated that a mode to draw curves would have been useful. Through discussions with each other, at the picture stage, they began to problem-solve. The program was particularly useful for demonstrating such concepts as symmetry and perspective, eg Bryan drew a sail blowing in the wind, Sonia a Christmas tree, Scott and Donna a Viking village. In each case it was easy to experiment with line length and angle size on the screen. It would have been difficult and frustrating to produce these effects with conventional materials. As the children became more confident and the workcards were operating, adult help diminished rapidly. I envisage them experimenting with modes more graphically, experimenting with different types of text in a design and with zoom mode to help attend to finer details. The program should continue to be thought-provoking and increase concentration and finer motor co-ordination. The workcards should provide a logical framework for use by the children and by the teachers who are not initially artistically-inclined. Indeed the program could prove an invaluable aid for teachers to create workcards.

'Edfax'

It is with the final program, 'Edfax', that we encounter the strongest differences of opinion as to *who* did and was responsible for *what*. Both writers acknowledge the difficulties of the program. There is no doubt that the fine detail involved is very difficult to assimilate. The experience also gives strength to the view that things only become easier once the teacher has been able to identify her own use for the program. However, Joan's account makes far less acknowledgement of Jane's involvement than would be acceptable to Jane herself. Perhaps Joan did not fully appreciate how much Jane was forced to modify her role in the classroom when working with this program. Certainly Jane felt that this was important to the extent that she suggests that the two teachers had very little real involvement. Let us start with Joan's account:

'Edfax' is a program offering a teletext format, combining both graphics and text. My main objectives in using the program were to introduce the children to computer graphics, showing how pictures are built up by using small blocks in squares, and to provide an insight into how teletext pages are put together.

I envisaged the program providing a lasting record of an event the children had participated in or of particular topic work the children may have done. It would not be destroyed or taken home as easily as books or art work often is and could be put on display in an attractive way for visitors and parents' evenings. This Autumn term's project was focussed on a visit to the Jorvic Centre in York on October 1987. Thus we commenced a course of study on the Vikings in September using books, both fiction and non-fiction, films, a television series of five programmes, posters and models from the museum service. By the time we visited Jorvik, the children had quite a knowledge of Viking life, and the visit enlarged and reinforced their knowledge, as well as giving an insight into searching for archaeological evidence. The work on Viking life has continued for the rest of the term, encompassing art and craft work in many media, and a certain amount of design technology as well as written work, both creative and factual.

I had in mind that 'Edfax' would provide a permanent record of our day in York. I have found in the past that although children often enjoy and learn a great deal from a field trip, their recorded work can be disappointing and not reflect their learning or enjoyment. On this occasion the children wrote good accurate accounts of the Jorvik centre, but there was too much in the day for it all to be recorded. I told the children of this program and how we were going to use it to make a record of our day. The children were to work in twos and each pair was to choose a different aspect of our visit to write a page for 'Edfax'. Some areas of the visit were covered by two pairs, but working independently. Each child wrote their own account and then discussed their work with their partner, after which a joint account was produced.

At this stage I showed the whole class the demonstration disc and gave them a brief idea of some of the possibilities available for the text (colour, double height, background, flashing) by creating a page of my own. We talked about centring the heading and how that could be achieved. The children then had to discuss with their partners what colours and functions they wanted to use and where.

As both teachers and researchers had found it a difficult program to come to terms with during our initial experiences, I anticipated using one of the researchers in the role of parent/helper. When I announced I was ready to use 'Edfax', both researchers were rather taken-aback. I prepared the disc with Derek's help, and organised the index pages. Pauline suggested that we could make a record of much of our term's work about the Vikings, so space was allowed for this. Although I had previously found the program difficult, once I had a purpose to use it I found it much easier to find my way around.

Jane helped the first two or three pairs to put their work on the computer. She began by allowing them to experience and experiment with the various functions, before embarking on the text of the page. As Jane had used the graphics facility she was able to show them how this could be used as a border. Once the first pair had typed in their text they were keen to make a picture of a helmet. We decided to give it a try and it proved very successful. The children seemed to adapt readily to the idea of making a picture from squares and once one pair had made a picture, everyone wanted to try the graphics. We decided to allocate each pair two pages on the disc so that it gave a page for a picture and any extra text that did not fit on the first page. These pages were then made to cycle together.

Soon after we had embarked on using 'Edfax' Jane was absent for a week. I was keen to continue the work so I used two reasonably able children, who had already produced their pages, as tutors. The process worked well. They used graphics for a frame and used the various text functions well. I have been able to continue with this process using Jane, mainly to assist with graphic pictures and with the less able children who require more help with their text.

I have been pleased with how well the children have coped with 'Edfax'. We adults seemed to find it such a difficult program initially that it quite surprised me how readily most of the children grasped the special aspects of the program, the idea of planning, and the hidden commands. Their pictures have been far more ambitious than I had imagined we could achieve. Of course, the super, creative ideas that children are always surprising me with have forced us to be more ambitious with the graphics. Probably the only function Jane did not quite achieve with the program was movement, although we understand the theory.

Of course, Jane's help was invaluable, but I now feel I could use the program by myself or with a real parent/helper in the classroom. It seems a good visual resource for recording children's work or even producing a kind of visual work card to display for children to work from. Certainly, I now feel confident in the program's use, and we have shown that children of this age (9–11 years) can produce good quality work with it, learning computer skills that will stand them in good stead in the adult world.

Now, by way of contrast, here is Jane's account:

Compared to the other programs introduced during the project, 'Edfax' required the longest assimilation period. To the teachers and research assistants, it appeared to be most complex and daunting.

Three months into the project, Derek demonstrated 'Edfax' to us at a practice session at the University where we practised on the computer using the handbook and some simplified notes which Derek provided. At the end of the session we all felt rather confused and not at all confident about using 'Edfax' in the classroom. The teachers said that they couldn't see an immediate use for the program despite attempts to encourage them to think of possible uses, for example:

To compile a collection of reference pages for the children to use in a project.
To present some of the children's work in writing and pictures.
To make a display for parents' evenings etc.

None of these suggestions stimulated the teachers to try the program out. We persisted with the suggestion that reference material be compiled for use in a proposed local studies project in the summer term. In order to prepare for this possibility I continued to practise with 'Edfax' during spare time in the classroom. In spite of having their own computers at home and the opportunity to practise, the teachers still avoided using 'Edfax' during the Summer term. The teachers finally decided to use 'Edfax' six months after they were first introduced to it. After a trip to York they recorded a diary of their visit using the program.

At the beginning of the Autumn term Sue and I practised 'Edfax' together in order to understand it thoroughly. At that point in time, it seemed to us that a new way of thinking was required. We had become used to the rules governing other programs and 'Edfax' seemed entirely different. Just as we were beginning to understand it, Joan announced that she was ready to use the program with her class that very morning!

I decided that the simplest way of introducing it to the children was to get them to look at the 'guide strip' placed above the keyboard. The strip contains most of the information that the children need. The children began by trying out various coloured text. Next they tried double height, background and flash, noting their order of precedence. They progressed to graphics characters in different colours, in double height and flash. Finally they tried the 'Conceal' function, noticing that a space had to be left for this control character and that it was added just before storing the page.

By using the strip as a starting point the children did not need to work their way through the handbook. From time to time, I used the handbook to clarify certain points, for example:- The order of precedence of function keys.

The children worked in twos, taking turns at the keyboard. They used contrasting colours, double height, background and flash to highlight certain words, phrases and the title. Some outlined the page with decorative lines and graphics borders. I returned after a day's absence to find that the children had composed pages of decorated text almost unaided. Joan was delighted. As one might expect, the children find it more difficult to produce a page of graphics without help. They are not yet able to compose a picture without some help.

Because of the more complex nature of 'Edfax', especially the graphics, my role has of necessity changed from that of a parent/helper–observer/recorder to that of teacher/initiator. Whereas the teachers have instructed the children in their use of the other programs, they have not so far become involved in teaching 'Edfax'. This is due to their lack of understanding the program and their consequent lack of confidence. They are happy that I take the initiative and act as teacher. Hopefully, roles will be reversed before the project ends.

It is only fair to say, however, that the preparation of pictures on graph paper noting spaces to be left for control characters, the careful matching of pencilled-in design to the 'Edfax' graphics shapes and the painstaking keyboard operation is quite demanding for nine to ten year olds. The handbook says that the program was designed for students aged nine to sixteen plus. It is therefore hardly surprising that many children in the younger age group find some aspects of the program difficult.

Most of the children who tried 'Edfax' found the text in its various modes easy to understand and operate. Simple graphics borders presented few problems. We discovered one or two peculiarities which needed to be taken into account when planning a design. These were:-

(1) Double height used elsewhere on a line caused gaps to appear in the border.
(2) It was impossible to delete background from line 20, column 40.
(3) We needed to repeat the appropriate command immediately before the right hand as well as the left hand border. If we didn't do this the right hand border was affected by other commands along the line and we had to correct this at the end.

Most of the children understood these minor idiosyncrasies. What they found more difficult was the creation of a graphics picture through its various stages. Each stage presented one or two problems:

(1) During the design on the graphics paper

    (a) Some children found it difficult to accept the discipline of filling in the small squares. e.g. they wanted to draw a round sun or a straight diagonal line unhindered by little steps.
    (b) Because they hadn't had enough experience of using the control characters, they obviously found it difficult to include enough spaces for these in their design plan. This problem should be resolved when they are more familiar with the program.
    (c) It had not registered with some children that black can only be obtained by leaving the background empty.

(2) Matching the drawing design with the appropriate graphics character

    (a) First of all, some of the children found it difficult to identify the groups of six pixels within their own drawings. Some found it easier if they outlined groups of six pixels with biro as they went along.
    (b) Less able children found it extraordinarily difficult to match their group of six pixels with the 'Edfax' plan. The usual matching problems presented themselves. For example, they confused left and right, top and bottom, black against white etc. More able children could usually match up quickly and accurately.

(3) Operating the keyboard

    (a) Most of the children were still not all that familiar with the keyboard. For example, they had to be reminded frequently that when a key shares two symbols the shift key must be used for the upper symbol.
    (b) The main problem in 'keying in' the graphics was 'remembering to do everything', that is, to put in all the control characters again on every line. Also, when using the HOLD GRAPHICS control remembering that the previous graphics character would be repeated in the 'space' occupied by the subsequent control character.

As one would expect, the more able children coped quite well with remembering what they had to do. The less able children found it extremely difficult.

So far I had been on hand to foresee and forestall difficulties. Time has not allowed for the children to play about and experiment with the program. They should have been allowed to go wrong more often and to resolve their mistakes – an extremely important part of the learning process. Because Joan has been anxious to produce an attractive record of text and graphics within a short space of time, I prompted the children more often than would be ideal.

Many of the problems mentioned above will be resolved when the children are allowed time to practise. The brighter children are well on their way to understanding the program. The less able children will need guidance for some considerable time. Will 'Edfax' become a part of the teachers' repertoire of resources? The answer to this question is yes it probably will because the teachers find the end result so attractive and the children are very enthusiastic about it.

The future success of 'Edfax' will depend on the teachers' willingness to take certain action. They have to arrive at a thorough understanding of the program. Based on my own experience, I have been willing to show the teachers how 'Edfax' works, but so far they haven't shown much interest.

It would have been helpful to have a trained parent to take over from the researchers when the project is over but so far the teachers haven't taken up this suggestion.

Again we must arrive at the same obvious conclusion that the success of a particular computer program in the classroom depends on the know-how and enthusiasm of the teacher.

The Headteacher's Reaction to the Project

Finally, who better to provide an overview of the whole enterprise than the headteacher herself. Mrs. Black started out as a complete novice as far as computing is concerned, but nevertheless was willing to accept us into her school on trust. She supported us in meetings with school governors and LEA officials. Towards the end of the project she, too, became drawn by the magic of the computer, participating in a small way with wordprocessing and the testing of Sue's work cards for 'Super Art'. In September 1987 she accompanied us to a European seminar at the University of Liège in Belgium, where she made a most creditable contribution alongside academics and fellow teachers from all twelve member countries of the EEC. Without her cooperation and support none of this would have been possible. Here is what she has to say:

When I was first approached to ask if I would be willing to allow two teachers to take part in the project, my immediate reaction was one of excitement. This seemed a golden opportunity to promote what had been a slow developing, half-hearted addition to the existing curriculum. We had no computer 'buff' in the school. Most attempts at working with the computer suffered from lack of training and time. The education authority's introductory training was woefully inadequate. People struggled in the dark with a handful of very simple programs.

Some time had been spent discussing the introduction to the curriculum of the microcomputer but we had only gone as far as deciding that it was important to spend time getting 'hands-on', and to avoid rushing headlong into something we did not fully understand.

When I approached Pauline and Joan, their reaction was tentative interest coupled with anxiety at the extra work it was going to produce. At this stage they could not be expected to see the advantage of integration. Indeed, with a particularly difficult group of 4th year boys that year, it was not surprising that they probably regarded the project as just 'one more thing to do'. Fortunately the two teachers are willing to 'have a go' at most things, and the project was under way.

Progress seemed slow initially. I felt both teachers were struggling to use the computer – as an afterthought – in their work planning. It was set up from time-to-time in their area – usually on a day when Derek was expected! However, as interest grew it did come out more often. For the first three months it was a burden and both teachers displayed some anxiety and stress. I felt guilty for imposing on them. My own absence from school for five weeks meant I was out of touch and unable to support and encourage.

On my return to school I was forcibly struck with both Joan and Pauline's obvious feelings of being under pressure. So it was with some relief that I listened to Derek's new training package, and the introduction of assistants to cope with the time-consuming task of supervising children using the computer. A residential visit provided the opportunity to collect data and use 'INFORM'. Before long, a very interesting wall display, which caught the eye of the whole school, was created. There were printouts of data collected in Quorn Churchyard, and children's written work describing the computer, the program, the entering of data and the computer questions. Suddenly, it seemed, the computer was beginning to be assimilated as an important aspect of the children's learning. The training package was giving the teachers the time they so desperately needed to 'play about' with the computer and to familiarise themselves with the software. Very quickly, they appeared to reject the less versatile software in favour of content-free programs like the database, wordprocessor and computer art. The walls of their class areas began to blossom with printouts, accounts written using the wordprocessor and computer graphics.

Both teachers became more relaxed as the summer term went on. They were obviously happy and justifiably proud of the work being produced. Interest was generated among the staff and the rest of the children in the school. Parents, who were in the school frequently, were impressed and began asking questions. It was suggested that a parent workshop could both inform them more fully and get them involved. This was planned for the beginning of the Autumn term.

The beginning of the new academic year brought no loss of impetus. The parent workshop was held, and offers to be trained as 'assistants' came from several mothers. These ladies now come into school several times a week to work alongside children. The wordprocessor is used by children of all ages, including infants. Parents have raised funds to purchase another computer. We now have three computers with disc drives and printers. A year ago we had only one of our own, the others were on loan from the University. Our parents' aim, over the next few years, is to provide each class in the school with its own computer so that each teacher can have the computer at the children's disposal at any time of the day.

We are now into the 'aftermath' of the project. The two teachers have a computer each. The children seem reasonably confident to work in pairs or on their own. Problems appear to be ironed out by the teachers fairly quickly, although 'hiccups' do occur occasionally. These always result in almost full-scale discussion and enquiry among the staff. In the event of non-resolution, Derek is always at the end of the telephone line! I cannot emphasise too strongly the importance of such back-up, and hope we can impose upon him for a long time to come.

7
PROFILES OF PROGRESS?

An Experiment in Changing Self-Images

In this chapter the term experiment is used in its conventional rather than its technical sense since neither did we employ random allocation in establishing the target group nor did a control group, as such, receive 'no treatment'. The pupil profiles that we collected during the first week of the study revealed a small number of children in both classrooms whose poor self-images as computer users were at variance with the views they held of themselves as reasonably competent and hardworking members of their respective class groups.

On the basis of their scores on the academic self-image, achievement motivation and computer-use profiles, six children (three boys and three girls) in each class were selected for special attention on the following basis. Each member of the experimental group achieved scores classified as average or above on academic self-image and achievement motivation, but below average on the total score of the image-as-a-computer-user profile. In selecting our target pupils, means and standard deviations were used to determine cut-off points on the frequency distributions in each of the class groups.

The names of the six boys and six girls were made known to their teachers who were then invited to participate in an attempt to change the rather negative images these pupils had of themselves as computer users. Discussion between teachers, observers and researchers resulted in agreement on a strategy for change. Without drawing special attention to target children, teachers would try to ensure that they worked at computer tasks with friends or with companions who were helpful and cooperative or with children who were better at the required tasks yet patient and willing to act as instructors. The teachers themselves were to pay particular attention to the progress of target children, intervening when necessary to help them with difficulties as they arose. Finally, the teachers were to give target children extra turns at the computer or longer periods at the computer as and when opportunities arose.

The exact form, duration and incidence of interventions were left to the discretion of the classteachers so as to ensure that strategies of change occurred as naturally as possible during the hurly-burly of classroom events. We as researchers and observers, however, were to monitor and record the frequency and nature of those interventions.

Quantitative Changes: Group Profiles

There are many problems in measuring change (Plewis, 1985), not least that on a number of the sub-scales of the computer-user profile several children (both target and non-target) awarded themselves 10/10 in their initial ratings, thus allowing for no further improvement. Our treatment of that occurring in the profiles of 48 children over a period of some five months is therefore cautious and qualified. We do no more than record the direction and degree of change found in the sub-scale profiles of target and non-target pupils, eschewing statistical analyses save for the '*t*' tests for correlated data, which examine the significance of change in the summated scores of each of the two groups over the total computer-user profile between the first and second testing sessions (see Table 7.1).

Table 7.1 Degree and direction of change on sub-scales of computer use between first and second tests

Computer user sub-scales	Target pupils $n = 12$	Non-target pupils $n = 36$
Pressing the right keys most of of the time	+11	−11
Doing well at computer games	+10	−19
Knowing all about how to use the computer	+4	+ 11
Understanding what the computer wants you to do	+12	+2
Getting the right answers to the computer's questions	+15	−11
Helping other pupils understand how to use the computer	+13	−22
Wanting to use the computer	+19	−11
Total change on overall computer-use profile	+84	(−61)

$$[t = 2.11 \; df = 11 \; p = 0.05] \qquad [t = 1.20 \; df = 35 \; p = \text{n.s}]$$

Overall, the target-children's ratings of themselves as computer users changed significantly in a positive direction between the January and the May testing sessions. Conversely, there were negative changes (albeit statistically non-significant) in the self-ratings of non-target pupils between the first and the second completions of the profiles. What can we make of these data? Even if the strategies for change had been undertaken under rigorous experimental conditions, threats to internal and external validity (Cohen and Manion, 1989) would prevent us from attributing the gain scores of the target children to the agreed-upon interventions of their teachers. Indeed, as we shall shortly show, qualitative data derived from observers' interviews and pupils' conversations suggest that plausible explanations of some target children's gain scores lie outside the classrooms of Broadwood School.

Quantitative Changes: Individual Profiles

Table 7.2 identifies individual gain or loss scores of target children on each of the seven sub-scales comprising the computer-user profile between the first and second testing sessions. Pupils are listed in descending order of gain. Table 7.2 shows that of the twelve children who were the focus of strategies of change, there were ten whose overall computer-user scores moved in a positive direction and two whose scores regressed ($p = 0.055$ one-tailed binomial test). In the case of one child, Maurice, the size of that negative shift is the object of more detailed discussion on pages 126–7. So, too, pages 124–6 present an extended account of Hannah, whose overall change score revealed the largest gain in the target group.

Table 7.2　Target pupils' changes between first and second tests

Target pupils	Computer-user sub-scales							Total change score
	Pressing right keys most of the time	Doing well at computer games	Knowing all about how to use the computer	Under-standing what the computer wants you to do	Getting right answers to the computer's questions	Helping other pupils to under-stand the computer	Wanting to use the computer	
Hannah	+4	+9	−1	+2	+4	+4	+4	+26
Tilusha	+2	+4	+1	+2	+2	+2	+2	+15
Sonia S.	+6	+1	+2	0	0	+2	+3	+14
Richard	0	+1	+2	+3	+3	+2	0	+11
Sarah P.	+2	+3	0	+4	+2	−1	0	+10
David	0	+1	0	+1	+1	+3	+4	+10
Robert	+1	+1	+1	+2	+2	+2	0	+ 9
Gregory	−2	−1	+1	+4	−3	+2	+5	+ 6
Krishna	+3	−6	0	−1	+7	−1	+2	+ 4
Sarah B.	+3	+2	−1	0	−2	0	+1	+3
Lindsey-Jo	−2	−2	+4	+2	0	−2	−2	−2
Maurice	−6	−3	−5	−7	−1	0	0	−22
Total	[+11]	[+10]	[+4]	[+12]	[+15]	[+13]	[+19]	[+84]

We said earlier that having agreed upon a strategy for changing the negative self-images target pupils had of themselves as computer users, the researchers would then leave the implementation of tactics to the teachers themselves. For our part, we would monitor and record the frequency and nature of the interventions that Pauline and Joan decided to employ.

Logbooks of computer use in both classrooms provided details of pupils' time at the computer and the specific programs on which they were engaged. The total number of minutes spent by each target pupil during the course of the project was counted. (For third-year pupils records cover January to December 1987; for fourth-year pupils records covered the period January to July 1987.) These were then summated to give an overall target-children score from which a mean time-on-computer was calculated.

A sample of 12 pupils, matched by sex and year in school, was randomly drawn from the 36 non-target pupils. Their records of computer use were calculated and compared with those of the target pupils. The results are set out in Table 7.3.

Table 7.3   Time on computer: a comparison of the exposure of (a) target pupils and (b) a matched group of non-target pupils

(a) Target pupils

January–December, 1987	Total time in minutes	January–July, 1987	Total time in minutes
3rd-year boy	812	4th-year boy	60
3rd-year boy	997	4th-year boy	240
3rd-year boy	150	4th-year boy	180
3rd-year girl	344	4th-year girl	240
3rd-year girl	380	4th-year girl	319
3rd-year girl	305	4th-year girl	262
	Σ = 2988		Σ = 1301
	$\bar{x}$ = 509		$\bar{x}$ = 217
	s.d. = 330		s.d. = 87

Total time on computer of all target pupils   = 4289 minutes
Overall mean time on computer of all target pupils = 357 minutes
s.d   = 273

(b) Non-target pupils

January–December, 1987	Total time in minutes	January–July, 1987	Total time in minutes
3rd-year boy	525	4th-year boy	180
3rd-year boy	210	4th-year boy	60
3rd-year boy	585	4th-year boy	175
3rd-year girl	250	4th-year girl	90
3rd-year girl	775	4th-year girl	60
3rd-year girl	887	4th-year girl	248
	Σ = 3232		Σ = 813
	$\bar{x}$ = 539		$\bar{x}$ = 137
	s.d. = 272		s.d. = 77

Total time on computer of all non-target pupils   = 4045 minutes
Overall mean time on computer of all non-target pupils = 337 minutes
s.d   = 284

t test between mean time on computer for *all target pupils* versus all *non-target pupils*: $t = 0.18$, d.f. = 22, p = n.s.

The results of the analysis surprised us. Until we undertook the calculations we had no idea that there was such a wide variation in the amounts of time on the computer allotted by Pauline and Joan to their respective target children. Nor had we realised that there was so little difference over the course of the school year between the average time on computer experienced by the target and non-target pupils.

Our initial reaction to these findings was to question the accuracy of the logbook records. However, we are reasonably certain that the great majority of children did record their periods at the computer faithfully and accurately. We must assume that if Pauline's and Joan's differential allocation of time on computer was based upon their perceptions of the individual needs of the target children (and there are grounds from informal conversation with the teachers' and observers' fieldnotes to support this view), then the variable, *overall time on computer* lacks explanatory power in accounting for the changes in the self-images we uncovered.

Changes in Self-Images as Computer Users Associated with Access to Out-of-School Computer Use

Table 7.4 shows two groups of pupils drawn from Pauline's and Joan's classrooms. They consist of those who had *very little* or *no access* to computers out-of-school (they scored either 0, 1, or 2 on the out-of-school computer-user questionnaire), and those who had *considerable access* to out-of-school computer use (scoring either 6, 7, or 8 on the questionnaire). Table 7.4 sets out the number of pupils in these high and low out-of-school computer user categories, together with the size and the direction of the changes in their summated self-image-as-computer-user scores between the first and the second testing sessions.

Table 7.4   Changing self-image as computer-user scores and access to out-of-school computer use

Access		*n*	Self-image changes	
Low				
Score	0	10	+46	
	1	2	+12	+88
	2	5	+30	
High				
Score	6	3	−7	
	7	5	+8	−35
	8	4	−36	

The data appear to suggest an association between positive changes in self-images as computer users and low access to out-of-school computer use or, conversely, negative changes in self-images and high access. We must treat these data with considerable circumspection. We referred earlier (page 115) to problems arising in connection with change score data not least the phenomenon of regression effect. Regression effect is simply the tendency of people scoring at the extremes to move towards a more moderate position on a second testing. It occurs on attitudinal-type measures such as ours, particularly when tests are low in their reliability. Our data in this respect are somewhat suspect. It is certainly the case that on initial self-image-as-computer-user tests, the high-access group scored significantly higher than their low-access classmates. Initial self-images as computer users were as follows:

High access $x = 60.25$; s.d = 8.30; $n = 12$;
$t = 3.66$; $p < 0.01$
Low access $x = 46.58$; s.d = 11.77; $n = 17$

Conceivably, regression effects could account for the change data reported in Table 7.4. However, two other pieces of information call for comment. First, of the seventeen children in the low-access group, eight are target pupils. (Target pupils' mean score on out-of-school computer access is $\bar{x} = 1.92$, s.d. $= 1.93$, as compared with non-target pupils' mean computer access score of $\bar{x} = 4.11$; s.d. $= 2.61$; $t = 3.10$; $p = <0.01$.)

Second, of the seven sub-scales comprising the self-images-as-a-computer-user questionnaire, it is on *wanting to use the computer* that target pupils register their largest, overall positive gain scores between test sessions 1 and 2. Arguably, it could be the case that those target pupils with very little or no access to out-of-school computers are, at first, understandably apprehensive when they compare their lack of knowledge with the sophistication and familiarity of their fellow classmates. Notwithstanding possible regression effects, could it be that given access to newly arrived school computers and carefully tailored initiations into computer use in companionable groups, target children change their self-images and their desire to work with computers significantly more than non-target pupils as the school year progresses?

In seeking to test this hypothesis we operationalised *companionable groups* in two ways, based upon pupil choice and 'pupil–teacher' membership. First, the sociometric data on children's choice of workmates enabled us to differentiate between computer-user groups recorded in the class logbooks in terms of (1) reciprocated friendship groups, (2) one-way friendship groups and (3) non-friendship groups.

Second, with the help of Pauline and Joan and the corroboration of observers' records, we could identify in the class logbooks those groups which had been constituted with specially selected, able and patient pupils as the 'teachers' of other group members.

Companionable Groups based on Pupil Choice

Because mean time on computer had failed to differentiate between target and non-target pupils groups (see Table 7.3), it was appropriate to adopt the following procedure.

- Three hundred discrete pupil groups were randomly selected from the total recorded in the logbooks of both classes.
- Initially they were classified as those containing a target pupil or pupils and those containing only non-target pupils. These were then broken down by reference to the sociometric data into reciprocated friendship, one-way friendship and non-friendship sub-groups. The data are set out in Table 7.5. (One-way friendship in the target group was defined as the target pupil initiating an unreciprocated choice of work companions.)

Table 7.5   Three hundred computer-user groups classified by target or non-target
status and by sociometric workmate choices

Status	Sociometric workmate choices			
	Reciprocated friendship	One-way friendship	Non-friendship	Totals
Target pupil(s)	26	5	56	87
Non-target pupils	39	31	143	213
Totals	65	36	199	300

$\chi^2 = 7.88$ d.f.2 $p < 0.05$

The analysis seems to suggest that Pauline and Joan may well have used their knowledge of the sociometric data we gave them at the beginning of the project to so constitute computer work groups that target pupils were more likely to work alongside reciprocated friendship choices than was the case for non-target children. At the same time, however, target pupils' unreciprocated choices of work companions seemed less likely to feature in their teachers' construction of companionable working environments.

Companionable Groups based on 'Pupil–Teacher' Membership

An exploration of the association of 'pupil–teachers' with target and non-target computer-user groups was undertaken as follows.

From the 300 computer-user groups used in the last analysis we drew out randomly the first 60 in which a 'pupil–teacher's' name appeared. These 60 groups were then classified according to their target group or non-target group status. The data are set out in Table 7.6. The data in Table 7.6 provide some support for the view that Pauline and Joan probably did have able and patient 'pupil–teachers' in mind when they assembled target pupils and others to work at the computer.

Table 7.6   Sixty computer-user groups classified by 'pupil–teacher' presence and
target or non-target status

Target pupil groups	Non-target pupil groups
22	38

$n = 60$

Taken together, the companionable-group pupil-choice analysis and the companionable-group 'pupil–teacher' analysis offer support for the view that part, at least, of the original strategy for change (see page 114) had been implemented.

Accounting for Change: Children's Explanations

We employed what has been described as 'structured eavesdropping' (Powney, 1988) in encouraging target children to talk about the changes they had noted in themselves as computer users between the first and the second administration of the profiles. Rather than interview them individually, we decided to let pupils talk informally in groups of three. It seemed to us that effective conditions for structured eavesdropping were in hand in so far as:

1. the children had participated in a common experience;
2. that experience was the focus of their conversations;
3. the children's talk involved genuine exchanges of knowledge, opinions and questions;
4. we constituted the conversation groups so that our participants had not worked in such close proximity that they had regularly exchanged information and ideas on the areas under discussion;
5. groups of no more than three permitted each child to contribute easily; and
6. the eavesdropper (one of the classroom observers) took a minimal role, sitting to one side of the conversation groups in order to take notes (Powney, 1988).

Somewhat to our surprise, the strategies for change, which teachers, observers and researchers had agreed upon, received only passing comment in pupils' conversations. Sonia thought she had improved because she got more turns at the computers. In actual fact, Sonia's 380 minutes of computer time was only slightly more than average for the target-pupil group (357) minutes.

> At first when I had a go I played a simple game but my typing wasn't very good. When Mrs. Green said 'Press SPACE BAR' or 'Press RETURN' I didn't know what she meant. I got better mainly because I had more practice. . . you see lots of people in our class have computers and they can help us. Teresa [a 'pupil–teacher'] and Sarah-Jane [a reciprocated friendship choice] used to get together. . .we've all been together on the computer.

Discussing his increased self-confidence, Robert appeared to discount the effects of extra turns at the computer, though the strategy of grouping friends and/or placing a more competent and sympathetic practitioner in the work group featured in his commentary: 'I don't think I had many extra turns in the classroom. I had a few more with the mouse. I get on with Gregory best. We worked on "Edfax" together. Erica told us all about "Edfax". [Erica, a bright, patient child, had acted as "pupil–teacher" in the group]'. Robert actually occupied the computer for 812 minutes, having received more time-on-computer than any other target pupil save for Gregory (997 minutes).

Lindsey-Jo went so far as to deny that she received additional attention. She was correct in her assessment, having been allocated only 150 minutes over the whole of the project, less than half the average time-on-computer enjoyed by the group as a whole: 'I didn't know where the keys were at first. I didn't have extra turns in the classroom. Only the people who were good at it had extra turns.'

An important explanation of increasing confidence in, and liking for, computer work was the access to a computer that several target children enjoyed outside of school – either a personal machine, one within the family or one belonging to a relative or a friend or in a parent's place of work. 'I got more used to the computer because I could practise on my brother's at home. He has a computer stored in his bedroom' (Lindsey-Jo). 'Well you see, part of the reason why is that we have got a computer at home. My uncle went off to Italy and he gave us his computer. I spent a couple of hours a day at home getting used to it' (Robert). Sarah thought that having her own computer accounted for her improvement: 'The boy who lives over the road – he's older than me – comes across and shows me how to use it. . . . I used to spend a lot of time practising on my old computer. I used to type on it.' (She now has one with a joystick.) Sarah liked doing the newspaper report using 'Front Page'.

Sonia found 'The Inhabitant' appealing because 'it was complicated and you had to think'. Lindsey-Jo: 'I liked the mouse ["AMX-Art"] best. I liked when we had to draw a snowman. Krishna helped me.' Krishna commented favourably, too, on the 'AMX-Art' programme: 'I liked the AMX mouse best of all. I liked doing the pictures.' Sonia's explanation was similar to Sarah's: 'Also I can practise at home and that's why I got better at it.' Krishna, too, thought that having access to a computer out-of-school had contributed to her progress: 'Because I practise at Dad's office. When we go shopping he takes me to the office and I practise on the computer.' Gregory's increased profile scores on understanding what the computer wants you to do (+4) and wanting to use the computer (+5) were not corroborated by anything he had to say in his discussions with two other target children:

> I only had one go with the mouse ['AMX-Art' program]. . . . I don't take much interest in computers really. You've probably noticed me sitting staring at the screen while the others get on with it. . . .
>   About a year ago I really wanted one but when Mum found out how much they cost – well, that put her right off!

Gregory was one of five pupils among the target-group children who neither possessed his own computer nor had access to one outside of school. His disappointment and dissatisfaction was plain for all to see.

As unobtrusively as possible, the focus of the children's conversations was directed towards their enjoyment of programs they had encountered during the course of the year.

We had expected to elicit assessments of the six programs used in the study. Once again we were surprised and somewhat chastened by pupils' particular enthusiasm for a program *not* included in our research repertoire! Boys, more than girls, were vociferous in their praise of a program that Mrs. Brown brought in as part of a study of the Viking settlement of Britain. This program was more akin to a computer game: 'You had to plan a raid, plunder villages and get treasure. You had a sheet to record on.' There were, however, some favourable comments about several of the programs in the study.

Accounting for Change: Researchers' Observations

The strategies for change we devised for the target children at Broadwood Primary were totally different from the drill-and-practice regimes initiated by our Belgian colleagues in their French language programs. At Crisnée, designated groups of learners rehearsed specific grammatical skills in regular shifts for fixed amounts of time. By contrast, the approaches at Broadwood Primary could only be described as unsystematic and irregular. An outsider would have been unaware that any strategies for change were being attempted. Small wonder that the target children themselves failed to recognise that they were objects of particular attention. In this respect the naturalness of our research cover was, in the main, successful. Observers' diaries reveal, however, that there was recognition in both Mrs. Brown's and Mrs. Green's classrooms that not all children received the same amount of time at the computer:

(25.5.87) Joanne and Garth who were new arrivals in Mrs. Brown's class complained that since coming to Broadwood School two months ago, neither had had a turn on the computer. When Robert retorted that he had had ten turns Joanne said, 'You've had ten turns because you're bright'. The observers confirmed that in both classrooms, some children associated extra turns at the computer with the better ability of the recipient.

The very different objectives of the Belgain and the British research projects were clearly manifested during exchange visits in March and May 1987. At Crisnée, we watched pairs of pupils who were assigned to one of seven or eight terminals practising a sequence of drills beginning with singular-subject agreements with singular-present indicative verbs and progressing to less familiar plural subjects attached to more complex verbs in even rarer moods. In contrast to such close prescription, readers will recall that our primary concern was with content-free programs. Belgian visitors saw British pupils using open-ended software such as wordprocessors, databases and a computer art program to help them experiment with new ways of expressing their ideas and tackling new problems in their work in environmental studies. These were our broad aims. Our objectives for the target children, however, were more specific. They were concerned with attitude change, in particular with changes in self-attitudes. In brief, how could we help these pupils to see themselves in a more positive light with respect to their skills with a computer?

However circumspectly we treat the evidence of quantitiative changes in the profiles of target pupils between the first and second testing sessions, the gains identified there are paralleled by the accounts of change we assembled from our systematic observations, interviews and conversations with adult and child participants. Our data contain numerous instances when one can almost 'see' changes occurring in the attitudes that both target and non-target children have of themselves as computer users. At times they literally grew in confidence before our eyes. Here are some examples.

1. At first *Gregory* was most concerned whenever he made a mistake on the keyboard. He became more confident when I laughed and said, 'It doesn't matter. Look how easy it is to change your mistakes.' *Gregory* keyed in *bear* instead of *beer* and laughingly recalled that his Mum had given his Dad a shopping list with 4 bears on it and cornflakes spelt with a k.

   Robert and *Gregory* were working at the computer. Erica and Michelle had shown them what to do the previous day. I asked *Robert* and *Gregory* if they had found the program easy and they said they had. The only problem had been when, 'We tried to put coloured writing against the background and the background colour kept changing'. However, they'd solved this themselves. . . . These two boys have gained enormously in self-confidence since the project began.

2. *Jill* kept asking questions about how a computer works. 'What do I do? What do I do?' *Jill* asked repeatedly. One item was inserted. *Jill* became highly excited as information appeared at the top of the screen.

   Jill was hesitant but Fiona gave clear instructions and plenty of time to respond. Fiona has a computer at home; she follows instructions easily and works out how to correct her work when editing. She discussed with *Jill* the most effective layout and they experimented. . . . *Jill* was thrilled with the results.

3. *Sonia's* rapid gains in confidence and skills can be deduced from the C.O.M.I.C.

systematic observation records and verbatim notes of the observers on two occasions separated by some three months. In the first record *Sonia* is paired with Erica, a competent computer operator. They are working on 'The Inhabitant'. During the first minute Erica had to be reminded to let her hesitant companion use the keyboard. *Sonia* starts to key in information from her notebook. She consults Erica at every turn, looking at Erica after every move.

Three months later (after the summer holidays) *Sonia*, now a fourth-year pupil, is paired with Carla, a third-year child who has joined Mrs. Green's class. They are working on 'Writer'. *Sonia* is now totally at ease with the computer. She remembers many details of her previous sessions. Carla is somewhat lethargic when dictating so *Sonia* has also to scan the notes. However, Carla has let quite a few mistakes slip by. No matter, *Sonia* does a thorough job of editing, remembering all the requisite procedures.

4. One of our main achievements was the article (on 'Front Page') produced by a boy of ten with severe learning difficulties. It is difficult to describe the sense of achievement that he obviously felt when, for once, perfectly executed work was put upon the wall display. His smile of pleasure said it all.

Demonstrating attitude change is one thing; accounting for it is quite another. For had we been able to cast our strategies for change within a traditional experimental framework in which the results of target children's exposure to strategic interventions could have been compared with the omission of those tactics in a matched group of pupils of average ability, average perseverance and low self-images as computer users, even then it would not have been possible to attribute demonstrable changes to such tactics of intervention and to those alone. This is not the place to pursue a discussion of threats to external and internal validity in educational research. Interested readers are referred to Chapter 13 in Cohen and Manion (1989). Suffice it to say that one of the most plausible of possible threats to external validity would seem to be the one to which several of the target children referred during the structured eavesdropping sessions recorded by the observers, namely, opportunities to get hands-on experience with a computer out-of-school.

Evidence that the so-called strategies for change agreed upon by teachers, researchers and observers at the beginning of the project had any influence on the target pupils is, to say the least, equivocal.

Target pupils, on average, did *not* experience any more time at the computer than their non-target classmates. Moreover, the wide disparity in time at the computer that was found to exist in the target group was mirrored by a similar wide range of exposure occurring among non-target pupils. At best, this represented a purposeful ploy on the part of the teachers in the light of their knowledge of the particular needs of individual pupils. At worst, it merely demonstrated that an agreed strategy had either been forgotten or neglected. There was, however, some evidence that Pauline and Joan had probably had pupils' preferences for workmates in mind when they constituted target pupils' computer groups and, in addition, that they had consciously tried to give target pupils the benefit of some exposure to patient and able 'pupil–teachers'.

A Profile of Improvement

Between the first and second administration of the computer-user profile, Hannah's score changed from 37 to 63, the largest gain recorded in the group of twelve target children.

When Mrs. Brown was asked in January and again in May to name the five most academically able and the five least academically able pupils in her class, the five most popular and the five least popular, the five hardest workers and the five who tried least hard, the five most capable computer operators and the five least capable, on neither occasion did the name Hannah appear on any of the lists that Mrs. Brown prepared for us. One could be forgiven for thinking that Hannah was probably one of those quiet, diligent girls who get on with their work, give no trouble and are rarely noticed by their teachers. This is not Hannah!

More typically (according to observers' reports) Hannah is better depicted standing arms akimbo, grim-faced, surveying the class group to which she has been assigned or, in the playground, setting herself up for confrontation. Hannah's school record-card describes her as 'getting off to a good start' when she joined Broadwood Primary at 5 years of age. The dominant traits, impulsiveness and verbal aggression that feature in teachers' comments as detrimentally affecting her later progress are already hinted at in the record of her earlier years in school. There are positive comments there too. Hannah is 'a good enthusiastic all-rounder'. She contributes well to class discussions and has a 'lively sense of humour'. In drama work she chooses dominant roles for herself (e.g. the teachers). Her teachers see her as 'uninhibited' and 'gregarious'. But the records of these latter years at Broadwood refer to Hannah's 'lack of progress at times due to impulsiveness'. She is 'in-and-out of friends'. Indeed, during the period of our study, Hannah's only close friend was Jasbir, a girl in Mrs. Green's class, an infrequent attender from a one-parent, ethnic-minority background.

In the January testing session Hannah received only one workmate choice (which she reciprocated). It came from Annette, described by one of the observers as 'the sort of little girl you would like to have in your class'. Hannah's low-choice status, the observers speculated, derived to no small extent from her dominance and verbal aggression. In the second testing in May, she received three choices.

Hannah does not have a computer of her own. Occasionally she gets a turn on one at the home of her close friend, Jasbir. Her initial self-ratings and comments seem to be thoughtful and realistic: 'I'm not very good at it. When I was using the computer with Carol we pressed *we* and pressed RETURN without writing the rest. It would be better if the keys were in alphabetical order.' On the January profile Hannah awarded herself 0 out of 10 on doing well at computer games, an appraisal that turned out to be based on her skills (or lack of them) at Jasbir's house: 'When I was at Jasbir's a gap came up in the floor and you have to jump through. It's easier said than done!' She is keen to have her own computer: 'I would like my own computer. I could write *Hannah was here* and it would come out on the screen. I like doing that in Boots.' Hannah is ingenuously open about helping other pupils understand how to use the computer: 'I can't explain to other people what I don't understand myself.' And she over-rated herself, first time round, she confesses, on knowing all about how to use the computer: 'I didn't know about commas. I got stuck on commas. They came below when you wanted them to go on top.'

By May, however, it is a very different story. Her natural assertiveness and self-confidence, her deliberate placement in computer groups with equitable partners (both boys and girls) and her own work-group choices of girls who can be manipulated, seem to have worked wonders for Hanna's computer-user image. At least, that is what we, as researchers, would like to believe. Our data, alas, allow only speculation. That she enjoys every opportunity to work at the computer is self-evident. She can more than hold her own when placed with two capable boys:

> Hannah had completed a full page of information to feed in. 'They all died together. They're a family. They're all in one place. Oh, that's good isn't it?'
>   All three argue over various points, eg. 'I'm supposed to press that'. Hannah works through fairly quickly. The checkers (both boys) are silent.

Inserting information on the database, 'INFORM', with Jonathan and Cheryl, a capable boy and girl respectively, Hannah insists on working out her own calculation after disagreeing with Jonathan's. It is Hannah's solution, not Jonathan's that is entered.

On another occasion Hannah is working with Cheryl (again) and with Donna, a zero-choice-status girl rated by Mrs. Brown as one of the least academically able and least hardworking in the class. Cheryl and Hannah, the observer records, do not explain fully to Donna. Hannah takes over the process of inserting information for Donna.

A Profile of Deterioration

There was one target child whose score on the second administration of the computer-user profile was found to have regressed by 22 points, the sub-scales, *understanding what the computer wants you to do* and *pressing the right keys most of the time*, accounting for some 13 points in that overall deterioration.

Maurice's declining self-image as a computer user called for further investigation. Taken together, his school record-card, an observer's diary entries of Maurice's activities and behaviour at the computer and her interviews with him about his changing self-image as a computer user, presented us with a picture of a very hesitant and unsure child; one who found the computer a source of growing concern.

Maurice is an angelic-looking boy. Socially gauche, he seems cut off from much of what goes on around him. His reading age has remained persistently below his chronological age throughout his school career. The baby-speech and tearfulness of the early years in school have disappeared; he is still, however, self-conscious and lacking in confidence. He is frequently tongue-tied over certain words and his bottom lip trembles when he is stressed. He is extremely nervous about new concepts; he lacks concentration, indulges in frequent day-dreaming; he is very quietly spoken.

C.O.M.I.C. profiles of Maurice's computer work on 'Front Page' and 'The Inhabitant' were compared with those of Teresa – a capable, confident girl doing identical work to that of Maurice. Teresa completed her 'Front Page' work with great gusto in 18 minutes. Maurice took 41 minutes. The interaction schedule shows Maurice's frequent questioning of the observer and/or the teacher about spellings when working on 'The Inhabitant'. He looks round at the teacher whenever she raises her voice to another child. After 15 minutes on 'The Inhabitant', Maurice suddenly becomes anxious when asked for a list of hobbies. He turns to the observer, 'We've got to list all our hobbies now. It's really boring. Mrs. Brown will kill us.' (He is concerned about the amount of time he has already taken to get to this point.) A few seconds later his anxiety surfaces again. 'Every time the others do maths, we've had to do the computer. I've got a lot of corrections to do.' (Maurice means maths corrections. He sees the computer as an unwanted intrusion upon his normal classwork, which presents him with enough difficulties in keeping abreast of his teacher's demands.)

Later on in the term, to the observer's questions about wanting to use the computer, Maurice replies, 'Not very much. I'd rather play with my mates.' Observation records show that he doesn't actually have any 'mates' in his own class but has found a friend in Ranjit – a social isolate in the other class. Here we are reminded of another study that exposed the limitations of sociometric measures in revealing pupils' true friendship choices (Denscombe *et al.*, 1986).

Maurice has computer games at home, he says, but adds, 'I'm not very good at answering ones with questions'. Asked about his low self-rating on *helping other pupils understand how to use the computer*, Maurice is only too ready to 'put himself down'. 'I don't know why. I just don't think I'd be any good at it.' In point of fact, both observers agree that Maurice is not as limited in his computer skills as he seems to believe. Mrs. Gray's records of Maurice working on the database, 'INFORM', show that having watched Sean, a very able boy and Ann, an equally able girl, keying in their gravestone data, Maurice is subsequently partnered by Ann and, without further ado, sets about his calculations, correctly entering his data within a short time.

Nevertheless, we are forced to conclude that in Maurice's case, the strategies for change were singularly unsuccessful. His records show that he received extra turns at the computer. On two occasions he had been placed with Sean, a capable and patient companion, one of Maurice's unreciprocated choices. On another occasion, Maurice spent time at the computer with Gary, in this case, a reciprocated choice of work fellow. Yet again, Maurice had worked with both Andrew and Anthea, a boy and a girl who were competent and pleasant with slower operators than themselves. Mrs. Brown, Maurice's teacher and both classroom observers had responded positively to his many requests for assistance; his long spells on the computer (in comparison to other users) had passed without adult comment. Despite all of this, Maurice's quantitative and qualitative data pointed unequivically to his increasing disaffection with the classroom computer.

8
MAINTAINING MOMENTUM

Assessing the effectiveness of an enterprise such as ours inevitably prompts the question, 'What methods of introduction and training were most successful?' In this final chapter we discuss those aspects of the research that offer pointers to teachers wishing to make information technology part of their world. In addition we suggest ways in which schools can 'maintain the momentum' once external support is withdrawn. Because the need for primary school teachers to become competent and regular users of information technology is brought into sharp relief by the requirements of the National Curriculum and made legally binding by the dictates of the 1988 Education Reform Act, it is appropriate to focus our discussion on the stipulations of the National Curriculum as detailed in Chapter 4, and to assess the extent to which Pauline and Joan feel the project activities have prepared them to face up to those demands.

The Project and the National Curriculum

Details of the National Curriculum were not published until some time after the fieldwork at Broadwood Primary School had been completed. When the guidelines became available we were not surprised to find several differences of emphasis between the proposals contained in the government documents and the specific objectives we had set for ourselves in designing the research project. Indeed, we were somewhat flattered to see the degree of common ground that existed between the National Curriculum requirements and our own intentions, especially with respect to the emphasis on the use of content-free programs and tools such as wordprocessors, databases and computer art and design packages.

Comparing official prescriptions with our own set of priorities, we were confident that the project had gone some way to prepare Pauline and Joan and provide them with sufficient confidence and general computer skills to enable them to tackle other kinds of computer-based activities as future needs might dictate.

A Checklist of Essential Skills

Close perusal of the National Curriculum requirements in Chapter 4 suggests minimum levels of knowledge, experience and skills that primary teachers must acquire in order to offer all the information-technology requirements of the curriculum to children up to the age of 11. After drawing up an initial list, we sought the opinions of colleagues involved in the training of primary PGCE students, other information-technology specialists, and Jane, one of our two part-time research assistants who had worked and trained alongside Pauline and Joan. The final result was the following checklist:

BASIC KNOWLEDGE AND SKILLS

1. Be able to set up, connect monitor, disc drive and printer to the computer.
2. Be able to switch on, insert a disc and run a program.
3. Understand how to handle discs safely and to avoid damage.
4. Be able to:

   format a disc, access a directory, copy a program, make a backup disc and write-protect a disc or individual program.

5. Know what to do when a program crashes.
6. Be familiar with the MOUSE or TRACKER BALL devices.
7. Be able to set up and use a CONCEPT KEYBOARD.
8. Use a computer for drill and practice and simulation activities.

USING LOGO

1. Understand the nature and purpose of LOGO.
2. Connect a BUGGY or TURTLE to the computer via the appropriate socket.
3. Understand how to give instructions to the turtle: in the immediate mode and by using simple procedures.
4. Understand LOGO primitives and the structure of the LOGO language.
5. Be able to WRITE, LIST, EDIT and RUN a procedure.
6. Be able to call a procedure within another procedure.
7. Understand and use RECURSION.
8. Be able to use SCREEN TURTLE to replicate all moves previously performed using the buggy or floor turtle.
9. Understand and use the MOVE primitive.
10. Understand what happens to the Turtle when it disappears from the visible area of the screen.

USING NON-COMPUTER BASED DEVICES

1. Set up and operate a cassette recorder, video recorder and a video camera.

USING COMPUTER-ART AND TELETEXT SOFTWARE

1. Understand the use PAINTBOX or COMPUTER-ART software to:

   create, store, edit and print pictures.

2. Understand and use TELETEXT Emulation software (e.g. 'Edfax') to create, store, access and edit pages of text and graphics.

USING DATABASES

1. Understand how a DATABASE works including the function of RECORDS and FIELDS.
2. Understand and formulate queries involving one field.
3. Be able to formulate queries involving multiple fields.

4. Be able to create a new datafile from scratch having defined fields and the kinds of questions to be asked.
5. Understand the need to consider the nature of the information to be collected, the limitations of the methods of collection and measurement, and the importance of accuracy.
6. Utilise information selectively retrieved from a database to make a graphical representation.
7. Use a database plot or graph utility to present data.
8. Understand how information is transmitted between computers by telephone.
9. Be able to use a MODEM to access and interrogate an external database, send and receive ELECTRONIC MAIL.
10. Be able to set up and access information from an interactive video system such as DOMESDAY.
11. Be able to access and use information retrieved from commercial Teletext systems such as PRESTEL, CEEFAX or ORACLE.

USING EXTERNAL SENSING DEVICES

1. Operate a simple input device attached to a computer to measure light, sound or temperature.
2. Be able to print out scientific data/results in tabular and/or graphical form.

USING A WORDPROCESSOR AND DESKTOP PUBLISHER

1. Operate a simple WORDPROCESSOR (e.g. Wordwise, View, Writer etc.) to create, format, delete and insert text, mark, copy, move and delete blocks of text, search and replace text, print out text. Load and save text files to and from disc.
2. In conjunction with a wordprocessor, use a SPELLING CHECKER, STYLE CHECKER, MAIL-MERGE, and THESAURUS program.
3. Operate a DESKTOP PUBLISHER to:

     a) create a variety of page layouts,
     b) enter text directly from the keyboard,
     c) import text files from a wordprocessor,
     d) import pictures and diagrams from a computer-art program,
     e) create and use a variety of text, paragraph and heading styles,
     f) print out the result.

It would be presumptuous and not a little naive to suppose that what Pauline and Joan now know about computers is solely attributable to their protracted involvement in the research project. None the less, it seems reasonable to expect that they might well display high levels of confidence in the specific areas of the checklist which describe activities in which they were frequently engaged during the eleven months we spent with them at Broadwood Primary School. For example, the programme of initial skills training designed by Derek Blease covered all of the basic knowledge and skills, 'Computer-Art' and teletext, some aspects of using databases, using a wordprocessor, and an elementary introduction to desktop publishing through the use of 'Front Page'. On the other hand, LOGO was not covered at all, nor were the use of a modem for communications, interactive video or external sensing devices for scientific experiments.

We asked Pauline and Joan to look at our checklist, indicating their level of confidence in doing each of the things contained there. Their responses more or less confirmed our expectations, sharply highlighting those areas where additional in-service training would be necessary. The results of our inquiry are set out in Tables

8.1–8.7. As expected, the basic skills and knowledge enumerated in the National Curriculum outline were fairly well covered. Both teachers were confident that they could handle all of the requirements without seeking help, though they might have cause to consult the manual from time to time.

Table 8.1 Basic knowledge and skills

Level of confidence expressed	Very high	High	Moderate	Low	Very low
Set up, connect monitor, disc drive and printer to computer	PJ				
Switch on, insert disc and run a program	PJ				
Understand how to handle discs safely to avoid damage	PJ				
Format a disc	P	J			
Access a directory		PJ			
Copy a program	P	J			
Make a backup disc	P	J			
Write–protect a disc or program		PJ			
Know what to do when a program crashes	J	P			
Use a mouse or tracker ball	PJ				
Set up and use a concept keyboard		PJ			
Use a computer for drill-and-practice exercises	PJ				

Table 8.2 Using LOGO

Level of confidence expressed	Very high	High	Moderate	Low	Very low
Understand the nature and purpose of LOGO		PJ			
Connect a buggy or turtle to the computer		PJ			
Give instructions in the immediate mode,				P	J
by using simple procedures				P	J
Understand LOGO primitives and the structure of the language				P	J
Call a procedure within a procedure				P	J
Understand and use recursion				P	J
Use screen turtle to replicate moves performed by the buggy or floor turtle				P	J
Understand the use of the move primitive				P	J
Understand what happens to the turtle when it disappears from the visible area of the screen		J		P	

LOGO had not been used in the project at all. Both Pauline and Joan, however, felt that they understood something of its purpose, needing to refer to the manual for further guidance. As was to be expected, Pauline felt the need for a lot of help with the rest; Joan was of the opinion that she would be unable to do it at all. Pauline's slightly higher overall confidence with LOGO may well have resulted from having a computer at home for her family to use.

Non-computer-based devices such as audio and video equipment were not covered by the project; but these resources are so much a part of school life anyway that they presented no problems. Both Pauline and Joan are fairly confident in using these programs, although Pauline still seems dependent on the sort of support we were able to provide with one of our researchers acting as a parent/helper in the classroom. The greater overall confidence in 'Computer-Art' is not surprising; both teachers spent much more time using it than they did with 'Edfax', which was introduced towards the end of the project.

Table 8.3   Using 'Computer-Art' and teletext software

Level of confidence expressed	Very high	High	Moderate	Low	Very low
Use 'Paintbox' or 'Computer-Art' to					
Create pictures	J	P			
Store pictures	J	P			
Edit pictures	J	P			
Print pictures	J	P			
Use a teletext emulation to					
Create pages		J	P		
Store pages		J	P		
Access pages		J	P		
Edit pages		J	P		

As one might expect following our extensive graveyard project using 'INFORM', Pauline and Joan demonstrate confidence in using a database in the classroom. Pauline's greater confidence with the modem and electronic mail was somewhat surprising since the school could not afford to buy a modem let alone pay for the use of a system such as TTNS. Joan felt that she would be unable to use these things at all. Commercial Teletext is, of course, available in many homes although neither teacher has the facility to use 'Prestel'.

It's interesting to note at this point a parallel between the behaviour of children and teachers in the class. We have already referred to the advantages of having a computer at home, especially when computer work in school begins. Those who have computers at home start off at an advantage and seem to progress well. Overall, however, it is the children who do not have computers at home who make the most rapid advances since they start from a much lower base. Pauline was in a similar position since by this time she seemed to be exhibiting greater confidence, possibly because the family has a computer at home and so her experience extended further than that of Joan. One result of this may well have been that she felt more willing to have a go at new things, expecting only to have to seek help from someone who knew what to do. This is evident in her responses to the use of external sensing devices, none of which are used in the school at all.

Table 8.4   Using databases

Level of confidence expressed	Very high	High	Moderate	Low	Very low
Understand how a database works including the function of records and fields	P	J			
Understand and formulate queries involving one field		PJ			
Formulate queries involving multiple fields	P	J			
Create a new datafile from scratch		P	J		
Understand the need to consider the nature of the information to be collected, the limitations of the methods of collection and measurement, and the importance of accuracy		P	J		
Utilise information selectively retrieved from a database to make a graphical representation		P		J	
Use a database plot or graph utility to present data	P			J	
Understand how information is transmitted between computers by telephone			P		J
Use a modem to access and interrogate an external database, send and receive electronic mail				P	J
Set up and access information from an interactive video system such as Domesday		P			J
Access and use information from Ceefax, Prestel or Oracle	PJ				

Pauline's greater confidence continues to be displayed in her response in using the wordprocessor. Both teachers had used it extensively with the children and for some of their own work. Pauline had used her home computer to write her accounts of computer use for us whereas Joan had stuck with writing out her accounts in longhand. Pauline's greater confidence still shows here, especially with regard to the spelling and style checkers, the mail-merge and thesaurus.

Table 8.5   Using external sensing devices

Level of confidence expressed	Very high	High	Moderate	Low	Very low
Operate a simple input device attached to a computer to measure light, sound or temperature			P		J
Be able to print out scientific data/results in tabular and/or graphical form			P		J

Table 8.6   Wordprocessor

Level of confidence expressed	Very high	High	Moderate	Low	Very low
Operate a simple wordprocessor to					
Create text	PJ				
Format text	PJ				
Delete and insert text	PJ				
Mark, copy, move and delete blocks of text	P	J			
Search and replace text	P	J			
Print out text	PJ				
Load and save text files to and from disc	PJ				
Use a spelling checker			P		J
Use a style checker			P		J
Use a mail-merge			P		J
Use a thesaurus program			P		J

Table 8.7   Desktop publisher

Level of confidence expressed	Very high	High	Moderate	Low	Very low
Operate a desktop publisher to					
Create a variety of page layouts		P			J
Enter text directly from the keyboard		P			J
Import text files from a wordprocessor		P			J
Import pictures and diagrams from a 'Computer-Art' program		P			J
Create and use a variety of text, paragraph and heading styles		P			J

When it came to the desktop publisher, Pauline seemed quite keen to give it a try; Joan, on the other hand, felt that she would be unable to do it at all.

Although we appear to have been reasonably successful in the introduction of our chosen programs with Pauline and Joan, it's important to avoid the suggestion that they might be typical of primary school teachers in general. Only Pauline and Joan participated in our training. Many other teachers have been trained in colleges, teachers' centres or in their own classrooms using similar programs to ours, but often doing very different things with their computers. It is self-evident that there is a wide range of expertise and competence within the teaching profession. What conclusions we reach about our own experience therefore can only serve as pointers for other in-service trainers in a very general way. It is our opinion, and it is only an opinion, that of the areas in which Pauline and Joan expressed the least confidence – communications, interactive video, external sensing devices and desktop publishing – would be the ones about which the majority of primary teachers would also express anxiety. The reason for this opinion is quite simple. These applications require resources that have so far been too costly for the average primary school to justify.

This is an issue which will not be resolved simply by including them in the National Curriculum. Nor are they the only things needing substantial additional resourcing before the statutory requirements of the 1988 Education Reform Act can be met. Making schools responsible for their own financial management may offer greater flexibility in the distribution of limited funds but, no doubt, individual headteachers and governing bodies will be reluctant to cut back on salaries, maintenance and basic resources in order to make way for the new technology unless they are convinced of its effectiveness and educational value.

What Did We Learn about Training?

Don't Try to Rush People into New Things

Probably the most important lesson to be learned about training that arises from our work at Broadwood School is that you cannot afford to rush people into things. This is particularly true when you are trying to introduce something totally new, something which is, for the most part, outside the normal experience of the learner. It's vitally important to provide breathing space, time to reflect on experience and time to identify one's own uses for the new technology.

Allow People to Pool their Experience

The most effective learning strategy proved to be common to both teachers and children. It involved a minimum of formal teaching or instruction and was based primarily on shared experience in small groups. The children responded well to small-group work at the computer with a distinct rotating division of labour. It consisted of more experienced children helping and teaching the less experienced, who in turn were able to pass on what they had learned to other less experienced children. The teachers responded best to a similar strategy. A new application or activity would be introduced; they would then be left with a problem to solve or an activity to perform for themselves. When difficulties arose, teachers and research assistants pooled their experience, different members of the group remembering different things. This strategy spilled over into the classrooms; if one teacher had a problem with the computer in her class area, she would call out to others nearby and they would all make suggestions as to how the problem might be avoided or solved.

Make the Activities as Visible as Possible

Helping one another had several advantages: the immediate problem was solved; it enabled others to share in the solution thus developing their own computer competence; and it provided an incentive to other teachers within earshot who were not yet involved with the computer in leading them to think that perhaps in such a non-threatening and friendly environment they too could become involved. This was an important factor in arousing interest around the school. As teachers saw Pauline and Joan learning alongside our two research assistants, Jane and Sue, and witnessed the enhancement of children's work through Joan's assembly and the various strategically place wall displays, demands for computer time increased dramatically.

Providing Adequate Support

What role did we play as computer competence progressed in the classrooms? In the early days it was necessary for us to be very accessible indeed. In fact it was important for someone to be on hand in the school or to be easily reached by telephone at any time. In order to make the most of the teachers' enthusiasm it was vital to drop everything when a problem arose and to deal with it as a matter of first priority. If the teachers had had to wait for any length of time for help, we suspect that they would soon have put the computer to one side as being more trouble than it was worth.

To start with at least, it required Derek Blease to spend a lot of time in the school until such time that the two research assistants could help sort out all but the most complicated of problems. As time went by the teachers' confidence increased; instead of their problems diminishing, however, they simply became different ones as teachers' expectations of what ought to be possible changed and were augmented by experience. Having said that, as the two teachers became more confident and competent they were able to help and train other interested colleagues in the school, including the headteacher.

Early on in the course of the project the question arose as to what could be done to ensure that the teachers maintained momentum after we had gone. Clearly, some support might be anticipated from the LEA advisory service. But like many other authorities there are relatively few advisers, and their time must be spread thinly over a large number of schools in the county. Although advisers' help and support is very welcome they would be the first to admit that they could not provide the intensity of support to which the school had become accustomed. As time went by we became increasingly aware of the need for extra provision from central government. Ultimately central government did pledge an 'Education Support Grant' of some £10.5 million for the period 1988/9 for the employment of advisory teachers who, through their LEAs and in collaboration with MESU, were to implement government strategy towards full integration of information technology at all levels in education. Noel Thompson, subsequently head of NCET, set the blueprint for such government strategy in a letter to all chief education officers in July 1987 (Thompson, 1987), outlining the provision needed in order to carry the strategy forward in the coming years. What he proposed went some way towards meeting what we felt was needed to help maintain the momentum at Broadwood.

To carry the strategy forward, provision is needed over the coming years under the following headings in particular:

i.   high quality curriculum materials and supporting software, which take full advantage of the new, more powerful machines now becoming available;
ii. in-service teacher training –

a.   to give all teachers at least a basic familiarity with the potential uses of IT in their specialism, **and**

b.   to ensure that, on the basis of roughly one teacher per average sized primary school and one per major department in each secondary school, there is a corps of key teachers who have more substantial, up-to-date training in the potential uses of IT in their specialism;

iii. advisory teachers with specialisms spanning the curriculum who can co-ordinate and lead throughout their LEA's the promotion of IT in application to their own and related specialisms;
iv. information and advice, both between central and local government and among LEAs about developments in hardware, in software, and in curriculum applications;
v.   technicians to ensure the maintenance of hardware, to set it up in classes and carry out general technical functions relating to both hardware and software, in order to free teachers from technical tasks for which few will be well-equipped, and to allow them to concentrate on developing the pedagogical applications of the technology.
iv. and – crucially – hardware – sufficient to make ready and frequent access a reality for all pupils.

(Thompson, 1987)

How Did the Teachers Cope with a Limited Number of Computers?

Our work at Broadwood was one part of a larger European study. It was useful, from time to time, to draw upon the experiences of our colleagues working independently in Paris and Liège. In fact, one of the most striking aspects of teacher behaviour observed during the project was the way in which French, Belgian and British teachers, within individual schools, independently devised their own strategies for managing the computer in the classroom. As novices to the new technology, they had to find ways in which to integrate a single computer, or at most a small number of computers, into their normal working procedures such that they could effectively manage the learning process. In the course of three school terms of classroom observation, five strategies emerged, several of which were common to all five teachers even though there was no formal communication or collaboration between individual schools.

Managing the Resource Single Handed

The Computer as one of Many Activities

In order to manage the computer single handed it was important for the teachers to come to see it as yet another classroom resource, or the centre of a particular and well-defined activity. The single computer does not easily lend itself to whole-class teaching. From the outset it was often seen as just one activity among many others. Although situations differed between the three schools, this strategy was observed in all three countries. The open-plan organisation of Broadwood School probably lent itself to this form of computer use most readily since group work, in which various activities are going on at one time in a class area, was already a common way of working. One group might be working on a mathematics exercise, another might be reading or writing, and another would possibly be involved in model-making or artwork. It was not difficult therefore for teachers to add yet another group activity involving the computer. In the Belgian school, small-group work was not uncommon, but children worked in a more conventional classroom setting, often with a small number of computers in a separate room. This arrangement created additional difficulties for the Belgian teachers who had to divide their time between two locations. In consequence they devised computer-based activities which were relatively self-contained. In the French school there was only one computer, housed in a separate classroom. To use it, the teacher had to take her whole class to that room and organise her group to work there. Since there was demand for the use of that room by other teachers, she found it difficult to rotate groups so that every child got computer experience within a short space of time.

Teacher Demonstrations and Discussions Using a Large Screen

On those occasions when a whole-class activity was considered appropriate, teachers chose to adopt the large screen TV in place of the conventional monitor. In general the picture quality was less satisfactory but this was offset by the greater visibility of the screen to the larger group. Joan introduced her class to the interrogation of a database, creation of a newspaper and the use of Teletext in this way. The major activities which followed these introductions, however, were always conducted in small groups of three or four children. In Belgium the use of one computer for a whole-class activity involved competing teams using the same program, and so visibility for the whole class was less important. In France, many lessons using LOGO started with the whole class. Some activities even started with work on the blackboard from which children copied into their books before taking it in turns to try out their solutions on the computer in front of the rest of the class. If other children disagreed with the solution they were encouraged to discuss and criticise it before the final version was put to the test.

Use of Short and Easy Exercises to Enable a Quick Rotation of Pupils when First Introduced to the Computer

When the computer was first introduced to the children, all the teachers felt it necessary to encourage excitement and motivation by making sure that early on everyone got the chance to try a short activity. The best example of this was in Belgium where one of the teachers commented:

> In view of the limited number of machines and the motivation of the children who were tackling them for the first time, it seemed a good idea to choose a short, easy exercise which allowed each pupil to get to a keyboard quickly. We organised a small competition between two groups of pupils, the objective being to develop a strategy whereby a higher score was achieved after each new exercise.

Eliciting the Help of Others

Children Teaching Children

One of the most effective teaching strategies adopted in English and Belgian classrooms was for more experienced children to act as tutors to others. This invariably took place in small group settings where composition of groups could rotate, a novice child being introduced every time a more experienced child left a group. The best example of this occurred at Broadwood School when the teachers introduced the database. Having collected data from gravestones in a local churchyard, the objective was to create a datafile which could be interrogated to find out as much about the inhabitants of the village in years gone by. Once a small number of children had been shown how to enter individual records, groups of three were arranged with a definite division of labour. One child operated the keyboard, one child read out the information to be entered whilst the third checked that screen entries were correct and performed calculations of ages and dates as required. As each child completed the entry of his/her own data he/she was replaced by a new child who was then taught what to do by the other two. This process continued until all data were entered and each child had performed each of the three tasks. In Belgium a similar method was used when using a wordprocessor. Moreover during the use of 'drill-and-practice' programs, the Belgian teachers found that this strategy helped solve the problem of having children working in two classrooms at the same time. A more experienced child was always paired with a less experienced one so that fewer demands were made on the teacher to solve minor difficulties.

Parents Used as Helpers in the Classroom

It's common practice for parents to help at Broadwood School. Traditionally they have listened to children read, worked alongside children when doing art and craft work or assisted with such things as cookery or swimming, all under the direct supervision of a teacher. Following a parents' evening to demonstrate what the children had been doing with computers, a small number of parents became involved with computer work with younger children in the school. This assistance continues to the present day.

Preparing Additional Resources to Save Teacher Time

Preparation of Simple Instruction Cards to Free the Teacher to Work with Other Groups

The introduction of 'AMX Super-Art' at Broadwood created organisational problems, not the least of which was that the instructions provided in the manual were difficult to follow. Although Pauline and Joan were quick to see its educational potential, they found the time required to become sufficiently familiar with all aspects of 'AMX Super-Art' usage burdensome such that even the simplest problems encountered by the children could not be dealt with expeditiously. This meant that the program was potentially a serious disruption in their classrooms. The problem was finally overcome when Sue, our second research assistant, created her own set of simple instruction cards which presented examples of the various modes of operation of the program accompanied by easy-to-follow instructions of how to achieve various effects. These cards were simple enough for the children to use and provided a means whereby parent/helpers could quickly become involved in the supervision of the work.

In France, additional resource acquisition took a rather different form in that the teacher prepared a series of twenty worksheets containing various exercises for her children to try out on the computer.

Facilitating the Planning of Work away from the Computer

Plan Screen Layouts on Paper First ('Computer-Art' and Teletext)

Much work involving graphics can benefit from layouts planned on paper before being tried on the computer screen. This was the way in which Pauline and Joan coped with demand for computer time when using 'Super-Art' and 'Edfax'. Designs were worked out on squared paper; in the case of 'Edfax', group decisions were made about how colours and other graphic effects were to be achieved. These were then plotted on to a specially prepared grid sheet.

Although wordprocessors are designed so that a writer can compose text at the keyboard, this is often not practical when only one computer is available in a classroom. Both British and Belgian children were encouraged to produce group compositions on paper, an activity which promoted cooperation, discussion and argument before final drafts were produced. Only then were texts typed, with special attention being given to layout and presentation.

Write it up First (e.g. LOGO) and Go to the Computer to See if it Works

In France, children were in constant competition for the computer to test out their LOGO procedures. To overcome this problem the teacher created a series of group activities which required verification at the computer at different times, thus staggering demand.

Using the Computer to Direct Children to other Activities

Much Work Done away from the Computer

Common to all five classrooms was the amount of work done away from the computer. Having a limited number of computers available made this inevitable, but lack of computers seemed to encourage good computer habits! In other words, other more appropriate resources were not neglected. Pupils were encouraged to research, plan, discuss, revise and edit; LOGO procedures were planned on paper first and then tried. In Belgium, a database activity involved five different 'off-computer' activities, oral expression, vocabulary and spelling, grammatical spelling, written composition and preparing a table, and only two 'on-computer' activities, namely, entering data and interrogation of files.

Move from Computer-Based Activity to other Methods and Media

It was often the case that computer programs themselves demanded that children look things up in books or tried an experiment. Much of the time spent away from the computer actually served to consolidate children's understanding of the strengths and weaknesses of the new technology. Experimenting with 'Super-Art' led one British pupil to discover how to achieve more dramatic effects when working with conventional paper and paint.

The Computer as Setter of Problems and Checker of Results

In the Belgian school they used a program designed to develop problem-solving skills. Children were divided into groups, each group being given a set of tourist pamphlets and travel books. The computer would set each team a problem such as finding the location of a particular town or city which they could only do by deduction and teamwork using the resources provided. The role played by the computer was simply to set the problems and check the responses. Another program actually set periodic tests to indicate pupils' progress in drill-and-practice language exercises.

Children Writing about Using the Computer to Consolidate their Understanding

Database activity at Broadwood led to a remarkable wall display of children's work, little of which was direct computer output. Pupils wrote about defining fields and collecting data. They described the process of entering records, formulating questions and interpreting results. The quality of the writing surprised us all. It's important to remember that such a high standard of work was possible because the teacher encouraged the children to think about what they had been doing and why, rather than simply managing the technical aspects of computing.

How will they Maintain the Momentum?

We are no longer working alongside Pauline and Joan and their pupils at Broadwood School. The question therefore arises, 'How will they manage to keep things going?' In some respects, the strategies which they devised for themselves during the course of the project will help. Children can, and still do, teach and supervise fellow classmates; indeed there are other educational advantages to this strategy as we have already suggested. We have shown, too, how with a little help and training, parents can act in support roles in classrooms, assisting both teachers and children with routine computer activities. Maintaining momentum, however, depends upon more than simply enthusiasm and skills on the part of individual teachers. Support and encouragement must be forthcoming from headteachers, parents and governors. At Broadwood there is no question that such support exists in abundance. But there is a limit to what can be achieved with limited resources. It is self-evident that the requirements of the National Curriculum for the application of information technology in primary schools cannot be met by goodwill alone. Holding jumble sales to raise funds for the purchase of computers and software may provide parents with opportunities to put something into the system, to create a feeling of all pulling together towards a common goal, but ultimately success will depend upon the level of resourcing provided by central government, either through MESU and the local education authorities, or directly to the schools themselves.

APPENDIX I

Categories for Observing Microcomputer use in Classrooms (C.O.M.I.C.) is an observation instrument specifically designed to describe children's behaviour when working at the computer. It was used to obtain a sytematic record of the actions of the keyboard operator both in an individual, one-to-one situation and when groups of children were working together.

The instrument can be used in either one of two ways, depending on the kind of information required:

1. To record the activities of a particular child on a number of different occasions when using the same computer, either with the same program or with a series of different programs, the objective being to see whether individual children develop their own styles of computer behaviour.
2. To record different styles of activity displayed by individuals or groups of children elicited by the demands of different kinds of programs.

In the event, given the time available and the relatively few occasions spent at the keyboard by individual children, it was impracticable to collect sufficient data on any one child to reach any conclusions about individual styles of use. It was possible, however, to obtain valuable information about styles of use elicited by the demands of different programs when used by many children. That notwithstanding, the quantity and type of information was still somewhat limited. We decided, therefore, to present our findings in this appendix as an example of how the instrument might be used in subsequent work. Where C.O.M.I.C. differs from other systematic observation instruments is in its provision for observers to note down details of context and actual interaction in between the regular recording of category numbers. Much of this sort of qualitative information has been incorporated into observers' accounts in previous chapters.

The Structure of C.O.M.I.C.

There are twelve categories of behaviour in all. These are further differentiated depending upon whether they relate to on- or off-task activities, system management, using software, performing computer-related tasks, interaction with others and performing non computer-related tasks.

The Twelve Behaviour Categories

Activities On-Task

A. *System Management*
1. Operating disc drive, monitor etc.

B. *Using software*
2. Using the keyboard.
3. Reading the screen.

C. *Performing computer-related tasks*
4. Writing or drawing.
5. Consulting a book or diagram.
6. Thinking.
7. Watching another person operate the computer.

D. *Interactions with others*
8. In conversation with the teacher (on-task).
9. In conversation with another child (on-task).

Activities Off-Task

E. *Interactions with others*
10. In conversation with the teacher (off-task).
11. In conversation with another child (off-task).

F. *Performing non computer-related tasks*
12. Doing something else.

On each occasion the observer sits where the children clearly can be seen and heard, the target child always being the one operating the keyboard. At the top of the tally sheet the observer records the name and type of program being used as well as the names of the children in the group. The number of the behaviour category best describing the behaviour of the target child is recorded on the sheet every ten seconds. An interval of ten seconds is chosen to provide sufficient time for the observer to record supplementary information about a group's activities concerning the context of their actions together with any comments made. This enables a fuller description of the interaction of the group members than would otherwise be possible. Clearly, the length of each session of systematic observation is dictated by the way in which the computer program is used. Observers should try to record pupil activity for the whole of a session wherever practicable. Typically sessions lasted from five to thirty minutes during the course of our project.

Rules for the Coding of Behaviour

Category 1: Operating Hardware

This category covers all activities which involve management of the system. Formatting of discs, loading and saving programs, adjusting the monitor, plugging in and unplugging peripherals, switching on and off, adjusting the position of the equipment etc. Reading instructions on how to operate hardware or software.

Category 2: Using the Keyboard

Any activity involving pressing keys on the keyboard while the software is actually running. Any other use of the keyboard should be coded as Category 1. If other input devices are in use, e.g. joystick, mouse, concept keyboard etc. these should also be coded as Category 2 while the software is running, otherwise Category 1.

Category 3: Reading the Screen

Looking at and/or pointing to the screen in order to obtain or check information, count or talk through a problem with him/herself. Talking through a problem with the teacher or another child whilst referring to the screen should be coded as either Category 8 or 9.

Category 4: Writing or Drawing

Tasks conducted in relation to demands made by the software. Filling in a worksheet or chart, writing notes, doing a calculation on paper, drawing or colouring a picture or diagram etc.

Category 5: Consulting a Book or Diagram

Tasks conducted in relation to demands made by the software. Reading a sheet of information, a book, a map or diagram. Reading information on the screen should be coded as Category 3. Reading instructions on how to operate the hardware or how to use the software should be coded as Category 1 whether on the screen or on paper.

Category 6: Thinking

This is the most difficult one of all. Temporary inactivity whilst engaged in using the software. It may be difficult to distinguish between this and 'day-dreaming'. Observers must try to assess whether this category applies from the context of the activity under observation.

Category 7: Watching Another Person Operate the Computer

While another member of the group or the teacher takes over operation of the keyboard as described in Category 2, or in the case of the single user, when another child or the teacher takes over the keyboard to demonstrate how the program works.

Category 8: In Conversation with the Teacher (On-Task)

Any discussion with the teacher about the software while it is in use. Discussion about using the hardware should be coded as Category 1.

Category 9: In Conversation with Another Child (On-Task)

Any discussion with another child about the software while it is in use. Discussion about using the hardware should be coded as Category 1.

Category 10: In Conversation with the Teacher (Off-Task)

Discussion with the teacher on any topic other than the program or hardware in use.

Category 11: In Conversation with Another Child (Off-Task)

Discussion with another child on any topic other than the program or hardware in use.

Category 12: Doing Something Else

Any activity at or away from the computer not involving or related to the program or hardware in use, e.g. fooling around, visiting another part of the room, doing a job for the teacher etc.

Analysis of the Data

Data were treated in exactly the same way as those obtained from using the Flanders Interaction Analysis Categories (FIAC) (Flanders, 1970; Wragg, 1973). Table AI.1 shows the tallies for the first five minutes of observation of two girls using a simple drill-and-practice program. Before the tallies can be tabulated they must be arranged into pairs so that each event becomes the second part of one pair and the first part of the next.

Table AI.1

		Seconds					
		10	20	30	40	50	60
	01	3	3	2	3	3	8
	02	8	8	8	8	8	8
Minutes	03	8	8	2	2	3	3
	04	3	2	3	3	3	10
	05	3	3	3	3		

The tallies in the first minute are 3, 3, 2, 3, 3, 8, which then become 3–3, 3–2, 2–3, 3–3, 3–8, 8– and so on. These individual pairs are then counted to obtain the total number of 1—1s, 1—2s and so on. They are entered on a 12 × 12 grid to reveal an overall profile of the types and frequencies of behaviour.

Looking at the whole five minutes of observation the pattern in Table AI.2 emerges.

Clearly the most common activity which occurred during this five-minute period was 3–3 (sustained reading of the screen) scoring 9 tallies. This was followed by 8–8 (sustained conversation with the teacher on-task), scoring 8 tallies. This pattern of events was confirmed by observers' informal notes. Obviously, observation periods of longer than five minutes are necessary to collect larger numbers of tallies.

Using information in the 12×12 grid we were able to find out other things about the ways in which programs were used. These included the total number of tallies and the percentage of time spent:

- operating the hardware
- operating the keyboard
- reading the screen
- writing or drawing
- consulting a book or diagram
- thinking
- watching another operator
- talking to the teacher on- and off-task
- talking to a child on- and off-task
- doing something else
- total off-task
- total on-task.

The complete 12×12 matrix and results for 'The Inhabitant', a simulation/drill-and-practice program, is shown in Table AI.3. Notice that there are 5761 tallies, representing approximately sixteen hours' observation in all.

Table AI.2

	1	2	3	4	5	6	7	8	9	10	11	12	Total
1													
2	1	3											4
3	2		9					1		1			13
4													
5													
6													
7													
8	1							8					9
9													
10			1										1
11													
12													

[27]

Results

The amount of time spent observing children working with individual programs varied considerably, being out of the control of the observers. It was the teacher who decided who would work on what program and for how long; indeed, it was a fundamental principle of the project that this should be so. The programs themselves can only be grouped very loosely in order to look for similarities. Even then, differences in time available for observation cast doubt on the validity of some apparent similarities and differences. For example, the two drill-and-practice programs are similar in structure and content, yet it is hard to suggest any real similarities in the time spent doing different things while using them (see Table AI.4).

Table AI.3

	1	2	3	4	5	6	7	8	9	10	11	12	Total
1	0	0	0	0	0	0	0	0	0	0	0	4	4
2	0	1003	563	0	29	10	17	85	205	0	5	14	1931
3	0	417	561	0	21	24	6	125	267	0	1	10	1432
4	0	3	7	6	0	0	0	0	3	0	0	0	19
5	0	44	23	3	107	0	1	6	4	0	0	3	191
6	0	25	9	3	0	28	1	10	20	0	1	1	98
7	0	16	8	0	0	0	9	1	5	0	0	2	41
8	0	122	89	4	12	15	1	681	56	1	3	13	997
9	0	292	148	3	13	18	6	80	277	3	5	7	852
10	0	1	3	0	0	0	0	0	0	5	0	0	9
11	0	4	2	0	0	1	0	3	5	0	13	0	28
12	4	8	9	0	6	2	1	12	12	0	0	105	159

Total number of tallies	5761
	%
Steady-state ratio	48.52
Operating hardware	0.07
Operating keyboard	33.52
Reading screen	24.86
Writing or drawing	0.33
Consulting a book or diagram	3.32
Thinking	1.70
Watching another operator	0.71
Talking to teacher on-task	17.31
Talking to a child on-task	14.79
Talking to teacher off-task	0.16
Talking to a child off-task	0.49
Doing something else	2.76
Total off-task	3.40
Total on-task	96.60

The proportion of time spent operating the keyboard when using 'The Inhabitant' and 'The Explorer' is quite different even though one might expect these to be similar. However, there is close parallel in respect of another child (on-task), ('The Inhabitant' 15%, 'The Explorer' 17%), which might well be expected when one considers the way in which teachers encouraged pairs of children to share ideas and discuss their responses to the programs' demands. This similarity is shared with the database which was the only other program where teachers encouraged discussion and group work.

Table AI.4

Program type	Title	Tallies	Observation time (minutes)
Drill and practice	'The Explorer'	1030	172
	'The Inhabitant'	5761	960
Database	'INFORM'	1173	196
Wordprocessor	'Writer'	2439	407
	'Wordwise'	426	71
Wordprocessor/DTP	'Front Page'	4271	712
Paintbox	'Super-Art'	501	84

Time spent in discussion with another child (on-task) was 20% when using the database, whereas when the children used 'Writer', a wordprocessor, it reduced to 7%. Discussion with another child (on task) did not feature at all with 'Wordwise' or 'Front Page'. Here, talking to the teacher (on task) featured more highly. ('Writer' 26%, 'Wordwise' 16%, 'Front Page' 15%). The greatest similarity, however, occurred in the proportion of time spent using the keyboard when the three wordprocessor programs were in operation ('Writer' 46%, 'Wordwise' 48%, 'Front Page' 48%). The only program where a non-keyboard input device was used was 'Super-Art'. There, a mouse controlled the movement of the pointer on the computer screen. This led to the highest proportion of time being spent actually inputting information (69%) as one might expect with a paintbox type of program. Even in this case, however, the proportion of time discussing the work with the teacher was relatively high (19%). Most of this involved seeking help with the rather difficult operating instructions.

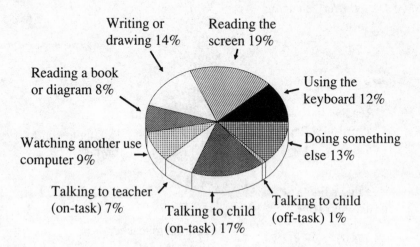

Figure AI.1   'Explorer' (simulation D & P)

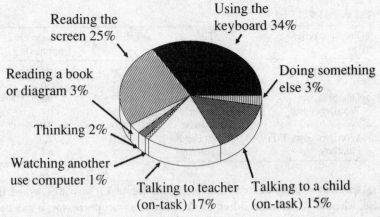

Figure AI.2   *'The Inhabitant' (simulation D & P)*

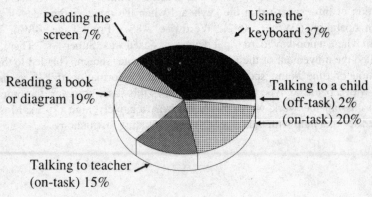

Figure AI.3   *'INFORM' database*

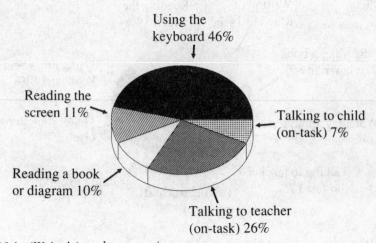

Figure AI.4   *'Writer' (wordprocessor)*

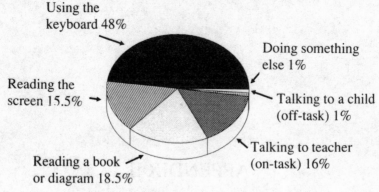

Fgure AI.5 '*Wordwise' (wordprocessor)*

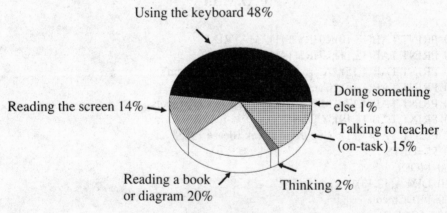

Figure AI.6 '*Front Page' (newspaper editor)*

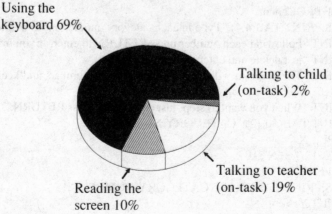

Figure AI.7 '*Super-Art' (paintbox)*

APPENDIX II

Computer Program in BBC BASIC to Process Data from 'C.O.M.I.C.'

```
10  CLS
20  PRINT TAB(13,10);CHR$(141);"MATRIX"
30  PRINT TAB(13,11);CHR$(141);"MATRIX"
40  PRINT TAB(1,15);"A program to process data from"
50  PRINT TAB(1,16);"Categories for Observing"
60  PRINT TAB(1,17);"Microcomputer Use in Classrooms."
70  PRINT TAB(14,19);"COMIC"
80  PRINT TAB(3,21);"Copyright Derek Blease 1987"
90  P$=GET$
100 MODE 3
110 DIM A(12,13)
120 PROCmenu
130 MODE 7
140 END
150 DEF PROCcount
160 CLS:PRINT TAB(4,4);"Type in each category number one at a time."
170 PRINT "Following each number press RETURN to enter. If you make a mistake"
180 PRINT "just delete and enter the correct number."
190 PRINT "The program will automatically pair the numbers and keep the tallies for you."
200 PRINT "When you want to stop, just enter 0 and press RETURN."
210 PRINT TAB(30,12);"CATEGORY NUMBER";
220 INPUT X
230 IF X>12 THEN 210
240 REPEAT
250 CLS:PRINT TAB(30,12);"CATEGORY NUMBER ";
260 INPUT Y
270 IF Y>12 THEN 250
```

```
280  A(X,Y)=A(X,Y)+1
290  X=Y
300  UNTIL Y=0
310  PROCsave
320  ENDPROC
330  DEF PROCprint
340  CLS:PRINT:PRINT:VDU2
350  FOR R=1 TO 12
360  A(R,13)=A(R,1)+A(R,2)+A(R,3)+A(R,4)+A(R,5)+A(R,6)+A(R,7)
+A(R,8)+A(R,9)+A(R,10)+A(R,11)+A(R,12)
370  NEXT
380  R=1
390  REPEAT
400  X=0
410  FOR C=1 TO 12
420   PRINT TAB(X);A(R,C);
430  X=X+6:NEXT
440  PRINT TAB(X);A(R,13):PRINT:R=R+1
450  UNTIL R=13
460  PRINT
470  C=13:T=A(1,C)+A(2,C)+A(3,C)+A(4,C)+A(5,C)+A(6,C)+A(7,C)
+A(8,C)+A(9,C)+A(10,C)+A(11,C)+A(12,C)
480  PRINT:PRINT "Total number of TALLIES ";TAB(40);T
490  @%=131594: PRINT
500  PRINT  "Steady  state  ratio";TAB(40);FNsteady(T);"%"510 PRINT  "Time
operating hardware ";TAB(40);FNhard(T);"%"
520  PRINT "Time operating keyboard ";TAB(40);FNkey(T);"%"
530  PRINT "Time reading screen ";TAB(40);FNscreen(T);"%"
540  PRINT "Writing or drawing ";TAB(40);FNwrite(T);"%"
550  PRINT "Consulting a book or diagram ";TAB(40);FNread(T);"%"
560  PRINT "Thinking time ";TAB(40);FNthink(T);"%"
570  PRINT "Watching other operator ";TAB(40);FNwatch(T);"%"
580  PRINT "Talk to teacher on task ";TAB(40);FNteachon(T);"%"
590  PRINT "Talk to child on task ";TAB(40);FNtalkon(T);"%"
600  PRINT "Talk to teacher off task ";TAB(40);FNteachoff(T);"%"
610  PRINT "Talk to child off task ";TAB(40);FNtalkoff(T);""%"
620  PRINT "Doing something else ";TAB(40);FNelse(T);"%"
630  PRINT "Total off task ";TAB(40);FNoff(T);"%"
640  PRINT "Total on task ";TAB(40);FNon(T);"%"
650  VDU3
660  @%=10
670  PRINT:PRINT "press any key"
680  G$=GET$
690  ENDPROC
700  DEF PROCmenu
```

```
710  PRINT TAB(20,10) "1 Create a new file"
720  PRINT TAB(20,12) "2 Add to an existing file"
730  PRINT TAB(20,14) "3 QUIT"
740  PRINT TAB(20,16) "4 Print out the DATA"
750  PRINT TAB(20,18) "CHOOSE A NUMBER AND PRESS RETURN";
760  INPUT N
770  IF N=1 THEN PROCcount
780  IF N=2 THEN PROCload
790  IF N=3 THEN 820
800  IF N=4 THEN PROCprint
810  CLS: GOTO 710
820  ENDPROC
830  DEF PROCsave
840  CLS:PRINT TAB(20,12);"Please type in the FILENAME ";
850  INPUT F$
860  X%=OPENOUT F$
870  FOR R=1 TO 12: FOR C=1 TO 12
880  PRINT# X%,A(R,C)
890  NEXT C:NEXT R
900  CLOSE#X%
910  ENDPROC
920  DEF PROCload
930  CLS:PRINT TAB(20,12);"Please type in the FILENAME ";
940  INPUT F$
950  X%=OPENIN F$
960  FOR R=1 TO 12: FOR C=1 TO 12
970  INPUT# X%,A(R,C)
980  NEXT C:NEXT R
990  CLOSE#X%
1000 PROCcount
1010 ENDPROC
1020 DEF FNsteady(T)=(A(1,1)+A(2,2)+A(3,3)+A(4,4)+A(5,5)+A(6,6)
     +A(7,7)+A(8,8)+A(9,9)+A(10,10)+A(11,11)+A(12,12))*100/T
1030 DEF FNhard(T)=A(1,13)*100/T
1040 DEF FNkey(T)=A(2,13)*100/T
1050  DEF FNscreen(T)=A(3,13)*100/T
1060 DEF FNwrite(T)=A(4,13)*100/T
1070 DEF FNread(T)=A(5,13)*100/T
1080 DEF FNthink(T)=A(6,13)*100/T
1090 DEF FNwatch(T)=A(7,13)*100/T
1100 DEF FNteachon(T)=A(8,13)*100/T
1110 DEF FNtalkon(T)=A(9,13)*100/T
1120 DEF FNteachoff(T)=A(10,13)*100/T
1130 DEF FNtalkoff(T)=A(11,13)*100/T
1140 DEF FNelse(T)=A(12,13)*100/T
```

```
1150  DEF FNoff(T)=(A(10,13)+A(11,13)+A(12,13))*100/T
1160  DEF FNon(T)=(A(1,13)+A(2,13)+A(3,13)+A(4,13)+A(5,13)
+A(6,13)+A(7,13)+A(8,13)+A(9,13))*100/T
```

Program to Merge Two Sets of Data

```
10  CLS
20  PRINT "This program enables you to merge two"
30  PRINT "sets of data."
40  PRINT "Just follow the instructions on the"
50  PRINT "screen and the program will do the work for you."
60  PRINT:PRINT "Copyright Derek Blease 1987"
70  DIM A(12,13):DIM B(12,13):DIM D(12,13)
80  PRINT "Type in the name of the first file"
90  PRINT:PRINT:INPUT F1$
100  X%=OPENIN F1$
110  FOR R=1 TO 12: FOR C=1 TO 12
120  INPUT# X%,A(R,C)
130  NEXT:NEXT
140  CLOSE#X%
150  CLS:INPUT "Type in the next filename ";F2$
160  X%=OPENIN F2$
170  FOR R=1 TO 12: FOR C=1 TO 12
180  INPUT# X%,B(R,C)
190  NEXT:NEXT
200  CLOSE#X%
210  FOR R=1 TO 12: FOR C=1 TO 12
220  D(R,C)=A(R,C)+B(R,C):NEXT:NEXT
230  FOR R=1 TO 12: FOR C=1 TO 12
240  A(R,C)=D(R,C):NEXT:NEXT
250  CLS:PRINT "Do you want to merge another file? (Y/N)"
260  INPUT P$
270  IF P$="Y" THEN 150
280  IF P$<>"N" THEN 250
290  CLS:PRINT "You must now save the new file."
300  INPUT "Type in the new filename ";N$
310  X%=OPENOUT N$
320  FOR R=1 TO 12: FOR C=1 TO 12
330  PRINT# X%,A(R,C)
340  NEXT:NEXT
350  CLOSE#X%
360  CLS:END
```

Table AI.5 Percentage degree of concordance between pupils'
self-images and their teachers' perceptions of those
attributes

	JOAN		PAULINE	
	% High	% Low	% High	% Low
Academic self-image	80	80	20	40
Determination to succeed	60	60	60	0
Popularity as work partner	60	60	20	40
Computer-user self-image	20	60	20	40

100% = perfect agreement

REFERENCES AND BIBLIOGRAPHY

Atkinson, P. (1980) Writing ethnography, cited in M. Hammersley (ed.) *The Ethnography of Schooling*, Nafferton Books, Driffield.

Ball, S. J. (1988) Participant observation, in J. P. Keeves (ed.) *Educational Research, Methodology, and Measurement: An International Handbook*, Pergamon Press, Oxford, pp. 507–10.

Ball, S. J. and Goodson, I. (eds.) *Teachers' Lives and Careers*, Falmer Press, Basingstoke.

Barker-Lunn, J. (1970) *Streaming in the Primary School*, NFER, Slough.

Beynon, J. (1983) Ways-in and staying-on: fieldwork as problem solving, in M. Hammersley (ed.) *The Ethnography of Schooling*, Nafferton Books, Driffield, pp. 39–53.

Bleach, P. (1986) *The Use of Microcomputers in Primary Schools* (interim report), Reading and Language Information Centre, School of Education, University of Reading.

Blease, D. (1986) *Evaluating Educational Software*, Croom Helm, London.

Brine, J. (1983) *The Microcomputer Threat to Classroom Order*, paper presented at the annual CSSE Conference, Vancouver, Canada.

Bryman, A. (1988) *Quantity and Quality in Social Research*, Unwin Hyman, London.

Burgess, R. (1985) *Strategies in Educational Research: Qualitative Methods*, Falmer Press, Basingstoke.

Carr, W. and Kemmis, S. (1986) *Becoming Critical*, Falmer Press, Basingstoke.

Cohen, L. and Manion, L. (1989) *Research Methods in Education* (3rd edition), Routledge, London.

Cox, M. V. (1987) Micro problems in the primary school, *Education 3–13*, June, pp. 17–22.

Crocker, A. C. and Cheesman, R. G. (1988) The ability of young children to rank themselves for academic ability, *Educational Studies*, Vol. 14, no. 1, pp. 105–10.

Culley, L. (1986) *Gender Differences and Computing in Secondary Schools*, Department of Education, Loughborough University of Technology.

Denscombe, M. (1983) Interviews, accounts and ethnographic research on teachers, in M. Hammersley (ed.) *The Ethnography of Schooling*, Nafferton Books, Driffield, pp. 107–28.

Denscombe, M., Szulc, H., Patrick, C. and Wood, A. (1986) Ethnicity and friendship: the contrast between sociometric research and fieldwork observations in primary school classrooms, *British Educational Research Journal*, Vol. 12, no. 3, pp. 221–35.

Denzin, N. K. (1988) Triangulation, in J. P. Keeves (ed.) *Educational Research, Methodology, and Measurement: An International Handbook*, Pergamon Press, Oxford, pp. 511–13.

DES and The Welsh Office (1988a) *National Curriculum. Design and Technology Working Group Interim Report*, HMSO, London, November.

DES and The Welsh Office (1988b) *English for Ages 5–11*, Proposals of the Secretary of State for Education and Science and the Secretary of State for Wales, HMSO, London, November.

Ellis, J. (1986) *Equal Opportunities and Computer Education in the Primary School: Guidelines for Good Practice for Teachers* (a project funded by the Equal Opportunities Commission, the Department of Trade and Industry and Sheffield LEA), London.

Evans, N. (1986) *The Future of the Microcomputer in Schools*, Macmillan, London.

Ewen, T. A. and Roberts, A. (1985) Microcomputer use, in I. Reid and J. Rushton (eds.) *Teachers, Computers and the Classroom*, Manchester University Press, pp. 38–59.

Fairbrother, P. (1977) Experience and trust in sociological work, *Sociology*, Vol. 11, pp. 359–68.

Fiddy, P. (1981) More professional software is needed, *Educational Computing*, June, pp. 41–2.

Flanders, N. (1970) *Analyzing Teaching Behavior*, Addison-Wesley, Reading, Mass.

Fletcher, B. C. (1985) Group and individual learning of junior school children on a microcomputer-based task: social and cognitive facilitation?, *Educational Review*, Vol. 37, no. 3.

Freeman, P. L. (1986) Don't talk to me about lexical meta-analysis of criterion-referenced clustering and lap-dissolve spatial transformations: a consideration of the role of practising teachers in educational research, *British Educational Research Journal*, Vol. 12, no. 2, pp. 197–206.

Gardner, A. D. (1984) CAL and in-service teacher training, *British Journal of Educational Technology*, Vol. 15, no. 3, pp. 173–6.

Geertz, C. (1973) *The Interpretation of Cultures*, Basic Books, New York, NY.

Gronlund, N. E. (1955) The relative stability of classroom social status with unweighted and weighted sociometric choices, *Journal of Educational Psychology*, Vol. 43, pp. 345–54.

Gronlund, N. E. (1959) *Sociometry in the Classroom*, Harpers, New York, NY.

Hall, J. and Rhodes, V. (1986) *Microcomputers in Primary Schools. Some Observations and Recommendations for Good Practice*, Educational Computing Unit, Centre for Educational Studies, King's College, London.

Halsey, A. H. (ed.) (1972) *Educational Priority: Volume 1 EPA Problems and Policies*, HMSO, London.

Hammersley, M. (1983) (ed.) *The Ethnography of Schooling*, Nafferton Books, Driffield.

Hawkins, J. (1983) *Learning LOGO Together: The Social Context*, Bank Street College of Education, New York, NY.

Heywood, G. and Norman, P. (1988) Problems of educational innovation: the primary teacher's response to using the microcomputer, *Journal of Computer Assisted Learning*, Vol. 4, no. 1, pp. 34–43.

High, J. (1988) A primary headteacher's view on information technology in education, *Computer Education*, June.

Hitchcock, G. (1983) Fieldwork as practical activity: reflections on fieldwork and the social organization of an urban open-plan primary school, in M. Hammerlsey (ed.) *The Enthnography of Schoooling*, Nafferton Books, Driffield.

Hollander, E. P. (1964) *Leaders, Groups and Influence*, Oxford University Press, New York, NY.

Holly, P. and Whitehead, D. (1986) *Collaborative Action Research*, Classroom Action Research Network, bulletin, Vol. 7, Cambridge Institute of Education.

Holmes, D. S. (1971) Self-appraisal of achievement motivation: the self-peer rank method revisited, *Journal of Consulting and Clinical Psychology*, Vol. 36, no. 1, pp. 23–6.

Holmes, D. S. and Tyler, J. D. (1968) Direct versus projective measurement of achievement motivation, *Journal of Consulting and Clinical Psychology*, Vol. 32, no. 6, pp. 712–17.

Kelly, H. H. (1983) Perceived causal structures, in J. Jaspars *et al.* (eds.) *Attribution Theory and Research: Conceptual Development and Social Dimensions*, Academic Press, London.

Kilpatrick, F. P. and Cantril, H. (1965) Self-anchoring scaling: a measure of individuals' unique reality worlds, in R. E. Hartley and E. L. Hartley (eds.) *Readings in Psychology* (3rd Edition), Thomas Y. Crowell, New York, NY.

Loftland, J. and Loftland, L. (1984) *Analyzing Social Settings*, Wadsworth, Belmont, Calif.

Lubeck, S. (1985) *Sandbox Society*, Falmer Press, Basingstoke.

Moore, J. L. (1987) Is using a computer at home more valuable than using a computer at school?, *Computer Education*, June, p. 13.

National Curriculum Council (1988a) *Science in the National Curriculum* (a report to the Secretary of State for Education and Science on the statutory consultation for attainment targets and programmes of study in science), NCC, York, December.

National Curriculum Council (1988b) *Mathematics in the National Curriculum* (a report to the Secretary of State for Education and Science on the statutory consultation for attainment targets and programmes of study in mathematics), NCC, York, December.

Olson, J. (1988) *Schoolworlds, Microworlds. Computers and the Cultures of the Classroom*, Pergamon, Oxford.

Opacic, P. and Roberts, A. (1985) Resistance to CAL implementation, in I. Reid and J. Rushton (eds.) *Teachers, Computers and the Classroom*, Manchester University Press, pp. 62–3.

Plewis, I. (1985) *Analysing Change: Measurement and Explanation Using Longitudinal Data*, Wiley, Chichester.

Pope, M. and Denicolo, P. (1986) Intuitive theories: a researcher's dilemma: some practical methodological implications, *British Educational Research Journal*, Vol. 12, no. 2, pp. 153–66.

Powney, J. (1988) Structured eavesdropping, *Research Intelligence*, Vol. 28, pp. 3–4.

Proctor, C. H. and Loomis, C. P. (1951) Analysis of sociometric data, in M. Jahoda, M. Deutch and S. W. Cook (eds.) *Research Methods in Social Relations Part II: Selected Techniques*, Dryden Press, New York, NY.

Richardson, T. (1986) Using micros to encourage pupil autonomy, *Education 3–13*, Vol. 143, no. 1, pp. 42–4.

Riding, R. J. and Buckle, C.F. (1987) Computer developments and educational psychology, *Educational Psychology*, Vol. 7, no. 1, pp. 5–11.

Schutz, A. (1964) *Collected Papers II: Studies in Social Theory*, Martinns Nijhoff, The Hague.

Shaw, D. G. *et al.* (1985) Children's questions: a study of questions children ask when learning to use a computer, *Computer Education*, Vol. 9, no. 1, pp. 15–19.

Shipman, M. D. (1974) *Inside a Curriculum Project*, Methuen, London.

Smith, D. and Keep, R. (1986) Children's opinions of educational software, *Educational Research*, Vol. 28, no. 2, pp. 83–8.

Stimpson, F. (1988) Content-free software in the primary curriculum, *Education 3–13*, March, pp. 13–17.

Stones, E. (1986) Towards a systematic approach to research in teaching: the place of investigative pedagogy, *British Educational Research Journal*, Vol. 12, no. 2, pp. 167–81.

Stowbridge, M. D. and Kugel, P. (1983) Learning to learn by learning to play, *Creative Computing*, Vol. 9, pp. 180–8.

Straker, A. (1984) Humpty Dumpty sat on a . . . micro?, *Computer Education*, November.

Taft, R. (1988) Ethnographic research methods, in J. P. Keeves (ed.) *Educational Research, Methodology, and Measurement: An International Handbook*, Pergamon, Oxford.

Tann, P (1981) cited in B. Simon and J. Willcocks, *Research and Practice in the Primary Classroom*, Routledge & Kegan Paul, London.

Thompson, N. B. W. (1987) New technology for better schools (a letter to all CEOs) Department of Education and Science, 21st July 1987.

Walker, D. (1983) Reflection on the educational potential and limitations of microcomputers, *Phi. Delta Kappan*, Vol. 65, pp. 103–7.

Walton, D. and Hannafin, M. J. (1987) The effects of wordprocessing on written composition, *Journal of Educational Research*, Vol. 80, Pt. 6, pp. 338–42.

Woods, P. (1986) *Inside Schools: Ethnography in Educational Research*, Routledge, London.

Wragg, E. C. (1973) A study of student teachers in the classroom, in G. Chanan (ed.) *Towards a Science of Teaching*, NFER, Slough.

Wright, A. (1987) The process of microtechnological innovation in two primary schools: a case study of teachers' thinking, *Educational Review*, Vol. 39, no. 2, pp. 107–15.